1989 Supplement

LEGAL RESEARCH

AND

LAW LIBRARY MANAGEMENT

Julius J. Marke
Professor of Law and Librarian
St. John's University School of Law
Professor of Law Emeritus
New York University
School of Law

Richard Sloane
Professor of Law Emeritus
University of Pennsylvania Law School
Law Library Planning Consultant

Law Journal Seminars-Press, Inc.
111 Eighth Ave.
New York, New York 10011

05572

(Rel. 5)

Library of Congress Cataloging in Publication Data

Marke, Julius J.
Legal research and law library management.

Bibliography: p.
Includes index.
1. Legal research—United States. 2. Law libraries—United States. I. Sloane, Richard, 1916- II. Title.
KF240.M24 340'.072072 81-19297
AACR

Table of Contents
1989 Supplement

---

*New in this Supplement

---

*New in this Supplement

CHAPTER 2A

A Guide to Reading and Writing for Lawyers

The following material comprises a new Chapter 2A for Legal Research and Law Library Management. *It is intended as supplemental material to the Main Text.*

WRITE IT IN ENGLISH:

Dreams of partnership crackled through the young associate's mind. His latest memorandum would make new law. It would keep a great company out of the grasp of an unwelcome suitor. It would save for the firm its most valuable client.

He entered the presiding partner's office with keen anticipation. Yes, there on the desk was the memorandum of his dreams. The great man picked it up, his nose quivering as though he had just smelled something foul.

He uttered only four words, "Write it in English!" Then he tore the offending memorandum in half and dropped the pieces into his trash basket.

The interview was over.

Generations of Americans—long before the advent of radio and television—developed considerable reading and writing skills without formal schooling beyond the fifth or sixth grade. After nineteen years of education, too many of today's law school graduates remain literary clods.

Law review articles are clothed in impenetrable phrases. They are studded with cliches. Vogue words abound.

"incoherence and indeterminancy of legal doctrine"
"antipositivist phenomenon"

"area of convergence"
"law was purposive rather than self contained"
"nondoctrinal interdisciplinary, behavioral research"
"classical doctrinal formalism"
"a normative pattern of recurrent and related operations yielding cumulative and progressive results"
"a deconstructive 'critique' of the text exposes the subjectivity of the linguistic assertion"

Does this "linguistic assertion" conceal wisdom, or is it plain fatuous writing? Court opinions, statutes and regulations are also subject to this type of cant.

[1]—A Cure for Cant

What one reads determines how well one writes. Since today's legal writers feed on one another, they are caught in a cycle of wretched writing. All the legal writing courses in the world will continue to fail unless they show by example what is good writing and what is not. To that end, and only as a first step, two groups of publications are recommended. *McGuffey's Eclectic Readers*[1] abound in examples of great writing, and the *Quarterly Review of Double Speak*[2] contains a distillation of deceptive writing, most of it by lawyers.

[a]—The *McGuffey's Readers*. *McGuffey's Eclectic Readers,* six in all, gave nineteenth century Americans an appreciation of great literature. They were "collections of well-chosen selections from the best English and American literature."[3] The *Sixth Reader* alone included writings of 111 different authors, among them Sir Walter Scott, Longfellow, Daniel Webster, Dickens, Samuel Johnson, Mil-

---

[1] The publishing house of Van Nostrand Reinhold has kept *McGuffey's Eclectic Readers* in print. In addition, the Conservative Book Club has offered facsimile editions at reduced prices as an inducement for joining. Adult readers will find the fifth and sixth *Readers* of more interest if less charm.

[2] Subscriptions to the *Quarterly Review of Double Speak* are available through the National Council of Teachers of English in Urbana, Illinois.

[3] Sullivan, *Our Times,* vol. 2, p. 47 (Scribner's 1939).

ton, Macaulay, Poe and Emerson. The *Readers* were "the very gates of literature ajar."[4]

With an uneven system of public school education and a population far below ours today, nineteenth century Americans bought more that 122 million copies of all the *Readers*. Some editions sold as many as one million copies a year. Though the covers were tattered from previous use, many brothers and sisters in a single family shared and treasured a single copy.

One historian wrote, "These textbooks constitute the most influential volumes ever published in America."[5] Henry Ford reprinted them all in the early part of the twentieth century, and they are still available from commercial publishers.[6]

[b]—The *Quarterly Review of Double Speak*. Many writers can express themselves clearly, but for reasons known best to themselves choose not to do so. Too often these people predominate as professional public spokesmen. Some of the most skillful among them are lawyers. To help translate the utterances of presidents, governors and mayors—the products of the country's Fitzwaters and their colleagues—one survival kit alone will serve. It is the *Quarterly Review of Double Speak*. This twelve-page newsletter abounds in linguistic perversions and distortions of the truth. Each issue includes extracts from a special branch of the writing profession—the "Doublespeakers." Once each year, the publishers gives what is known as the Orwell Award.

The editor of the newsletter has defined "doublespeak" as "language which pretends to communicate but really does not. It is language which makes the bad seem good, something negative appear positive, and something unpleasant appear attractive, or at least tolerable."[7] A few examples:

"The bodies of the astronauts killed in the Challenger disaster

---

[4] *Id.*

[5] So noted by Herbert Quick in *One Man's Life*, as quoted by Sullivan, N. 3 *supra.*, at p. 14.

[6] See N. 1 *supra*.

[7] Editor William Lutz, Professor of English, Rutgers University, in the January 1987 issue of the *Quarterly Review of Double Speak*, p. 10.

were referred to by NASA as "recovered components," and their coffins were called "crew transfer containers."[8]

Asked what he was doing to put a halt to the purchase of $400 hammers by the military, a Deputy Secretary of Defense replied, "We must turn our attention to the logistics tail of spare parts acquisition as we fine-tune our initiatives and push them down to the operating level."[9]

Speaking of the reported firing of two American missles at an Irani jet, presidential spokesman Martin Fitzwater told the press, "At this point, I will not confirm any part of the incident." He also said that President Reagan had been informed "soon after the incident happened." When asked what incident he was talking about, Fitzwater replied, "The incident that I'm not confirming."[10]

The Chairman of the President's Council of Economic Advisors gave the following testimony before a Senate Committee: "[I]t is a tricky problem to find the particular calibration in timing that would be appropriate to stem the acceleration in risk premiums created by the falling incomes without prematurely aborting the decline in the inflation-generated risk premiums."[11]

The Defense Department has defined "preemptive attack" as meaning that the United States attacked first; to "engage the enemy on all sides" is an ambush; and "tactical redeployment" is a retreat.[12]

"Revenue enhancement" is a tax increase,[13] and "poorly buffered precipitation" is a positive way of referring to acid rain.[14]

"Traumatic amputation" is the United States Army's way of saying that someone's arms or legs were blown off.[15]

Each issue of *Double Speak* seems to outdo the previous one providing examples of euphemisms, jargon, gobbledygook and inflated language.

---

[8] *Id.*, at p. 2.
[9] *Id.*, at p. 5.
[10] See the April 1988 issue of the *Quarterly Review of Double Speak*, p. 4.
[11] See the January 1987 issue of the *Quarterly Review of Double Speak*, p. 11.
[12] *Id.*, at p. 12.
[13] *Id.*
[14] See the April 1988 issue of the *Quarterly Review of Double Speak*, p. 6.
[15] *Id.*

[2]—Formal Writing Instruction

Law publishers rarely let a month go by without issuing some new text on the subject of legal writing instruction. Yet law firm associates regularly complain that the firm's library has virtually nothing on the subject. The complaint should be taken as a compliment to the librarian because so little exists that is helpful.

There are, however, two exceptions. One is a full volume by Bryan A. Garner entitled *A Dictionary of Modern Legal Usage*.[16] The other is a short article called "Elements of Legal Style" by George D. Gibson.[17]

Garner's work is modeled after Fowler's *Modern English Usage*. It is no mere legal writing primer. Rather, it is a mature legal dictionary that sparkles with extracts from court opinions, briefs, and all forms of legal writing. This is a valuable source for learning usage, style and choice of words. The volume includes some 200 short essays on matters of style and grammar. Of particular value are the writings on cliches, euphemisms, gobbledygook, legalese, misplaced modifiers, obscurity, tautology, vogue words, and weasel words. *A Dictionary of Modern Legal Usage* is a work worthy to stand beside Fowler's *Modern English Usage*.

Gibson's short article shows lawyers how to communicate with brevity, clarity and style. His essay is recommended over the dozens of books and hundreds of articles that purport to teach lawyers how to write. Gibson simply does it best and in the shortest space.

[3]—The Inspiration of Biography

A few men have devoted a lifetime to the study of words, their meanings and their uses. Three names stand out and their lives are an inspiration to all writers.

James Augustus Henry Murray spent thirty-six years of his professional life compiling the mammoth *New English Dictionary* which was subsequently published as the *Oxford English Dictionary*. The most remarkable feature of Murray's work is the extracts from thou-

---

[16] Garner, *A Dictionary of Modern Legal Usage* (Oxford University Press 1988).

[17] Gibson, "Elements of Legal Style," Bus. Law., pp. 547-555 (April 1967).

sands of works of literature to help demonstrate the meanings of particular words as they changed throughout the ages. A biography of Murray's life, *Caught in the Toil of Words,* has been written by his grand niece.[18]

Before the typewriter was in general use, Murray corresponded by hand with hundreds of scholars. The wealth of quotations in his dictionary—drawn from that correspondence and from his own reading—is unmatched by any other dictionary in any language.

Another dictionary maker was Peter Mark Roget, who, for most of his professional life, was a noted London physician and scientist, and a frequent contributor to the *Encyclopedia Britannica.* He only began work on the Thesaurus when he was in his seventies. It was first published in 1852 and he lived to edit its first twenty editions. His biography, entitled *Peter Mark Roget, the Word and the Man,* was written by D.L. Emblen.[19]

Finally, there is Noah Webster, an American and the only member of this trio who was a practicing lawyer. Webster's dictionary, first published in 1828, is the predecessor to the now standard Merriam-Webster dictionaries. His biography, *Noah Webster,* is by H.P. Warfel.[20]

---

[18] Murray, *Caught in the Toil of Words: James Murray and the Oxford English Dictionary* (Yale University Press 1977).

[19] Emblen, *Peter Mark Roget, the Word and the Man* (Longmans 1970).

[20] Warfel, *Noah Webster* (Macmillan 1936). Warfel also published a collection of Webster's *Letters* in 1953.

CHAPTER 4A

Jump Cites and Computer-Assisted Legal Research

The following material comprises a new Chapter 4A for Legal Research and Law Library Management. *It is intended as supplemental material to the Main Text.*

One of the first citation rules we learn in law school is that when citing a particular assertion or quotation in a case rather than the case generally, the page numbers on which it occurs must be indicated, as well as the first page on which the case begins. For example: *Tunis Bros. Co. Inc. v. Ford Motor Co.*, 763 F.2d 1482, 1498 (3d Cir, 1985).

This is known as a jump cite. Similarly, in citing material within a concurring or dissenting opinion we were taught to give both the initial page of the case and the page on which the specific material appears rather than the initial page of the concurring or dissenting opinion. For example:

> *Tunis Bros. Co. Inc. v. Ford Motor Co.*, 763 F.2d 1482, 1503 (3d Cir. 1985) (Hunter, J. dissenting).

It is a simple matter to pinpoint these pages when the case is reported in book form. The pages are clearly noted and can be accurately recorded. But how does the researcher meet these requirements when a federal circuit court or district court case is retrieved electronically through LEXIS or WESTLAW? Until recently both of these computer-assisted legal research systems provide pagination only for the first page of the case and not for the succeeding pages of the case which the researcher may wish to quote. And—therein lies the tale of *West Publishing Co. v. Mead Data Central Inc.* (Civil File No. 4-85-937, U.S. District Court, District of Minnesota, Fourth Division, 1985).

The decisions of the United States Circuit Courts and the United States District Courts are not officially published. Instead, they are selectively reported in the *Federal Reporter* and the *Federal Supple-*

ment by West Publishing Co. as part of its National Reporter System. As they are the only comprehensive reporters of the decisions of those courts published in book form, they are accepted by all courts as though they were officially sanctioned.

When a federal court decides a case, it sends an authoritative copy of its decision to the West Publishing Company. The West editors then carefully check the wording of the decision, the authorities it refers to, and prepare it editorially for publication in its reporters. When a case is published in the *Federal Reporter* or in the other reporters of West's National Reporter System, it is sequentially numbered as to volume and pages. For citation purposes, and for obvious reasons, the reference to the exact volume and page number is a *sine qua non*. There is no other way those cases can be cited in the courts.

Mead Data Corporation owns and operates Lexis, a computer-assisted legal research tool containing decisions of state and federal courts in its data base. West Publishing Company owns and operates Westlaw which similarly provides the full text of state and federal court decisions. By reason of the manner in which these cases are entered into their system, both Lexis and Westlaw note only the citation to the first page of the judicial opinions as reported in West's Federal Reporter and Federal Supplement. This was done by displaying at the top of the computer screen the volume number and page number on which the opinion begins. To be able to cite the exact page or pages to be quoted from within the body of the opinion, however, it was necessary to check additionally the specific volume and pages of the reporter in which it is initially reported in book form.

Obviously, if this second step can be eliminated, the value of Lexis would be enhanced for Lexis users. Recognizing this potential value, Lexis announced in June, 1985 that it will include "star pagination" within the texts of its court reports. "Star pagination" was widely used in 19th Century America to reprint privately official federal and state court reports, including the U.S. Supreme Court Reporter. Each star represents the start of a new page in the edition being reprinted. "Star pagination" would add the official page cites to the full text of online case law material. In essence, therefore, "star pagination" meant the insertion of page numbers from West's Federal Reporter, page by page, within the body of Lexis reports. This would permit Lexis users to determine the exact pages of the text of a case reported in West's *Federal Reporter* coinciding with the text of a Lexis report of the same case, taken from the Lexis screen or computer printout without physically referring to West's reporters.

The implementation of this program would be highly desirable in the interest of computer-assisted legal research because it would eliminate the second step of referring to the West Reporters. On the other hand, West might suffer economic harm since many practitioners and law libraries might reduce the number of subscriptions they carry to West's Federal Court reporters, possibly eliminating them altogether.

Alleging that Lexis's intended "star pagination" program constituted an appropriation of West's comprehensive arrangement of its case reports, in violation of its copyright, West moved in the U.S. District Court of Minnesota for a preliminary injunction enjoining that use. The essence of West's claim was that its National Reporter System arrangement of volume and page numbers is protected by copyright. Both West and Mead Data agreed that some parts of West's National Reporter System were appropriate subjects of copyright protection and some were not. The court focused on which portions of those publications were protected by copyright, especially the pagination used by West.

Relying on the 1888 Case, *Callaghan v. Meyers*, 128 U.S. 617, the court found that West's arrangement of pages was copyrightable and granted the injunction. *West Publishing Co. v. Mead Data Central, Inc.*, 616 F. Supp. 1571 (Minn. 1985). It noted with approval the holding in *Callaghan* which delineated the copyrightable portions of law reports, separate and apart from the opinions of the court.

> "Such work of the reporter, which may be the lawful subject of copyright, comprehends. . . . The order of arrangement of the cases, the division of the reports into volumes, the numbering and paging of the volumes, the table of cases cited in the opinions (where such table is made), and the subdivision of the index into appropriate, condensed titles, involving the distribution of the subjects of the various headnotes, and cross-references where such exist." 128 U.S. at 649.

It is interesting to note the court's reaction to the fact that Lexis has long noted at the beginning of each of its cases the "cite" according to the West Publishing Company's arrangement. "This West acknowledges is a fair use of its copyrighted material. It should be noted parenthetically, that this is not necessarily altruism on West's part. That cite calls a researcher's attention to West's books—which they are in business to sell as well as create. But this case turns on whether or not the succeeding page numbers themselves are protected by copyright, even if the overall arrangement is a copyrightable entity. This court holds that they are so protected."

The so-called "jump cite" (i.e., 479 F.2d 701, 702) infringes on West's copyright because it goes beyond fair use. Once one has access to the MDC data base, using the LEXIS keyboard, one has access to the copyrighted—protected overall arrangement as delineated by West Publishing Company.

How is the bar affected by this injunction? Lexis's attempt to introduce star pagination into its own database would enhance its position commercially. It might eliminate a substantial use of West's hard bound volumes of reporters. But what LEXIS attempted to do could have proved a boon to legal research and is highly desirable. As Mead Data argued before the court, the introduction of star pagination would give judges, lawyers and citizens freer access to the entire body of the law and that would be in the public interest.

It must be noted in this context that Westlaw also did not provide a star pagination feature. Mead Data argued before the court that if the preliminary injunction were issued, West would have time to develop such a feature for Westlaw and as a result, Lexis would lose the market supremacy it has achieved over Westlaw. The court found this claim to be speculative at best and added "even if West were to introduce a star pagination feature, it should be noted that West would be referring to its own page numbers, from its own volumes of law reports, from its own National Reporter System publications."

On appeal, the District Court decision below granting the preliminary injunction, was affirmed by the United States Court of Appeals for the Eighth Circuit. In its "analysis", Judge Arnold, speaking for the Court (Judge John W. Oliver, Senior District Judge sitting by designation, concurred in part, and dissented in part), concurred in the District Court's conclusion that West's arrangement is a copyrightable aspect of its compilation of cases, that the pagination of West's volumes reflects and expresses West's arrangement, and that Mead Data's intended use of West's page numbers infringes West's copyright in the arrangement.

Noting that the case came to the appeals court from an order granting a preliminary injunction, and that the case has yet to be tried he added, "We trust it will be tried soon." . . . when it is tried, and when judgment is entered, another appeal can be filed. At that time it will be our duty to examine anew, on the basis of the full record, the issues discussed in this opinion . . . The District Court's findings and our observations as to the governing law made in this opinion, are tenntative and provisional, in the sense that different findings or conclusions might be warranted after a trial on the ments." 799F.2d at 1229.

In the interim, Mead Data has announced that it will use its own citation system, it calls "LEXIS Cites", available on line by early 1988. This system will make it possible to cite specific pages (screens) of all federal and state cases and administrative decisions appearing in

LEXIS. Additionally, this citation system will be incorporated into Auto Cite, making it possible to locate parallel citations for LEXIS documents. A LEXIS citation will consist of three parts: (1) the year of the decision; (2) an abbreviation for the source of jurisdiction; (3) the document accession number (renumbered consecutively each year in the order put on line). A LEXIS page equals 1200 characters or approximately one computer screen. Initially, all 1987 federal cases in LEXIS will be assigned LEXIS citations and cites will be assigned prospectively to all new documents (case and administrative decisions) entered into LEXIS during 1988. LEXIS citations will also be added retrospectively to older LEXIS documents.

Almost simultaneously with the LEXIS announcement, West Publishing Co. announced that it would add star pagination to WESTLAW.

WESTLAW's star pagination feature gives users parallel cites to the National Reporter System or the official U.S. Reports for any WESTLAW case that appears in the bond values of one of these reporters. The feature can be turned on or off by entering "star" or "x star".

As noted in the "AALL Newsletter":

Compared to LEXIS Cites, WESTLAW's star paging system offers users the advantage of being able to cite to traditional printed sources for most of the cases appearing in the WESTLAW databases; however, WESTLAW's star paging system excludes the many cases not published in the bound volumes of the National Reporter System. On the other hand, LEXIS Cites will offer users citations to all new cases entered into the LEXIS system as soon as they appear in Lexis, even though these citations will not be to traditional printed sources and will not immediately extend to cases decided prior to 1987; however, should West lose its copyright infringement case against Mead, a star paging system similar to WESTLAW's might be added to LEXIS Cites.

A basic need in legal research today is accessibility to legal and law-related information and documentation. To achieve this objective, innovative programs reflecting the tremendous potential of the new technology, such as Lexis and Westlaw, are being developed with striking success. The traditional tools of legal research are giving way to the hardware and software of this new technology to such an extent, that the law library of the future could be unrecognizable to researchers of today. Both Lexis and Westlaw should recognize the significant effect of these technological developments on their own programs, especially in the field of case reporting, and work out some sort of accommodation that reflects their best interests.

CHAPTER 6A

The Search for Comparative State Legislation

The following material comprises a new Chapter 6A for Legal Research and Law Library Management. *It is intended as supplemental material to the Main Text.*

It has been estimated that "as many as 130,000 different bills are introduced and up to 250,000 actions take place in the states and the federal legislatures in any given year." By reason of the disorganized manner in which information about these bills and actions is made available to the public, and the inadequate extrinsic finding aids that must be depended upon, lawyers who seek relevant comparative state legislation, both pending and in force, find the search an almost insurmountable task.

If only information about the laws in force of a specific state is sought, it is possible to check the subject indexes of the session laws or annotated code of the state, but they vary significantly in comprehensiveness, organization, and editorial effectiveness. However, if similar information is sought about the laws of other states, for comparative purposes, often the amount of time involved could be prohibitive.

A reference tool which offers a working index to the laws of the states in force on selected topics is the *Law Digest* volume of the annual *Martindale-Hubbell Law Directory.* This volume, however, only gives a brief digest of the law of the various states. It does provide citations to current statutory sources, so that the researcher then can check the full text in the state code involved. *The Annual Survey of American Law* (published annually since

1942 by New York University School of Law) is a good source for discussions of current state law on selected subjects. Its subject index, cumulated intermittently, is quite helpful. There are also annual surveys of the laws of a number of states, published usually by a law school in the state. The *Index to Legal Periodicals* refers to them under the name of the state. If a "uniform law" is involved, *Uniform Laws Annotated, Master Edition,* published by the West Publishing Company, publishes every uniform law adopted by at least one state, along with notes of the Commissioners on Uniform State Laws on these laws. The text of each act is set forth and is annotated section by section. A table of adopting states with statutory citations precedes every act. Under a section entitled "action in adopting jurisdiction," the editors indicate where the text of the uniform law varies from the text as adopted by a state. Annual pocket part supplementation keeps the set current. For comparative purposes, *Shepard's Acts and Cases by Popular Name, Federal and State* is valuable, as are some of the annotated state codes. *West's Louisiana Revised Statues,* for example, cites under various sections of the Code, similar legislation in other state codes.

Topical looseleaf services provide, at times, full texts of state laws in force on specific subjects. Digests of these laws with citations are usually given when the full text is not set forth. For example, Prentice-Hall, *Wills, Trusts and Estates Reporter, Commerce Clearing House, State Tax Reporters,* and Bureau of National Affairs, *Environmental Reporter* provide the full text of all state laws on the subjects they cover. The advantages of the looseleaf series in locating comparative state laws on specific topics is that their indexing is usually more comprehensive and detailed. In addition, they also provide relevant decisional law pertaining to the statute. Their weekly supplementation adds to the currency of the research. Then again, they also selectively provide information about pending legislation. The Bureau of National Affairs with its fifty or so daily, weekly, bi-weekly and monthly information services in legal, economic, business, labor, environmental and tax management fields, among others, attempts to provide comprehensive information on the legislative histories of these laws as well. Prentice-Hall and Commerce Clearing House provide similar information.

Commerce Clearing House, particularly, provides looseleaf services of significant value in the state and federal legislative fields. The *Congressional Index,* published by CCH in two volumes, is published weekly while the U.S. Congress is in session. Biennial editions at the beginning of each Congress, trace actions on all Public Bills and Resolutions from introduction to final disposition. It is indexed by topic, author and bill number. CCH *Congressional Legislative Reporting* allows the subscriber to select the subjects, and then provides the texts of bills, fast action reports, and official texts of laws. For comparative state legislation, the CCH *Advance Session Laws Reports* is a valuable research service. It provides periodic reports while the state legislatures are in session and includes full text reprints of pertinent new business and tax laws passed at regular and special sessions of the state legislatures. Reporting by subject and by state, its subscribers receive material officially released by the state. Another valuable, but highly priced service, is the CCH *State Legislative Reporting System.* For a minimum contract of $9,000 for two years, covering at least ten states, CCH allows the subscriber to select legislative subjects. CCH then issues periodic reports on those subjects from introduction to enactment, with bill texts, action reports, amendment texts and full texts of laws.

Straight, comprehensive indexing by subject to all state laws, both pending and current, is a much desired service legal researchers would welcome. There once was one entitled the *State Law Index* which was compiled and published biennially from 1925 to 1948 by the Legislative Reference Service of the Library of Congress. The service was discontinued when Congress failed to provide funds for its publication. It was not only a valuable service, but for most purposes the only comprehensive source of information for identifying by subject, laws enacted by various states during the period concerned. Entries were alphabetical by subject with a great variety of cross-references. Citations were to state, date of approval and inclusive pages, chapter and section of the acts. Entries under each subject heading were alphabetical by state. Unfortunately, the biennial volumes were not cumulative and each two year period had to be examined separately. But the wealth of information was such that law librarians to this day mourn its demise.

In the fields of social science, economics and sociology, many important new laws published by the states are indexed by *Public*

Affairs Information Service Bulletin (PAIS). A weekly bulletin, PAIS entries are by subject but not by jurisdiction. It offers some help in locating comparative state legislation. Then there is the *Monthly Checklist of State Publications,* known as the "Monthly Checklist." This is a rather good listing, but incomplete as it indexes only those state documents received monthly by the Library of Congress. There is an annual author and subject index.

For a while, an attempt was made to provide a similar service as that offered by the *State Law Index.* From 1963 to 1970, two new publications were started, but they died aborning. *Current State Legislation,* which was prepared by the American Bar Association, was superseded by the *Automated Statutory Reporter* and the *Aspen Computerized Law Index. Aspen* was replaced by the *Monthly Digest of Current Legislation,* which carried all currently enacted state and federal legislation of general application with brief abstracts of these laws. It also listed every word of substantive value in the abstracts as an index entry, alphabetically arranged. Unfortunately, its first issue appeared in July, 1971, and its last in March, 1972.

As part of this account of multi-state indexing by subject, Schultz, *Comparative Statutory Sources* (1973) should be noted as a guide to comparative sources for approximately 300 types of statutory provisions. Another excellent reference tool in this context is Foster and Boast, *Subject Compilations of State Laws* (1981). Subtitled a "Research Guide and Annotated Bibliography," it provides a comprehensive index to the statutes of all the states and an annotated bibliography of state laws arranged by subject.

The *Book of the States* is published biennially. It does not provide citations, but its Tables summarize the laws of the various states by subject, such as Sunset legislation, voting, marriage laws, medical malpractice and many other subjects. *American Jurisprudence 2d Desk Book* (1979) features tables covering state statutes of limitations for common actions, automobile guest laws, marriage and divorce laws and others. Unfortunately, citations to the statutes are not given. Law review articles can also be helpful in this context and they can be checked in the *Index to Legal Periodicals.*

Both Lexis and Westlaw provide full text coverage of state laws. But at this writing neither service covers all states of the United States.

Subscribes to *LEXIS* can also subscribe to *NEXIS*. This is a full text library of general and business news and information. The *NEXIS* library presently comprises a core group of leading publications and wire services and is being enlarged with additional newspapers, magazines, wire services, newsletters and other sources of information. Typically, newspapers are available the day after publication, weekly magazines one week after publication, monthly magazines three weeks after publication and wire services twelve to forty-eight hours after they are carried over the wire. As they appear in full text, references to current state legislation can be easily identified.

A new electronic legislative search system offered by Commerce Clearing House, and available to subscribers since February 1981, finally appears to be the answer for comprehensive searching of pending and current state law and federal law. Entitled *Electronic Legislative Search System* (*ELSS*), it provides on-line timely information on all types of legislative actions. Its computer containing its legislative data base, CCH claims, is probably compatible with most office electronic typewriter-printers or video-screens or computers. Contact with the CCH computer for the information needed is by telephone

ELSS monitors bills by subject and action taken on them in the committees and on the legislative floors of all of the fifty states and the U.S. Congress. It performs the legislative research and updates the subscriber daily on legislative actions. The *ELSS* database is available for research on a twenty-four hours-a-day, seven days-a-week basis. It provides on-line information about the introduction of bills, including bill descriptions, committee assignments and other action on bills, latest status reports, legislative histories of bills, subject searches, notice of enactment or defeat of bills, and hearing dates. Subscribers can select the legislative subjects and jurisdictions to be monitored. In addition, subscribers are provided direct "computer to computer" link up with CCH's legislative data base, permitting a search of any subjects selected in one or the other states and federal jurisdictions. As indicated above, CCH provides looseleaf services in its legislative reporting system. Now as Donald J. Hill of CCH notes, "This is the first time that we have been able to prepare and deliver our products electronically . . . the system gives our customers a good deal more flexibility; greater opportunity for information; and capabilities we couldn't offer until now." ELSS is indeed an electronic breakthrough, reflecting the enormmous potential of the new technology in legal research. It appears to be in the vanguard of the new "paperless" society.

CHAPTER 6B

Legislative Retrieval Systems—The New York Experience

The following material comprises a new Chapter 6B for Legal Research and Law Library Management. *It is intended as supplemental material to the Main Text.*

Lawyers who monitor current developments in the statutory law of New York will welcome a new on-line service. It is an outgrowth of an electronic information system created for the New York State Legislature by The New York State Legislative Bill Drafting Commission. Known as the *Legislative Retrieval System* (LRS), it allows the subscriber, with the use of its own computer hardware, to access official legislative information from selected portions of the computerized data bases of The Legislative Bill Drafting Commission.

This new service was authorized by Section 21 of Chapter 257 of the Laws of 1984, after proving successful on a trial basis in 1984. It provides timely, precise and accurate information tracing the course of a bill from introduction to enactment.

Of particular significance is the bill status service of LRS. As expressed by the Commission, "bill status is at your fingertips." The official and complete status of every bill and resolution is updated daily in the data base within a period of ten to fifteen minutes after any action occurs on the bill. Another advantage of LRS is that the search for bills and laws can be made by subject and it is not necessary to know the bill number of initiate the search. When necessary, a search can be made by sponsor, committee name, bill number or topic. Current Senate and Assembly floor calendars and schedules of public hearings can also be retrieved almost spontaneously. The Legislator's (Prime, Co-sponsored, Multi-sponsored) Introduction Records are also available through the master data base. A researcher can also locate a bill which has been reintroduced into the current session of the legislature although the researcher knows only the bill number from a previous session of the legislature.

Another unique feature of the LRS service is its capability of storing searches so that the subscriber can create its own files on groups of special interest bills or research bills by subject matter through a cross-reference system. A researcher is capable of following one hundred bills in a self-created file, which can be checked each day, week or month for current status, without punching in each bill every time its status is to be checked. Another advantage of the system is that currently introduced and amended bills can be obtained through LRS even before they are available at the respective document rooms.

In addition to checking the status of the bills, the LRS also provides full text of all current legislation immediately upon introduction of the bill, including sponsorship information. Unfortunately, the LRS data base as yet, does not include Governor's Memoranda or Governor's Bill Jackets. The Bill Drafting Commission, however, is prepared to provide this service if the demand warrants it.

Another commendable feature of the LRS service is that a combination data base allows the researcher to search current Chapter Laws and Consolidated Laws in one operation. Of significance too for research purposes that the full text of the Consolidated Laws of New York, selected Unconsolidated Laws and the complete Administrative Code of the City of New York can all be searched.

Access to the service is provided to the subscriber between the hours of 8:00am and 7:30pm, or one-half hour after the adjournment of the last adjourning house of the legislature, if later, every day except Saturdays, Sundays and legal holidays. In the event the Legislature or either house is in session on week-end days or holidays, access is provided on those days.

Subscribers are charged an annual connection fee of $1500 for initial access and $1000 for each additional terminal sign-on to be used by the subscriber.

Following are LRS data bases which can be accessed by the subscriber and the use charges computed on the basis of the amount of connection time used by it during each month:

Data Base	*Hourly Rate*
(a) Text of the Consolidated Laws and such other laws as the Commission may add from time to time	$ 25
(b) Text of the chapters of the Session Laws	$ 18
(c) Text of the Administrative Code of the City of New York and the New York City Charter	$ 25
(d) Bills:	
(i) Text of bills	$ 25
(ii) Bill status data	$ 15
(iii) Record of bills introduced by each member of the Legislature	$ 15
(iv) Summaries of all bills	$ 18
(v) Legislative calendars and schedules of public hearings for both houses of the Legislature	$ 14
(vi) On-line bill status	$ 17

It should be noted that these rates do not include long distance telephone charges which amount to approximately 58¢ for the first three minutes and 35¢ for every minute thereafter. However, when a subscriber has paid for a cumulative total of at least 200 hours of connection time, the rates are reduced by 10%. Then again, a subscriber is given ten complimentary hours of connection time per month to the on-line bill status data base as part of the annual fee of $1500. After the original ten hours of connection time are used, the hourly rate of $17 is charged monthly for additional connection time.

The New York State Legislative Bill Drafting Commission conducted a study to determine how much it would cost to use the LRS for a period of twenty-six weeks for four hours a day and concluded that it would amount to approximately $2000. To this sum must be added the initial connection fee of $1500, usage time and telephone charges.

It is important to note that the subscribers' equipment must be compatible to interface with the LRS computer system. The terminal or microcomputer (with software) must look like one of the following:

ADDS	Regent 20, 25, 40, 60, 100 and 200 Viewpoint*
DEC	VT52 and VT100
IBM	3101
Lear Siegler-	ADM 1A, 2, 3A, 3A+, 5*, 31, 32* and 42
Hazeltine	1400, 1410, 1420, 1421, 1500, 1510, 1520, 1552, Esprit, Executive 80 and Modular 1
Telex	310
Colographics	-MVI-100*
Northern Telecom-	Displayphone*
Tymnet	Scanset 410* and 415*

*In case of a micro-computer installation, the subscriber must add software which will make its computer look like one of the above. In addition to the above, a telecommunication modem compatible with the Bell 212A capable of data transmission at 1200 baud and a RS232 cable of no longer than twenty-five feet are required.

This is another example of how the traditional tools of research are giving way to the new techniques of electronic document-storage and computerized information retrieval systems.

Of course, timely information about laws currently being enacted and proposed in New York, can still be obtained in the traditional manner.

The New York Legislative Record and Index, from 1902 to 1984 provided a comprehensive history of each bill introduced in the Senate and Assembly. It presented summaries of all bills in order of introductory numbers, with detailed record of action, printed number tables, subject index of resolutions, bills and laws, bills vetoed by the Governor, standing committees of Senate and Assembly and other relevant information about the legislative process.

Beginning with the 1985 term of The New York State Legislature, a new legislative service took its place, entitled *The State of New York Legislative Digest,* distributed by the Hamilton Printing Company. *The Legislative Digest* is published by the New York State Legislative Bill Drafting Commission as part of its program to prepare and monitor the legislative activities of both chambers of the N.Y. State Legislature. In essence, the *Legislative Digest* is the Commission's official version of this activity. The Commission has recently announced that the 1985 *Legislative Digest* contains more information than was available in *The New York Legislative Record and Index*—and is being offered at a new low price.

The daily sheets and weekly cumulative bound volumes comprising the *Legislative Digest* contain copies of the documents officially distributed to the members of the Assembly and the Senate. They are mailed to subscribers the same day they are delivered to the legislature for distribution. They contain a concise summary of each bill and resolution introduced that day in the legislature as well as a journal of action taken thereon by the legislature. The summary of the bill includes the name of the introducer, bill number, section numbers of the law or laws affected if the bill is passed and the committee to which the bill is referred. The daily journal sheets contain one line descriptions of the bills for reference and the action taken thereon by the legislature on that day.

The weekly bound cumulative volumes not only add a compilation of all bills and resolutions introduced to date, but also the following information:

Assembly action on Senate bills
Assembly bills passed by Assembly
Senate bills passed by Assembly
Assembly bills delivered to the Governor
Assembly bills signed by the Governor
Assembly bills vetoed by the Governor
Senate action on Assembly bills
Senate bills passed by the Senate
Assembly bills passed by the Senate
Senate bills delivered to the Governor
Senate bills signed by the Governor
Senate bills vetoed by the Governor
Members' introduction record
Subject index of resolutions introduced
Subject index of bills introduced
Subject index of laws of 1985
Print number table
Cross reference table of 1985 laws
Chapter effective dates

Bills vetoed by Governor (including veto messages)
Public hearings
Senate confirmations
Executive orders
Memorandums of approval
Proposed amendments to constitution

It should be noted that approval memorandums, veto messages and executive orders are also included in the Digest's weekly volumes. The weekly volumes also feature a helpful subject index of bills introduced and its annual companion subject index of laws. Although these indexes facilitate the search for bills and laws of specific interest to the researcher, they can be improved. The subject categories used in the index are much too broad. A more liberal use of "see" and "see also" references could help pinpoint the search process. For example in the January 9 to January 18, 1985 issue, unless the researcher knew that residential rent control references could be found under the subject, *New York City Administrative Code*, they could only be identified by carefully scanning the Bill Summaries for the Assembly and Senate.

A critical note: the computer print-out used as copy for the contents of the weekly *Legislative Digest* is barely legible. Compared with any West Publishing Company product, on a scale of one to ten, it rates a weak "two."

An annual cumulative bound volume is being published as part of the service.

Daily Amendment Sheets, which include the full text of amendments to bills, are available as a separate service. The cost for this service is $150 for an initial twenty weeks, plus a $10 additional weekly charge for each week the legislative session continues beyond May.

Recapitulating, the complete *Legislative Digest* service consists of three components:

—The daily legislative information sheets
—The weekly bound volumes; and
—The annual bound volume.

The complete Digest Service costs $1000 for a twenty-week subscription. If the legislative session continues beyond May, the subscription will be extended on a week-to-week basis at a cost of $50 per week.

The components of the service can also be purchased separately as follows:

—Daily Sheets (Summaries and Journals $450.00 plus $20.00 a week beyond May 2)
—Weekly Bound Volumes and Annual Bound Volume with supplements. ($600.00 plus $30.00 a week beyond May)
—Annual Bound Volume with supplements, $100.00

The *New York Legislative Service* should also be noted in this context as a central legislative information service for New York State and New York City. It services its subscribers by providing general research service as well as bill copies and memos, Legislative Documents (1934 to present), opinions of the Attorney General and the Comptroller (prior and current) and the opinions of the Court of Appeals. Its weekly report lists bill introductions, weekly actions, Committee and Commission hearings and other state legislative activities. Its *New York State Legislative Annual* compiles primary source material on New York State Legislation, such as pertinent memoranda prepared by agencies or individuals initiating or recommending particular legislation, as well as the Governor's approval messages and veto messages.

For those who subscribe to a general membership, other services are provided, such as Governors' Bill Jackets and Veto Jackets, at a discount. Its Legislative Service for New York State costs $600 plus $15 per day for each day that the legislature is in session after July 1. Its Legislative Service for New York City costs $475 annually. Its Bill Jacket Service requires an initial payment of $500, which includes thirty bill jackets. After the first thirty, bill jackets will be furnished at a reduced rate of $30, plus 30¢ a page. Non-members are charged $70 per bill jacket plus 40¢ per page. Its New York City Local Law Index costs about $150 annually.

Of course, no general recital of legislative services in New York can be complete without referring to *McKinney's Session Law News of New York*, published by West Publishing Company. It features "authentic text of the laws together with other valuable legislative and executive materials," such as legislative memoranda, Governor's memoranda and messages and judiciary memoranda. The *New York Consolidated Law Service*, published by the Lawyer's Cooperative, offers a similar service.

CHAPTER 11

Access to Public Records

The following material comprises an addition to Chapter 11 of Legal Research and Law Library Management. *It is intended to be read in conjunction with the material in the Main Text.*

The Fourth Annual Report of the New York State Committee on Public Access to Records was issued pursuant to Section 89(1)(b)(V) of the Public Officers Law on December 3, 1981. Besides its other valuable information on the New York State's Freedom of Information Law, it is an excellent reference source for lawyers concerned with the legal effect of the law.

When the Committee on Public Access to Records was created by the enactment of the Freedom of Information Law in 1974, New York joined a number of states and the federal government in the trend toward ensuring open and accountable government.

As the Committee believes that one of the more important functions it can offer is the preparation of written advisory opinions on the implementation of the Freedom of Information Law, an official record has been created which is of significant research value to lawyers. To suggest the scope of this service, during the initial years, approximately 200 advisory opinions were written annually. In 1980, 496 written advisory opinions were prepared. As of November 4, 1981, 429 written advisory opinions were rendered by the Committee. Based upon that figure, it is anticipated that nearly 500 written advisory opinions will have been prepared under the Freedom of Information Law in 1981.

Among the 429 opinions prepared by November 4, 1981, the total by groups is as follows:

Public	309
State Agency Officials	29

Local Government Officials	73
Representatives of the News Media	18

These written opinions were rendered in addition to 4,118 oral communications regarding the interpretation of the Freedom of Information Law by November 4, 1981.

The Committee believes that part of the success and the utility of the Freedom of Information Law is due to the activist role that it has taken, especially with reference to the facility with which it offers guidance to the public, state agency officials, local government officials and representatives of the news media on the implementation of the law. In addition, the Committee rightfully asserts that due to the thousands of oral and written opinions given each year, the Committee has acted both directly and indirectly as a mediator and educator. By mediating when disputes arise, the Committee has often helped to avoid litigation, thereby saving money for individual taxpayers who might otherwise seek judicial review of a denial of access to records, and for taxpayers generally, who must pay for the government's legal representation in court.

Of research value to lawyers, in this context, is the fact that the Committee publishes a subject index to its written advisory opinions. Until 1979, the index identified opinions by means of approximately 200 "key phrases." Due to the substantial volume of opinions, which total more than 2,200, and the need for greater specificity of the subjects involved, the index has been updated on an ongoing basis. The current index identifies written opinions by means of nearly 375 "key phrases" and is attached as Appendix II to the Committee's Report rendered to the Governor.

Copies of the opinions in their entirety are distributed monthly to various libraries across the state and are also available from the Committee directly. To suggest the wide variety of subject matter to be found in these advisory opinions, note the following "key phrases" describing the subject content of the Committee's opinions in interpreting the Freedom of Information Law.

Abandoned Property
Accident Reports
Adopted Children
Appraisals

Assessment Information
Attendance Records
Attorney-Client Privilege
Attorney, Compensation of
Attorney, Disciplinary Proceeding Against
Attorney Work Product
Autopsy Reports
Birth Records, Relating to Adoption
Confidentiality, Assertion of
Constriction with Other Laws
Creation of Records
Examination Questions and Answers
Governmental Privilege
Home Address, Public Employee
Hospital Records
Interest of Applicant
Law Enforcement Purposes
Litigation, Records Related to
Medical Records
Payroll Information
Police Blotters
Privacy
Statistical or Factual Data
Time Limits for Response
Trade Secrets

Another valuable reference service provided by the Committee in its Report is designated as Appendix III. It is an alphabetical listing of judicial determinations involving interpretations of the Freedom of Information law of which the Committee is aware. The listing includes a brief summary of the determinations as well. Citations to the reporter, the New York Law Journal or the identity of the court when the case is unreported, add to the value of this case summary. Because the Freedom of Information law was amended effective January 1, 1978, the Committee warns that determinations made prior to 1978 may in some instances be subject to reversal or modification under the revised provisions of the law. Therefore provisions of the law, both in its original form and as amended are cited and distinguished as the ''original law'' and the ''current law.'' Following are some samples:

People & C. v. Billy Billups, Sup. Ct., Queens County; Criminal Term, N.Y.L.J., July 13, 1981—Freedom of Information Law could not be used by litigant, in this case a convicted criminal defendant, to circumvent proper times and procedures for criminal discovery set forth in Art. 240 of the Criminal Procedure Law; see also *Burke v. Yudelson*. Current Law.

New York Public Interest Research Group v. Greenberg, Sup. Ct., Albany City, April 27, 1979.

Office of District Attorney is subject to the provisions of Freedom of Information Law. Agency has the burden of proving that the records sought fall within the exclusionary scope of §87(2); *in camera* inspection made, records found available since investigation terminated. Current Law: § 87(2)(e), § 84, § 89(4)(b), § 86(3).

Useful notes are added as well. For example, with respect to a case *Doolan v. Boces*, 48 N.Y.2d 341 (1979), in which the Court of Appeals held that salary and fringe benefit data compiled by one agency for the use and information of another are available,[1] the Committee notes:

> "Court of Appeals appears to have abolished the 'governmental privilege' (see *Cirale v. 80 Pine Street, Corp.*, 35 N.Y.2d 113 (1974), stating that '[T]he public policy concerning governmental disclosure is fixed by the Freedom of Information law. The common-law interest privilege cannot protect from disclosure materials which that law requires to be disclosed. Meeting the public's legitimate right of access to information concerning government is fulfillment of a governmental obligation, not the gift of, or waste of, public funds.')"

Often an advisory opinion prepared by the Committee is highly persuasive authority, useful in avoiding litigation. There have been numerous situations in which advice prepared by the Committee following a determination on appeal has resulted in a settlement, negating the necessity of litigation. In this role as a

[1] Doolan v. Boces, 48 N.Y.2d 341 (1979).

mediator, the Committee provides a useful service resulting in settlements rather than litigation in the matter involved.

The Committee on Public Access to Records has much to be proud of as it continues providing such excellent basic support to the implementation of the Freedom of Information Law as required by the Law. It is with good reason that James T. O'Reilly in the 1981 edition of *Federal Information Disclosure* commends the work of the Committee as models for other jurisdictions:

> "New York's Committee, a low budget operation, is both a pioneer and a state role model. It is a pioneer in resolving state-level questions, and it can provide the federal agencies with precedents of useful thinking on questions similar to those which will arise before the federal agencies. The Committee's reports of cases are a helpful source to relevant case law and are exceptionally well organized."

The Committee on Public Access to Records will provide a copy of its annual report on request. Address requests to 162 Washington Avenue, Albany, New York 12231. (Tel:) (518) 474-2518, 2791.

CHAPTER 11A

Public Access to Federal Government Data: A Saga of Reduced Services, Increased Charges and Lost Information

The following material comprises a new Chapter 11A for Legal Research and Law Library Management. *It is intended as supplemental material to the Main Text.*

Public access to government information is in greater jeopardy today than at any time since the founding of the Republic. The dictator countries suppress information through censorship, expropriation of publishers' property, imprisonment and torture. The "American Way" is more subtle. Taxpayer-funded information is simply "buried." The federal government has reduced publishing services, increased charges for those limited services, and all too often, lost information.

Item: The *Second Annual Report on Eliminations, Consolidations, and Cost Reductions of Government Publications* released on January 6, 1984 by the Office of Management and Budget, (OMB) reported the elimination of 2,387 federal government publications and the proposed consolidation of another 561. The total of eliminations and consolidations equaled 3,848 publications or one-fourth of the total inventory. These publications accounted for over 150 million copies or 15% of all copies printed by the federal government. In addition, federal agencies proposed 5,020 cost-reduction actions on 3,070 other publications including reducing the volume, frequency of issue, use of color, and other printing and distribution cost reductions. Thereafter, the OMB planned to establish new publication elimination and cost reduction goals for the remaining 9,000 publications in the government inventory of 15,900 publications by issuing new guidelines.

Item: A 300 percent increase in the cost of an annual subscription to the *Federal Register*—from $75 to $300—went into effect in March, 1982. In 1981, the price of a year's subscription to the *Congressional Record* increased from $75 to $208.

Item: Many federal government publications formerly distributed free are now available only for a fee and government agencies are being persuaded by OMB to start charging prices high enough to recover their costs. As an example, the Agriculture Departments' Economic Research Service, because of budget costs, stopped free distribution of its publications and made these reports available only on a paid subscription basis.

Item: The government's two biggest collectors of statistics, the Census Bureau and the Bureau of Labor Statistics have cut programs because of budget reductions. The *Washington Post* in a news article of May 4, 1982 quoted a business leader testifying at a congressional subcommittee hearing in March 1982 to the effect that "a million dollars saved today through short-sighted reductions in the budgets for statistical programs could lead to erroneous decisions that would cost the private and public sectors billions of dollars over the long run."

Item: In November 1981, the Securities Exchange Commission discontinued publication of the *Securities and Exchange Commission News Digest*. The SEC continues to print it for internal use, but does not make it available to the public by subscription or through depository library distribution. Instead, a private firm publishes it at a 50% increase in price from $100 to $150 per year.

Item: After being published by the Commerce Department's Office of Federal Statistical Policy and Standards for forty-five years, in July 1984, *The Federal Statistical Directory* was published by a private publisher. When the Government Printing Office sold the 1979 edition, the most recent then available from the government, it charged $5.00. The private publisher updated the 1979 version, added an index and appendix and charged $14.95.

Item: Federal agencies are publishing notices in *The Federal Register* announcing increased fees to the public for record retrieval including Freedom of Information Act requests. The increased fees implement the policy to recover the direct costs of document search and duplication, but can be high when an individual requests information which must be retrieved by computer. For example, the U.S. Postal Service published standard charges for system utilization services in the October 29, 1984 *Federal Register* (p. 43468). The service charges ranged from $189 to $1,827 per hour. Dedicated use of a 370/135 costs $15,704 per accounting period. Peripheral charges vary from $.01 per frame for office microfilm processing to $2,960 per accounting period for inspection service processing. Even the cost of a manual search can be high when an agency charges a $9 per hour search fee and estimates that a search will require 100 hours.

Item: In November 1984, the *Chemical Information System* (CIS), with its twenty chemical databases of physical and regulatory data, which the Environmental Protection Agency (EPA) has operated since 1973, was given to two private contractors. Each contractor operates a different system, hence users will be forced to subscribe to both to ensure access to what they could previously get from the CIS. Users also are concerned that unprofitable but scientifically valuable components of the system are likely to be dropped.

Item: The Merit Systems Protection Board no longer publishes the full text of its decisions in bound volumes. Users are referred to private sector sources for MSPB decisions. The *Federal Register* for March 4, 1985 (p.8684-8685) lists private publishers which offer the MSPB decisions in various formats, not all of which include the complete decisions, at prices ranging from $250 to $498 per year. The bound volumes in the past were provided at no charge to 472 depository libraries, including thirty-seven federal libraries.

Item: The Bureau of Labor Statistics has reduced the *Monthly Labor Review* to a quarterly publication. It has also eliminated the *Handbook of Labor Statistics and Productivity and Manufacturing*.

Item: The former U.S. Court of Claims published its *Cases Decided* through the Government Printing Office. As a result, copies were distributed to 557 depository libraries and about 300 copies were sold by the Superintendent of Documents for about $82 in 1982, the last year they were published. The reports of the U.S. Court of Claims are now being published commercially for $219 for six volumes to make the set current. It is estimated that it will cost $102 per year for new issues.

Item: Bechtel North American Power Corporation was awarded a contract to record SEC filings onto microfilm and disseminate them. Starting October 1, 1985, Bechtel is providing an estimated 250,000 microfiche annually to the SEC's public reference rooms. Bechtel, according to the *Washington Post* for May 29, 1985, is expected to earn between $4 million and $6 million a year from sales of the information, depending on the number of filings.

Item: *The Deficit Reduction Act of 1984* required that all federal agencies reduce their publication expenditures and output by 29.7% in fiscal 1985. As a result important federal publications were eliminated or distributed in such limited copies that adequate national coverage is impossible. For example, National Bureau of Standards (NBS) Handbook 133, entitled *Checking the Net Contents of Packaged Goods*, provides information required by the *Fair Labeling and Packaging Act*. In the past, NBS issued a *Field Manual* to the *Handbook* for the use of weights and measures officials in the fifty states. Both the *Handbook* and the *Field Manual* were delivered to depository libraries. In 1985, however, because of the *Deficit Reduction Act's* mandate to reduce government publications by 29.7%, NBS photocopied fifty copies of the *Field Manual* and sent one to each state. Depository libraries did not receive a copy, nor is it available as a formal NBS publication. Carol Turner, Head of Government Documents at Stanford University Libraries, advised a Congressional Subcommittee on July 17, 1985 that:

> "If the NBS examples are indicative of the cuts in other federal agencies, it will not take long before state and local government officials will find themselves deprived of essential federal information formerly available in publications issued on a regular, consistant, and long-term basis. . . . Because of the Act and OMB policy on restricting government publications and information dissemination activities, it will take nothing short of a minor miracle to assure future continuity and stability in the flow of information and publications from executive agencies to the American public."

This litany of reduction and elimination of federal government publications and accessibility to government generated information has aroused the library and academic community. The American Library Association has taken on a "watch-dog" role in monitoring this emerging trend, recognizing how significant the impact will be on the quantity and quality of federal information which will be available to policy makers and to the public. It also is concerned with the accelerating tendency of federal agencies to use computer and telecommunications technologies for data collection, storage, retrieval and dissemination. "While automation clearly offers promises of savings," it warns, "will public access to government information be further restricted for people who cannot afford computers or cannot pay for computer time? A few of the factors which will influence the answer to this question are: contractual arrangements with commercial firms to disseminate information collected at taxpayer expense, increased user charges for government information, the trend toward having increasing amounts of government information available in electronic format only and the elimination of the printed version."

And now—we have OMB Circular No. A-130, which provides a general framework for Management of Federal Information resources. The *Circular*, issued by the Office of Management and Budget Executive Office of the President, implements provisions of the Paperwork Reduction Act of 1980 (P.L. 96-511, 94 Stat. 2812, 44 U.S.C. Ch. 35), as well as other statutes, executive orders and policies concerning general information policy, information technology, privacy and maintenance of federal records. The Paperwork Reduction Act delegates authority to the OMB to develop and implement uniform and consistent federal information resources management policies. OMB Circular No. A-130 is based on OMB Draft Circular on the Management of Federal Information Resources which appeared in the March 15 1985 *Federal Register*. At that time, the OMB invited the public to comment on the draft proposal. It received about 350 letters. Of that number 52% came from the library and academic community, 28% were from other members of the public and 20% from federal agencies and members of Congress. Although the OMB was urged to revise the draft and issue the revision for another round of public comment because of the perceived serious deficiencies in the draft circular, it decided instead to publish a final version, OMB Circular No. A-130, in the December 24, 1985 issue of the *Federal Register* with corrections in the January 6, 1986 *Federal Register*. Circular No. A-130 went into effect on December 12, 1985.

In essence, the thrust of the circular is to achieve a sharp reduction in the federal government's efforts to collect and distribute statistics about all aspects of American life. Federal agencies are limited by the OMB to "create or collect only that information necessary for the proper performance of agency functions and that has practical utility, and only after planning for its processing, transmission, dessemination, use, storage and disposition [*8(a)(i)*]; Seek to satisfy new information needs . . . through commercial sources, where appropriate before creating or collecting new information [*8(a)(2)(ii)*]; In order to minimize the cost and maximize the usefulness of government information activities, the expected public and private benefits derived from government information, insofar as they are calculable, should exceed the public and private costs of information [*7(d)*]."

The OMB claims that Circular No. A-130 as revised, accommodated valid criticisms and objections addressed to the Draft Circular. The library and academic community, on the contrary, continues to take issue with the obvious effect of the policy reflected in the circular which "would likely reduce," as expressed in an editorial in the *Washington Post* of December 23, 1985, "the number of printed government publications available in libraries or at low cost and increase the already widespread practice of private outfits interfacing with government computers and providing printouts for users at hefty fees."

Although OMB Circular No. A-130 does reflect some of the criticisms addressed to the Draft circular, still, as expressed by the American Library Association (ALA) it "establishes official government policy which will sharply reduce the federal government's efforts to collect and disseminate information to the public, and will accelerate the current trend toward the commercialization and privatization of government information."

The ALA also cautions that there are other factors which are likely to restrict federal government information, such as OMB Circular A-3, entitled *Government Publications*, which requires federal agency heads to submit annually to OMB for approval a list of current and proposed periodicals, with detailed justification for proposed periodicals. Also, to be watched carefully, is the manner in which the revision of other OMB Circulars will be accomplished, especially those closely related to Circular A-130, such as Circular A-76 (Performance of Commercial Activities) and Circular A-25 (User charges).

What is of deep concern to the library and academic community is that despite its strong condemnation, Circular No. A-130 still requires cost-benefit analysis of government information activities, "maximum feasible reliance on the private sector" for the dissemination of government information products and services, and cost recovery through user charges when appropriate.

Although Circular No. A-130 is not a regulation and therefore does not have the force of law, still it is a presidential policy directive to executive agencies which provides a general policy framework for the management of federal information resources. As expressed by the

ALA, "agencies ignore it at their peril. The Director of OMB will use fiscal budget reviews and other measures to evaluate agency compliance with the circular."

This government policy must inevitably have an adverse effect not only on scholarly research generally, but on the research of the legal profession. The concerns of the ALA with Circular No. A-130 should become those of the legal profession. These are:

(1) The circular directs agencies to disseminate information only when it is either required by law or necessary for the proper performance of agency functions and only when it will not duplicate current or potential similar products or services provided by other government agencies or private sector organizations. These restrictive conditions can place insurmountable barriers between the public and government information.

(2) Agencies are to place maximum feasible reliance on the private sector for dissemination of the products or services, a reliance that can lead to the dissemination of only that information with strong profit potential in the market place. The private sector is under no obligation to make government information available to the American public at an affordable price, nor to keep that information easily accessible and readily available. A gap based on ability to pay between information "haves" and "have-nots" can easily evolve. Such a gap unfairly limits individual opportunity in a free and democratic society.

(3) The circular states that access would be provided consistent with the Freedom of Information Act (FOIA). Yet there are members of the legislative and executive branches who have been trying to broaden the exemptions to FOIA, increase fees for its use, and make it more difficult for the public to use the Act.

(4) The circular directs federal agencies to create or collect *only* that information necessary for proper performance of agency functions. Will information not mandated by agency mission no longer be available? If so, government information needed by citizens will be cut off effective at the source.

Another major objection to the circular is the uncertainty over the application of the information management principles that it sets forth. As expressed by Congressman Glenn English, Chairman of the House

Subcommittee on Government Operations, in a letter addressed to the OMB dated, May 15, 1985:

> "Overall, I find the principles set out in the circular to be very general and therefore very difficult to evaluate in the abstract. There is nothing in the circular that indicates how the principles would be applied by agencies in practice or what specific programs would be affected. . . . Someone who relies regularly on a government publication can find nothing in the draft that constitutes reasonable assurance that the publication will be continued. This uncertainty extends to all government publication programs, major and minor."

The issue, as the Director of the Boston Public Library, Arthur Curley, sees it, in the address he gave to the *Annual Congress for Librarians* at St. John's University on February 17, 1986, is that society is at a point of crisis. Modern technology has brought us closer and closer to the point of universal access, but a conflict of interest exists. The largest collector of information, the United States Government, is also the disseminator of that information. Therefore, the government might be tempted to limit or exclude embarrassing information. Under the authority of the Paper Reduction Act, the government has shifted the responsibility of information dissemination to the private sector. At present there are no built-in safeguards to protect against price-gouging by a contractor who has a monopoly over a particular database. The private contractor operates on the profit motive. He is not required to set democratic social goals. The government will not pay for the incurred user charges. How can a price be placed on the value of an informed democracy? Paying lower taxes cannot be our only social goal.

Appropriately, the theme of the 1986 Annual Congress for Librarians, sponsored by the Division of Library and Information Science and the School of Continuing Education of St. John's University was "*Information Poverty: Unequal Access to the World's Information.*"

CHAPTER 11B

Hidden Sources of Law and Lore: Local, State and Federal Rules and Regulations

The following material comprises a new Chapter 11B for Legal Research and Law Library Management. *It is intended as supplemental material to the Main Text.*

Lurking in some 300 dry, legal tomes is a remarable literature that helps to catalog and tries to control the nonviolent wickedness of the human race. These sources are three in number: (1) a vast array of rules and regulations of New York City agencies, issued in a variety of formats from looseleaf binders to simple typescripts; (2) the New York State *Official Compilation of Codes, Rules and Regulations* (NYCCRR); and (3) the 185-volume *Code of Federal Regulations* (CFR).

These three collections are more than compilations of establishment rules. They contain bibliographies, job finding aids, and specialized training for lawyers. In addition, they are a *World Almanac* of unexpected facts, particularly on scientific subjects—air and water pollution, food additives and prescription or generic drugs.

[1]—Local Regulations

More than fifty separate New York City agencies have promulgated rules. One compilation alone has been selected for comment here. It is a veritable encyclopedia of human wickedness and a worthy battery of rules to combat it. That is the best way to describe the huge red binder and its contents, titled *Laws and Regulations, City of New York Department of Consumer Affairs.*[1]

---

[1] Issued by the Department in early 1988, it can be consulted in numerous libraries in New York and at the Department's offices at 80 Lafayette Street, New

In one sense this publication is the collective biography of Fagin, Ponzi and the inventor of Three Card Monte. However, in fact, it is New York's valiant effort "for the protection and relief of the public from deceptive, unfair and unconscionable practices, for the maintenance of standards of integrity, honesty and fair dealing . . . for the protection of the health and safety of the people of New York City. . . ."[2]

The Department wisely chose "Fingerprinting" for its first regulation in Chapter One.[3] It covers some ten trades, peopled one must assume by occasional artful dodgers and confidence persons. Three of those trades: TV service dealers, home improvement contractors (including sales people), and process servers.

Members of these ten trades, after fingerprinting, may be licensed for two years, the term being staggered for each trade. On February 28, each year all process servers must renew their licenses. Anyone who has a complaint about "sewer service" (this is akin to postal carriers' consigning the contents of their mailbags to a trash can) should mark a big red circle around that date on the calendar.

Reading forward a few hundred pages one reaches Chapter 3, "Weights and Measures."[4] Bearing in mind one's childhood memories of a smiling butcher with his thumb pressing down innocently on the scale, it is reassuring to peruse this twenty-three-page section.[5] A few extracts:

> "A hanging scale shall be suspended from a stationary support, so that the face or dial of the scale is in full view of the public."[6]
>
> "'Customer Scales' shall be color-striped in red in such a manner as to permit them to be readily located. The stripes shall be no less than one half inch nor more than two inches in width."[7] This

---

York, N.Y. 10007. It can be purchased at Citibooks for $50 either in the Municipal Building, Room 2223, or at 47 Chambers Street in New York.

[2] Section 20-101 New York City Administrative Code.

[3] of this compilation.

[4] *Id.*

[5] *Id.* The Bible calls this ancient practice an "Abomination"—Deuteronomy 26, Verse 16.

[6] *Id.*, Ch. 3, Reg. 3(a).

[7] *Id.*, Ch. 3, Reg. 3(f)(4).

is part of a series of rules requiring that those scales used to check on a butcher's accuracy be both accesible and visible.

To justify use of the term "Jumbo", a dozen eggs must weigh 30 or more ounces. If "Extra Large"—27 to 30 ounces, "Medium" —21 to 24 ounces. The Department specifies six gradations of egg sizes.[8]

"There shall be no colored lights or spotlights in, on near or above the meat display case or showcase which make the food products contained therein look better than they actually are."[9]

Chapter 4 is designed to protect consumers from various nefarious practices in the sale of solid fuel, hamburgers and chopped meats, prepackaged meat and perishable foods.[10]

It is Chapter 5 "Unfair Trade Practices"[11] that has the most human appeal. Here are regulated "Deceptive Classified Ads" (Regulation 205), "Limited Editions" (Regulation 206) and "Refund Policy" (Regulation 407).

The rules go intro great specificity as to goods temporarily in short supply.[12] They carefully distinguish between "deceptive" and "unconscionable" practices.[13] Jewelry dealers and appraisers get strict attention[14] as do mail-order sellers,[15] deliverers of furniture and major appliances,[16] and repairers of consumer goods.[17] On a lighter note, there are even rules relating to "Out of Context Quotes" (Regulation 520). Let the play producer or publisher beware if he subtly exaggerates or rearranges a critic's "language in a way that alters the critic's meaning.[18]

For a panoramic view of human wickedness—and even wretchedness—caused by deceptive and unconscionable commercial behav-

---

[8] *Id.*, Ch. 3, Reg. 23.
[9] *Id.*, Ch. 3, Reg. 44.
[10] *Id.*
[11] *Id.*
[12] *Id.*, Ch. 5, Reg. 408.
[13] *Id.*, Subparagraphs (c) and (d).
[14] *Id.*, Ch. 5, Reg. 502.
[15] *Id.*, Ch. 5, Reg. 503.
[16] *Id.*, Ch. 5, Reg. 505.
[17] *Id.*, Ch. 5, Reg. 509.
[18] Id., Ch. 5, Reg. 520, Subparagraph (b).

ior, first prize goes to the big red watchdog books: *Laws and Regulations, City of New York, Department of Consumer Affairs*. It is a model storehouse of regulatory facts.

[2]—State Sources

In addition to the numerous layers of city rules, the State of New York has issued its own sixty-one volume set of rules and regulations that occupies fourteen feet of shelf space and is supplemented every three months. It carefully spells out the requirements for conducting business, professional, farming, government and educational affairs. It appears to regulate almost every other phase of human activity as well.

Looking at the ABC's of it, the State regulates abandoned property, barber shops and beauty parlors, the bacterial count of dairy products, cable TV, and the cultivation and marketing of cherries. In the WXYZ's it regulates wrestling, the use of X-rays, the protection and conduct of youth and the problems of zoning in connection with fire protection. However, its hidden sources provide an education on a variety of subjects that rival the offerings in the New School catalog. Some examples:

Case Notes. Appearing at the end of each volume, some are unique and not even to be found in *Shepard's Citations to New York Codes, Rules and Regulations*.

Civil Service Exemptions. There are hundreds of jobs that one may obtain in New York State government without competing for them through a civil service examination. These are the jobs for which ". . . examinations or other qualification requirements are not practicable."[19] An appendix to this title lists the kinds of jobs that are "free" or noncompetitive for each state agency. Among the "free" jobs are agriculture promotion specialists, public relations officers and assistants in Audit and Control, Commerce Department directors for various cities, even stenographers and affirmative action officers in the Motor Vehicle Department. The Thruway Authority even exempts electricians, welders, minority business specialists, trainees and secretary-stenographers (regarded as confidential).[20]

---

[19] NYS Off. Comp. of Codes, Rules and Regulations, Title 4, Civil Service 2.1.
[20] *Id.*

Forms. An imaginative lawyer could learn how to practice before a number of specialized New York courts simply by studying the forms reproducted in this work. As an example, there are 600 pages of "Forms of the Family Court and Surrogate's Court of the State of New York"[21] alone.

Freedom of Information. Every agency in the State is required to spell out the rules for public access to its records. In most cases, a statement of the subject introduces the rules. See for example the statement of the Medical Care Facilities Finance Agency.[22]

Water Resources. The State takes great pride in its water quality. The Conservation title includes a fascinating list of 1,664 rivers, streams, brooks, rivulets and ponds.[23] The precise location and water quality is given for each together with a map.

Insurance. This title includes a "Publications Price List."[24] A reading of all thirteen items might qualify one as an insurance agent or broker. Many of these are free to residents of the State. The cost of the others is nominal. Of particular interest to insurance lawyers is the Department's "Circular Letters." A currently effective set lists at five dollars.

[3]—Federal Rules

The 185-volume *Code of Federal Regulations* and its daily (Monday to Friday) supplement, the *Federal Register*, are the main sources of federal rules. The Code is reissued—replaced in its entirety—each year.

Its finding aids (the locater and updating keys) and its indexes have been improved and expanded through the years. A few titles provide separate, enlarged indexes—more detailed than the master index at the end of the set.

Its fifty titles parallel but do not match the fifty titles of the *United States Code*. There is a statutory table that lists the rules under each U.S. Code provision for which rules exist. Like its local and state counterparts, the CFR also furnishes a panoply of encyclopedic fea-

---

[21] *Id.*

[22] *Id.*, Title 21 (B) Miscellaneous 2300 (Public Access to Records).

[23] *Id.*, Title 6, Part 941.5 (Assigned Classifications and Standards of Quality and Purity).

[24] *Id.*, Title 11, Insurance, Appendix 6.

tures in addition to its regulations. Among these are guidelines and interpretations that expand on the rules themselves.

Federal Trade Commission (Title 16). It includes "Guides" that prescribe standards of conduct for particular industries. These are similar to the New Deal NRA Codes: "Guides for the Nursery Industry" (Part 18); "Tire Advertising and Labelling Guides" (Part 228) and "Guides for the Law Book Industry" (Part 256) are three examples.

Securities and Exchange Commission (Title 17). Part 231 contains a list of several hundred interpretative releases issued under the Securities Act of 1933, with release numbers, dates and citations to the *Federal Register* issues where they may be found. However, the CFR does not reprint them. Parts 241, 251, 261, 271 and 276 contain lists of interpretative releases issued under subsequent acts administered by the SEC.

Protection of Environment (Title 40). "Notice to School Employees—a Guide for Reducing Asbestos Exposure" is of timely interest. It appears in Part 763.111.

So too is "Interim Method for the Determination of Asbestos in Bulk Insulation Samples" in Part 763, Appendix A to subpart F. This appendix contains a long list of references to scientific articles.

CHAPTER 13A

AIDS: Medico-Legal Research Sources

The following material comprises a new Chapter 13A for Legal Research and Law Library Management. *It is intended as supplemental material to the Main Text.*

ISN'T IT SAD . . . ?

On the Saturday after Thanksgiving in 1942, some 491 merrymakers were killed in a fire at the Coconut Grove, a popular nightclub in Boston. Few people carried credit cards at that time. Yet strangely it was discovered the next morning that none of the dead had any money in their pockets or purses. Few had watches on their wrists or rings on their fingers.

When AIDS patients die, their gold crowns will remain in their mouths, their watches and rings will be found in place and their other personal effects intact. Isn't it sad that people are afraid to rob *these* dead?

The disease AIDS (acquired immune deficiency syndrome) has stirred more interest and controversy than any other disease since the plague in London during the years 1165 and 1166 and the Black Death that killed some 25,000,000 people in Europe during the 14th century.

On the legal side, AIDS raises questions that range from the right to hospital care, job retention, school admission, patent law and privacy through landlord and tenant matters to basic constitutional issues.

On the research side, AIDS requires a broad knowledge of both legal and medical research methods and research sources. Late in 1985 some 300 lawyers, doctors, union officials and law librarians attended the first in a series of conferences, "AIDS: Legal Aspects of a Medical Crisis", which was held at the Association of the Bar of the City of

New York.[1] The sponsor was Law Journal Seminars-Press. Each speaker recognized the consequences of fear and near-panic on current legal developments in AIDS-related matters.

Fear of this disease is so widespread that one even encounters roadblocks in the way of identifying and using medical-legal research sources. Ordinarily cooperative librarians, for example, suddenly become unhelpful. "Stay away from it," they urge. Such is the aura of fear that permeates this subject.

Even under circumstances unclouded by emotional issues, lawyers have difficultly gaining access to some medical institutions, and non-lawyers encounter resistance when they attempt to enter a law library.

What follows is a guide to medical sources in major cities throughout the country—both institutions and publications—that are accessible to almost anyone.

[1]—Institutions

[a]—Library Directories. An excellent guide to New York libraries is *Library Resources in New York City*, edited by Cornelia Marwell, and published by Columbia University School of Library Service, 1979. It shows for each library the general nature of the collection and the access rules for the public. Similar information appears in the current directory of the New York Chapter of Special Libraries Association and for the country at large in the *SLA Directory of Special Libraries and Information Centers*.

[b]—Medical Libraries.

[i]—New York Area.

- **New York Academy of Medicine**, 2 E. 103d St. This library is open to the public and stays open during working hours Monday through Saturday (Not open on summer Saturdays). Its collection is broad, containing all the important indices, medical journals and other guides one might need in doing AIDS research.

---

[1]Subsequent conferences were held in New Orleans, Washington, D.C., Chicago and Los Angeles during 1986. The Law Journal Seminars-Press remained the sponsor. The University of Pennsylvania Law School, together with ALI-ABA and the City of Philadelphia, held a similar conference at the Law School early in the same year.

• **New York Public Library.** While it does not collect extensively in the fields of medicine or law, its Research Department (5th Ave. at 40th St.) in the old Arnold Constable Department Store building, does include selected medical periodicals, such as the *New England Journal of Medicine* and *Lancet* and the major scientific indexes including *Index Medicus*.

As a government depository, the Research Libraries of the New York Public Library (Economics Division, 5th Ave. at 42d St./Room 228) maintain holdings of transcripts of most Congressional hearings, and copies of reports, documents and Committee prints. These papers are assuming increased importance in medical research. Virtually all law school libraries, the New York Law Institute and the Association of the Bar of the City of New York are depositories of government documents.[2]

By statute and regulation, those libraries are obliged to admit the general public to use depository documents, no matter what their other restrictions on admission may be.[3] The remaining New York medical libraries are listed in alphabetical order below. All are in Manhattan, except as indicated.

• **Blue Cross and Blue Shield of Greater New York-Corporate Reference Information Services**, 3 Park Avenue. The collection includes health insurance. Has NEXIS, and DIALOG. Open to the public.

• **Brooklyn Public Library—Ingersoll (Central Library)** Grand Army Plaza, Brooklyn. The Science and Industry Division has a collection on biological sciences. Open to the public.

• **College of Insurance (Insurance Society of New York) Library**, 101 Murray Street. The insurance industry has begun to monitor all phases of this disease. The collection can be expected to contain statistical materials and forms of insurance policy restrictions and coverage generally. Open to the public for reference.

---

[2]A complete list of Depository Libraries appears in the September number of the Government Printing Office Monthly Catalog. Some 32 New York libraries were so designated in 1985, including 15 in Manhattan and the rest distributed throughout that city's remaining four boroughs (at pp. D16-D-17).

[3]44 U.S.C.A. § 1911. The Superintendent of Documents attempts to enforce his use rules by sending an inspector to each Depository Library periodically.

• **Cornell University Medical College—Samuel J. Wood Library**, 1300 York Avenue. A good general collection. Has Medline and BRS. Open to the public by appointment only, with identification and letter of reference or prior telephone approval. Reference use only. To apply, telephone (212) 472-5300.

• **Memorial Sloan-Kettering Cancer Center—Lee Coembe Memorial Library**, 444 East 68th St. Resources cover cancer, virology cytology, biochemistry, immunology and related subjects. Has Medline. Open by application only. Telephone: (212) 794-7393.

• **Merck & Company, Inc.—Merck Sharp & Dohme Research Laboratories, Literature Resources**, Rahway, N.J. Collection includes works on biochemistry, immunology sciences. Has some 900 serials. Open to the public with prior clearance by management.

• **Trudeau Institute Immunobiological Research Laboratories Library**, Algonquin Ave., Saranac Lake, N.Y. Specialty: Immunobiological research. Public welcome with permission.

• **United Hospital Fund of New York Reference Library**, 3 East 54th St. Resources: Hospital management and health care management. Approximately 200 periodical titles. The issue surrounding the rights of access to medical and nursing care are likely to be covered by publications in this collection. Open to graduate students, researchers, staff. Appointment is required.

• **W. Alton Jones Cell Science Center, George and Margaret Gey Library**, Old Barn Road, Lake Placid, N.Y. Collection includes works on cell culture, cytology, cancern research, virology, biochemistry and immunology. Has Medline and Dialog. Open to the public with permission.

• **Yeshiva University Albert Einstein College of Medicine**, 1300 Morris Park Ave., Bronx. Subjects: Biochemistry, Immunology among many others. 2,345 serial subscriptions. Has MEDLARS and BRS. Open to the public with restrictions.

• **Haven Emerson Public Health Library**, 125 Worth Street, Room 223. The collection covers public health, environmental health, vital statistics, general medicine and related topics. A depository for all New York City health-related documents. An important source for regulatory research. Open to the public.

[*ii*]—*Philadelphia Area.*

• **University of Pennsylvania Biomedical Library**, 36th Street at Hamilton Walk, Philadelphia. Has a comprehensive medical collection, with subscriptions to some 2,300 serial publications and the leading computer information services. Open to the public for reference use only.

• **College of Physicians of Philadelphia**, 19 South 22nd Street, Philadelphia. A fine collection, with 2,450 serial subscriptions and the main computer services in medicine. Open to public for reading and photocopying.

• **Jefferson University Hospital Library**, 11th at Walnut Streets. Has 1,643 serial subscriptions and several computer services. Open to public with restrictions.

• **Pennsylvania Hospital Medical Library.** Some 540 journal subscriptions. Open to public by appointment.

• **Free Library of Philadelphia**, Government Publications Department, Logan Square. The best local source for government documents at all levels. A federal depository.

[*iii*]—*Boston Area.*

• **Harvard University, Schools of Medicine, Dental Medicine and Public Health, Boston Medical Library**, 10 Shattuck Street. Has upwards of 500,000 volumes, 4,976 journal and other serial subscriptions, and the main computer services. Open to those with a vocational interest in the technical literature of the health sciences.

[*iv*]—*Chicago Area.*

• **University of Chicago—John Crerar Library** (Science Technology; Medicine), 5730 S. Ellis St. Subscribes to about 10,000 journals and the main computer services. Open to public with restrictions.

• **University of Illinois at Chicago, Health Sciences Center Library**, 1750 W. Polk St. Has 4,585 journal subscriptions, many computer services. Open to public for reference use only.

[*v*]—*Houston Area.*

• **Houston Academy of Medicine-Texas Medical Center Library**, 1333 M.D. Anderson Blvd. Subscribes to 4,602 journals, the majority of which are on computer. (Open to public with fees for borrowing and other services).

[*vi*]—*Los Angeles Area.*

• **University of California at Los Angeles-Biomedical Library, Center for Health Sciences.** Has holdings of nearly 400,000 volumes, subscribes to 6,891 journals and other serials. Provides most medical computer services. Publishes for sale its serials holdings list, brief guide to the biomedical library, recent acquisitions list and similar catalogs. Inquire as to public access: (213) 825-5781.

• **University of Southern California-Health Sciences Campus**, Norris Medical Library, 2025 Zonal Avenue. Has 2,147 journal subscriptions, the major computer services. The library is open to the public for reference use only.

[vii]—San Francisco-Berkeley Area.

• **University of California at San Francisco-Medical Library**, Parnassus Avenue. Has 3,923 journal subscriptions and the major computer services. Open to public with restricted circulation.

• **University of California at Berkeley-Public Health Library**, 42 Earl Warren Hall. Has 2,080 serial subscriptions and the major computer services. Specialities include epidemiology, biostatistics, environmental health and biomedical science. Open to public for reference use only.

[c]—National Libraries. Recourse can be made to the National Library of Medicine in Bethesda, Maryland should the local institutions fail to include needed materials. The MEDLARS tapes (Medical Literature Analysis and Retrieval System) are based on the holdings of this library.

Finally, the Center for Disease Control (U.S.) maintains two important libraries in Atlanta: its CDC Library and the Chamblee Facility Library, both at 1600 Clinton Road. The former includes microbiology, public health and virology among its specialties and is open to the public with restrictions. It is the more likely of the two to contain Aids-related material. The Chamblee library is somewhat smaller and is open to the public by appointment.

[2]—Publications

[a]—Medical Research Manual. A single reference manual adequately surveys the field of medical literature: *Introduction to Reference Sources in the Health Sciences* by Fred W. Roper and Jo Anne Boorkman, 2d ed. Chicago Medical Library Association, Inc, 1984. Its fifteen chapters give an overview of the reference collection, provide an explanation of particular biographical sources for monographs, periodicals, indexes and abstracts, data bases, government documents and conferences, and analyze the main features of various information guides. These include dictionaries, handbooks, audiovisual sources, statistical guides and directories.

[b]—Dictionaries. Terminology, whether in law, medicine or any other technical field, offers major challenges to the researcher. Included here are three standard medical dictionaries and one annotated medical-legal dictionary.

• **Dorland's Illustrated Medical Dictionary.** 26th ed. Philadelphia, W.B. Saunders & Co., 1981. In a visit to four doctors' offices during the past two years, this was the only dictionary visible in three of them. It is one of two medical dictionaries used in general reference courses at Columbia University School of Library Service for more than forty years. *Stedman's* is the other. It is indispensable to any medico-legal research.

One of its idiosyncrasies: Descriptions of all diseases, operations and syndromes (there are some 400 of these) are collected under "d," "o" and "s" rather than being entered, for example, under Alzheimer's disease, Albert's operation or Aarskog's syndrome. Cross references guide the user to the entry being used. There are numerous illustrations and color plates.

• **Stedman's Medical Dictionary.** 24th ed. Baltimore, Williams & Wilkins, 1982. An equally important medical dictionary. Both *Dorland's* and *Stedman's* appear innumerable times in the cases, as shown by Lexis and Westlaw searches.

• **Attorney's Dictionary of Medicine and Word Finder** by J.E. Schmidt, N.Y. Bender. Current, looseleaf, 4 Vols. Originally issued in 1962 and last updated in 1986. Its definitions are clear, concise and easy to understand. For purposes of court use, *Dorland's* and *Stedman's* still have greater acceptance.

• **Sloane-Dorland Medical-Legal Dictionary** by Richard Sloane, St. Paul, West Publishing Co., 1987. The first dictionary to include thousands of case annotations, each associated with a particular medical term.

[c]—Indexes and Abstracts.

• **Index Medicus.** Bethesda, Md., National Library of Medicine. Monthly, cumulated annually. This is the main source for periodical literature in the field and copies will be found in virtually all medical libraries. Each month's issue is about the size of the Manhattan telephone directory. A clear explanation of how to use this index appears at the beginning of each issue. A helpful adjunct is *Medical Subject Headings* (MeSH) which appears in the January issue and is revised each year.

• **Biological Abstracts.** Philadelphia, BioSciences Information Services. Biweekly, cumulated twice a year. Covers many of the journals indexed in *Index Medicus*, but many others as well.

• **Biological Abstracts/RRM (Reports, Reviews and Meetings).** Same publisher. Semimonthly. Covers publications shown in its title and, in addition, pertinent government documents and chapters in books.

[d]—Catalogues.

• **Medical Books and Serials in Print.** New York, Bowker, Annual. A typical Bowker catalog similar to their *Books in Print*. Covers books issued or distributed in the United States. Its serials list is international in scope.

• **National Library of Medicine Current Catalog.** Bethesda, Md., the Library. Quarterly, with annual and five-year cumulations.

• **National Library of Medicine Current Catalog Proof Sheets.** Chicago, Medical Library Association, Weekly. Useful for very current material, particularly useful in a rapidly developing branch of medicine.

[e]—Bibliographies. Three outstanding bibliographies cover the fields of medicine, nursing and allied health sciences. All three were compiled by the same two medical specialists: Alfred N. Brandon, a medical library consultant in Daytona, Florida, and Dorothy R. Hill, Assistant Professor of Medical Education and Collection Development Librarian at the Gustave L. and Janet W. Levy Library, Mount Sinai School of Medicine of the City University of New York.

• Selected List of Books and Journals for the Small Medical Library, 73 *Bulletin*, Medical Library Association 176-201 (April 1985). The 11th revision of this selection guide, it is classified under some 48 medical specialties from "allergy" to "urology" and lists as well the leading dictionaries, directories and encyclopedias. Includes price information for each of its 583 books and 138 journals.

• Selected List of Nursing Books and Journals, 34 *Nursing Outlook* 74-82 (March/April 1986). Similar in format to the medical list, this is a third revision. It too contains price information.

• Selected List of Books and Journals in Allied Health Sciences, 72 *Bulletin*, Medical Library Association, 373-391 (October 1984). A classified list of 450 books and 67 journals. Even though many of the subjects covered in the medical list are included in this one, there is little overlapping in book titles. Price information is included.

[f]—Medical Data Bases. Medicine and the sciences in general preceded law in their development of computer research sources. The data bases listed below are available in most medical libraries. More important, most can be brought into the office through one's own personal computer or other terminal. There is significant overlapping among the vendors of computer services and *Medline* is basic to them all.

• **Medline.** Bethesda, Md. National Library of Medicine. *Medline* is a computerized bibliographic retrieval system, the *on-line* segment of MEDLARS. MEDLARS (MEDical Literature Analysis and Retrieval System) is the computerized bibliographic system of the National Library of Medicine, from which *Index Medicus* is produced. Through *Medline* (which is MEDLARS on line) one gains references to articles in more than 2,500 journals, some proceedings of conferences and chapters in books for which the authors were several contributors.

• **Catline.** Bethesda, Md. National Library of Medicine. *Catline* is the National Library's on-line catalog of monographs and serials. It includes more than 400,000 entries and is currently supplemented.

• **Biosis Previews.** Philadelphia, Bio-Sciences Information Services. This is the on-line version of the same company's *Biological Abstracts* and Biological Abstracts/RRM, listed above.

• **BRS/Saunders Colleague.** A joint venture of Bibliographic Retrieval Services and the medical book publisher, W.B. Saunders Company, New York and Philadelphia. Includes *Medline, Medical and Psychological Previews, International Pharmaceutical Abstracts and Health Planning Administration*, all in the form of indexes or abstracts on line; a small collection of biomedical books in full text; and the full text of several leading medical journals, among them *The British Medical Journal, The Lancet* and the *New England Journal of Medicine*.

• **PAPERCHASE.** A joint venture of two hospitals and Harvard Medical School. It searches the MEDLINE database from 1977 to date, covering the 3,400 journals indexed by Medline (earlier described as "more than 2,500 journals"). Available in many medical libraries, this is apparently the most economical searching system.

[g]—Statistical Compilations. The incidence of disease is likely to have direct effect on legislative and regulatory action at all levels of government. Notifiable or reportable diseases must be reported to Boards of Health by doctors or hospitals. The volume of cases of AIDS can be expected to be included in the *Statistical Abstract of the United States*. However the 1986 edition, issued in December 1985, does not mention AIDS, even though Table 184 (Specified Reportable Diseases—Cases Reported: 1960 to 1983) is a routine item in this compilation.

• **Morbidity and Mortality Weekly Report.** Atlanta, Center for Disease Control. Each issue summarizes case data collected throughout the United States and, in addition, contains special features of which "Current Trends" is the one to watch for our purposes. This *Report* is cumulated in the Center's *Annual Summary*.

• **New York (City) Vital Statistics**, Weekly. N.Y. Department of Health. Contains a record of the incidence of AIDS cases. The Department also publishes an annual *Summary of Vital Statistics*.

With these publications, most of which can be found in the libraries listed above, any researcher should be able to collect sufficient background information for any study of AIDS and its medico-legal problems.

CHAPTER 13B

Human Experimentation and the Law

The following material comprises a new Chapter 13B for Legal Research and Law Library Management. *It is intended as supplemental material to the Main Text.*

What is the appropriate role for the artificial heart in its current state of development? Should it be used as a permanent implant in selected patients or as a temporary means to keep patients alive until a human heart can be implanted in its stead?

The experts cannot agree and it appears that the eventual decision will be made by the Food and Drug Administration (FDA). The FDA, for example, has allowed only one surgeon, Dr. William C. DeVries, to implant artificial hearts as a permanent device, although other surgeons have been given similar permission to implant temporary artificial hearts in limited numbers of patients. Upon completion of these experiments, the FDA will decide whether further temporary or permanent implants should be allowed based on a review of the medical, ethical and financial costs involved. These decisions are being made by the FDA's division of cardiovascular devices, an advisory panel of experts in the field.

The public accepts and approves this control over such human experimentation. Yet it is to be noted, that although physicians and scientists have conducted experiments involving human beings for over 2000 years, it is only since the early 1960's that such experimentation has been subject to any form of official regulation beyond the ethical, moral and professional judgment of individual researchers and research institutions. As a result, although such discretion allowed to researchers did benefit society on occasion by finding cures to disease and relieving human pain and suffering, it was accomplished at the expense of horrible physical or mental harm suffered by the human research subjects involved.

This theme is professionally documented in a well organized and researched work entitled *Human Experimentation: Federal Laws, Legislative Histories, Regulations and Related Documents*, edited by Bernard D. Reams, Jr. professor of law and director of the law library at Washington University in St. Louis, and Carol J. Gray, assistant law librarian of the same law school and published by Oceana Publications, Dobbs Ferry, N.Y. The work combines in-depth coverage in microform of statutes and regulations with analyses and indexes in looseleaf format, both of which will be periodically updated. It is a unique combination of microform and looseleaf hard copy on a current and controversial subject.

The microform portion is released in segments and will cover the post-World War II period to the present. It will include statutes and regulatory history, current congressional action, current regulations, reports from federal agency publications, congressional and agency studies that have been used as background for laws and regulations. Presented historically, it follows the problems in governmental regulation of research on humans. Access to the collection is obtained through author and title and subject indexes and chronological directories of hearings, *Federal Register* regulations and notices and *Congressional Record* statements—all to appear in the looseleaf binder. A legal, ethical and historical analysis will also appear in that looseleaf binder, together with analysis of major laws and regulations, with references indexed to the microform portion.

The scope of subjects covered by the set includes all topics related to the protection of subjects of human experimentation. "Protection" includes issues of informed consent, privacy, rights to research results, compensation for injury and rules governing supervision, administration and performance of research on human subjects and their enforcement. "Experimentation" means biomedical, behavioral and social research.

The set does not cover recombinant DNA research, and research that inadvertantly affects human populations. Although the set does include statutes, congressional material, current and historical regulations, agency studies and guidelines and commission reports, federal court cases are not included because they are beyond the statutory and regulatory focus of the set. The court cases are listed, however, in a "Table of Cases Cited" and the case law is reviewed in the looseleaf text.

The researcher concerned with case law can refer to the *Bioethics*

Reporter; Ethical and Legal Issues in Medicine, Health Care Administration and Human Experimentation, published by University Publications of America, Frederick, Maryland. Each month the *Bioethics Reporter* examines a major issue, or a related group of issues, for which a collection of papers is presented. They discuss the current state of the question, providing both historical and contemporary views. Frequently, the editorial advisors provide an analysis or commentary which attempts to explore and to advance the issue under discussion. Issues are up-dated every two years.

Some of the issues covered by the *Bioethics Reporter* are experimentation with human subjects, institutional review boards and human subjects research, hospital ethics committees, rights of the fetus, organ donation and transplantation, informed consent to therapy and experimentation, genetic engineering, the determination of death, and the artificial heart. The *Bioethics Reporter* provides full-text briefs and opinions of current federal, state and local court cases in its field. It also reviews recent legislation, bills, hearings, and special reports from federal, state and local sources, and includes selected documents and codes concerning professional responsibility and human subjects research.

Another standard work is *Experimentation with Human Beings; The Authority of the Investigator, Subject, Professions and State in the Human Experimentation Process*, by Jay Katz of Yale University, published by the Russell Sage Foundation in 1972. This is an able discussion of such issues as how and by whom should research policy be formulated and administered, and the consequences of research reviewed. Of equal significance is what consequences to subjects should affect the authority of the investigator. In this context, the author considers what constitutes harm and the relevance or choice of and attitude toward human subjects, disclosure of risks, pursuit of knowledge, the interests of society, limitations inherent in informed consent, and most significantly today with AIDS victims, experiments with dying subjects.

Also worthwhile is *Human Experimentation and the Law* by a lawyer, Nathan Hershey, and a medical doctor, Robert D. Miller, published by the Aspen Systems Corporation, Germantown, Maryland, in 1976. It discusses the scope of law relating to investigation with human subjects, state as well as federal, and provides professional codes and guidelines, federal regulations and a bibliography. The authors comment on responsibilities of the Institutional Review Board as well as its responsibilities to human subjects. They also provide guidance for the investigator presenting a research study for approval by an institutional board—(e.g., protocol preparation, written consent forms and protocol for research study).

Of value too, is *Clinical Investigation in Medicine: Legal, Ethical and Moral Aspects*, edited by Irving Ladimer and Robert Newman and published by Law-Medicine Research Institute of Boston University in 1963. This is actually an anthology of seventy-three articles selected not only from medical journals, but from publications of other disciplines—anthropology, biology, biostatistics, history, hospital administration, law, penology, pharmacy, philosophy, physiology, psychology, public health, religion and sociology. In essence its articles embrace the legal, ethical, moral and philosophical aspects of experimental medicine and clinical investigation. In this book are collected important contributions to the philosophy of human testing in clinical medical research. Because the editors recognize that the anthology represents only a selective, quite arbitrary sample of what has been written on the subject, they have added a bibliography of about 500 items in order to make a more useful reference and guide book for the professional medical researcher or administrator, as well as for scholars in related disciplines, such as law. Despite the age of the publication, it is a valuable reference work, although a new edition is in order.

Then there is *The Human Body and the Law*, written by Charlotte Levy, and published in 1983 by Oceana Publications as part of its *Legal Almanac Series*. The style is more popular, but it provides sound and relevant information on the legal and ethical considerations involved in human experimentation, such as sterilization, fetal experimentation, transplantation, the Uniform Anatomical Gift Act, and mind and behavior control. A well selected-bibliography adds to the value of this little work.

As brought out by Professor Reams in his *Human Experimentation*, "Over the course of the last quarter-century, congress and several administrative agencies have sought to regulate the conduct of experiments involving human subjects, thereby walking a tight-rope pulled taut by the competing demands for scientific progress and individual protection. In drafting the laws and regulations governing human experimentation, efforts have been made—with varying degrees of success—to protect the welfare of research subjects without substantially impeding physicians and scientists in the conduct of legitimate and ethically acceptable medical research."

Despite the obvious need for additional regulatory action, conflict exists on two opposed subjects: (1) whether current regulations are excessive in that they conflict legitimate and significant research with costly and unnecessary administrative details; and (2) whether the government has been lax in that it has afforded inadequate protection to human subjects of experiment. Experimentation in the practice of medicine is as old as medicine itself. The answer, perhaps, lies in the thought expressed by the late legal philosopher, Edmond Cahn: "though laws and regulations governing the distribution of experimental drugs are indispensable, their efficacy will largely depend on the fundamental attitudes of those who administer them, those who are subject to them and those for whose protection they are enacted."

CHAPTER 13C

Products Liability Research Without Computers

The following material comprises a new Chapter 13C for Legal Research and Law Library Management. *It is intended as supplemental material to the Main Text.*

A gas leak disaster that occurred in Bhopal, India in December 1984 sent lawyers scurrying to New Delhi and kept office lights blazing in several cities across the United States and in West Germany and France. The proof-of-damage claims and defenses to them will occupy lawyers and their researchers for many months or even years.

Some of the questions they will try to answer.

- What chemicals were involved and what is known about them?
- How did the accident happen?
- How could it have been avoided?
- Who or what was at fault?
- Was anyone recklessly careless?
- When did company officers learn of the dangers or when could they reasonably be expected to know of them?

Some of the answers will be found on the spot. Computer searches will turn up *recent* information. But an examination of court papers and opinions in other accident and product liability cases discloses that most answers are buried in "literature" that is not yet recorded in computer data bases.

That "literature" consists of scientific studies, seminar lectures, medical journal reports, popular and technical magazine articles, even in the daily press; in books, dissertations and pharmaceutical company handouts that "detail" men distribute to doctors.

What starts out, for example, as a laboratory study is often announced publicly in the *New England Journal of Medicine* or in *Lancet*. Soon the wire services or news reporters hear of it. The item will appear next in *The New York Times* or *Washington Post*. Then *Time* or *Newsweek* may report it. So will the trade papers in an industry that uses the offending product. *The New Republic* or *I. F. Stone's Weekly* may have editorialized about it.

This Chapter provides a basic checklist of a single source of this kind of information: the main newspaper and periodical indexes. There are many other sources. Experienced librarians—especially the pre-computer generation of librarians—are familiar with them.

One significant fact about those indexes is the span of years that they cover. Some like the *Times Index* began publishing near the opening of this century—long before computer coverage became available.

[1]—Newspaper Indexes

- *New York Daily Tribune Index*, 1875-1906. This covers all but six years before the much more detailed *New York Times Index* was started.
- *The New York Times Index*, 1913 to date. Complete runs are on open shelves at the New York Public Library, the New York Law Institute and most college libraries.
- *Wall Street Journal Index*, 1958 to date. Divided into two main parts: a company index and a subject or general index.

All three indexes are cumulated annually, except that the *The New York Times Index* was published only in quarterly cumulations from 1913 into the early 1930's.

[2]—Periodical Indexes

- *Applied Science and Technology Index*, 1913 to date. This was originally issued as the *Industrial Arts Index*, A typical H.W. Wilson product, except that it is purely a *subject* index to more than 200 of the periodicals of interest to products liability lawyers. Sets are available at major libraries throughout the country. Cumulated annually. Prior to 1958, use the *Industrial Arts Index*.
- *Business Periodicals Index*, 1958 to date. This is an offshoot of the *Industrial Arts Index* which, in 1958, was divided into the *Applied Science* (*supra*) and this index. Prior to 1958, look for the thick

black volumes of *Industrial Arts*. It is kept in most business libraries throughout the United States. Cumulated annually.

• *Engineering Index*, 1906 to date. Covers most industries and industry products. The period from 1884 to 1905 was covered by the *Descriptive Index of Current Engineering Literature*. Cumulated annually. Copies are in most major American libraries.

• *F & S Index of Corporations and Industries*, 1960 to date. Titled *Funk & Scott* . . . 1960 to 1967. Covers about 750 periodicals, indexing news of particular companies, industries, products and technical developments. Looseleaf and cumulated annually. Starting in 1967, *F & S Index International* picked up coverage outside the United States.

• *Index Medicus*, 1879 to 1899 and 1903 to 1927; *Bibliographia Medica (Index Medicus)*, Paris, 1899 to 1902; *Quarterly Cumulative Index Medicus*, 1927-1956; *Current List of Medical Literature*, 1950-1959; and *Index Medicus*, 1960 to date.

These five indexes, with some overlapping years of coverage, provide a key to most medical periodical literature of the past 100 years. Sets are in medical school and medical society libraries. An annual cumulation has the title: *Cumulated Index Medicus*.

• *Poole's Index to Periodical Literature*, with Supplements, 1802 to 1881 and 1882 to 1906. A purely *subject* index to major periodical writings, mainly in the United States, during the 19th century. Found in the larger public and college libraries.

• *Readers' Guide to Periodical Literature*, 1900 to date. This is the "flagship" of the H.W. Wilson Company indexes, cumulated both annually and again biennially. It has gradually expanded its coverage from fifteen popular magazines until about thirty years ago when it became the major index of popular, scientific (but not technical) and literary magazines. Includes authors and subjects. Available at most public and college libraries in the United States.

Cautionary notes: Like the West Publishing Company Descriptive Word Indexes, each of these newspaper and periodical indexes has been compiled by a different team of indexers. The result: The *same* ideas or the *same* products may be indexed under *different* headings in each of these publications. Moreover, the personnel of the "teams" change from time to time with a consequent change in their use of headings.

Accordingly, before sending paralegal assistants off on a wild goose chase, it is important for lawyers to learn first the technical language in each field of his or her interest; and then the terms employed by the respective indexers. That is the better way to ensure effective use of each index. The best way is to send your sharpest librarian.

CHAPTER 13D

Law of the Sea Publications

The following material comprises a new Chapter 13D for Legal Research and Law Library Management. *It is intended as supplemental material to the Main Text.*

When the United Nations Convention on the Law of the Sea was finally signed in December 1982 at Montego Bay, Jamaica, by more than 120 countries, and subsequently by twelve other countries, it marked a singular development in international law in the post-World War II period. Although the United States refused to sign UNCLOS III (as the Convention is now popularly called), except for the provisions pertaining to deep seabed mining, it does accept a few of the Convention's major provisions, such as those relating to international navigation and the rights and duties of coastal states, on the theory that they have by now become independently binding, customary international law. This policy was reflected in April 1983, when President Reagan proclaimed a 200 mile-wide exclusive economic zone based on the thrust of UNCLOS III and proclaimed that it would respect similar zones established by other states, subject to reciprocity. "Consequently," notes Professor Louis B. Sohn in his perceptive Nutshell book on the Law of the Sea,[1] "it seems that, with the exception of the part relating to deep seabed mining, the provisions of the Convention have become the best evidence of the emerging new international law of the sea, and have become the law of the United States on the subjects covered by them.[2]

---

[1]Sohn and Gustafson, *The Law of the Sea in a Nutshell*, St. Paul, Minn. West Publishing Co., 1984. 264p.

[2]In support he quotes from *The Paquete Habana*, 175 U.S. 677, 700 (1900); "International Law is part of our law, and must be ascertained and administered by the courts

The need for UNCLOS III, resulted from a realization that the old rules that had governed the uses of international waters for centuries had become obsolete by reason of the political, economical and technical developments that had ensued. The International Law of the Sea particularly had to respond to the political confrontation between developed and developing nations over the increasing need for minerals, energy and food which the new technology could retrieve from the waters of international seas.

In the course of the process that has come to be known as UNCLOS III, occupying easily the better part of ten years, there were many conferences, congresses, symposia, workshops and seminars that discussed and analyzed the proposed convention as well as treaties and agreements affecting the law of the sea. Such a vast amount of documentation was created that research in this dynamically developing situation cannot be accomplished without a comprehensive up-to-date knowledge of the literature involved. Bibliographical control has become a necessity.

A unique approach to organizing and publishing that documentation has been the program of Oceana Publications of Dobbs Ferry, N.Y. Initially conceived in a conference program held in 1971, Oceana published over the years an indexed eleven volume documents compilation titled *New Directions in the Law of the Sea* (edited by K.R. Simmonds). The hard-bound set terminated with the adoption of the UNCLOS III convention, but has been continued as a looseleaf service under the same title. It is designed to provide ongoing coverage of developments in all phases of the law of the sea.

Contemporaneous with *New Directions*, and under the general editorship of Kenneth R. Simmonds, Dean of the Faculty of Laws at Queen Mary College, University of London, a grouping of looseleaf regional services was developed to bring attention to regional compacts and national legislation (in English). The publications in this field include *Latin America and Development of the Law of the Sea* (by A. Szekely, 2 looseleaf binders), *The U.S.S.R., Eastern Europe and Development of the Law of the Sea* (by W. E. Butler, one looseleaf

---

of the justice of appropriate jurisdictions, as often as questions of right depending upon it are duly presented for their determination. For this purpose, where there is no treaty and no controlling executive or legislative act or judicial decision, resort must be had to the customs and usages of civilized nations. . ."

binder), *Western Europe and the Development of the Law of the Sea: National Legislation* (by F. Durante, 3 looseleaf binders), and *North America, East Asia, and Pacific Islands and Development of the Law of the Sea* (by M. Nordquist and C. H. Park, 2 looseleaf binders). These services reflect the work product of specialists in the field and provide the changing law in various regions of the world in reaction to the adoption of UNCLOS III.

Oceana has also published a four volume set entitled *Cases on the Law of the Sea*, edited by Professor Simmonds, which presents a systematically organized selection and commentary on leading cases drawn from established reports which are scattered and often difficult of access. Later selected material will be included in digest form in the *New Directions in the Law of the Sea* looseleaf service. Oceana also has published a ten volume set of documentary materials concerned with UNCLOS III, which contains the complete legislative history of the conference including proposals and papers from various working groups, under the title, *Third United Nations Conference on the Law of the Sea: Documents* (by Dr. R. Platzoder). It is much in demand by delegations to UNCLOS, as well as by researchers and academicians.

Important as is the availability in consolidated and accessed form of primary source materials, coverage of specific topics is also essential for the business professional and the lawyer. A good overview of the subject can be found in the West Nutshell Publication, *The Law of the Sea* (Sohn and Gustafson, 1984). Not only does it summarize the current principles and rules of the law of the sea, relying strongly on the parts of UNCLOS III which have been accepted by the United States, but it also takes into account other relevant treaties of the U.S. (including the four 1958 conventions on the law of the sea ratified by the United States), Congressional legislation and the jurisprudence of the United States courts on this subject.

The following specialized publications should also be noted: *Pollution of International Watercourses: a search for substantive rules and principles of law* (by J. G. Lammers, 1984, M. Nijhoff) which searches for the substantive rights and duties of riparian states of an international watercourse in respect of pollution as a problem of international law; *Deep Sea Mining and The Law of the Sea* (by A.M. Post, 1983, M. Nijhoff) which analyzes the salient features and risks involved in the various aspects of ocean mining; *Origin and Development of the Law of the Sea-History of International Law Revisited* (by

R.P. Anand, 1982, M. Nijhoff) which examines the history of international law, particularly the law of the sea, as it developed in Asia over the years in a well documented and scholarly treatise; *Resource Management and the Oceans: The Political Economy of Deep Seabed Mining* (by K. M. Shusterich, Boulder, Westview Press, 1982) in which the author competently "analyzes the various domestic and international issues that have been raised about the management of the global commons. It provides an analysis and history of the major issues and the development of the United States and international laws on marine policy and resource management. The book focuses on the case of deep seabed mining, while pointing to the broader range of political implications involved that may influence exploitation for other resource commons."

Also to be examined are: *Straits in International Navigation*: Contemporary Issues (by Khen-Lian Koh, 1982, Oceana); *The Lawfulness of Deep-Seabed Mining* (by T. KronMiller, 1980, 3 v. Oceana) [Although this work is not an official version of the United States position, it does present a legal analysis of what has essentially come to be this country's position on deep seabed mining]; *Land-Locked States and the UNCLOS Regime* (by Mpazi Sinjela, Oceana, 1983) in which a former advisor to the land-locked states articulates their viewpoint as to their rights to the resources of the sea; *Ocean Oil and Gas Drilling and the Law* (by P.N. Swan, 1979, Oceana), which addresses legal problems on the development of offshore oil with a focus on American Law; and *The International Control of Marine Pollution* (by Gr. J. Timagenis, 1980, 2v. Oceana), which is based on diplomatic documents that are often difficult to locate.

Oceana is also publishing an *Ocean Policy Study Series*, a periodic publication of the Center for Oceans Law and Policy of the University of Virginia, consisting of scholarly studies, conference papers and readers' comments on papers previously published. Booklet 2 is entitled *Establishing the Non-Seabed Provisions of the UNCLOS III Treaty as customary International Law*. It reflects the policy objectives of the United States and other nations seeking orderly development of the law of the sea. Other issues are on international fisheries, oceans industry and regulatory reform. Finally, there is *U.S. Law of the Sea Policy: Options for the Future*. Six issues a year are planned.

The volume of publication on the law of the sea is so overwhelming and practically unmanageable that the researcher will welcome *The*

New Law of the Sea: International Law Bibliography, (Prepared by Blanka Kudej, Assistant Law Librarian, New York University, 1984, Oceana). This bibliography is a practical reference tool which highlights the research materials in the field published in English. It is also designed to serve as a guide for building a sizeable and manageable library collection with an in-depth research capability. The entries selected date from 1958 to the present with the exception of a few classics. It covers primary sources and the various subject facets of the law of the sea.

Another classified bibliography which should be noted is the *International Law of the Sea and Marine Affairs, a Bibliography Supplement to the 1980 edition* (by Nikos Papadakis and Martin Glassner, M. Nijhoff, 1984), which not only brings the first edition up to date but greatly expands it through inclusion of German, Spanish, Italian, Yugoslavian and Russian material. Both the Kudej and the Papadakis-Glassner bibliographies list relevant bibliographies, references, directories and dictionaries.

CHAPTER 15A

The Index to Legal Periodicals

The following material comprises a new Chapter 15A for Legal Research and Law Library Management. *It is intended as supplemental material to the Main Text.*

The Index to Legal Periodicals has played a significant role in legal research since it was first published in 1908. Over the years, it has been the best known and most popular index for researchers seeking references to current legal periodical literature. It provides international coverage in every area of law and indexes periodical articles of interest to the diverse research needs of judges, attorneys, scholars and others concerned with evolving principles of law and the administration of justice. It is staffed by professional indexers with law degrees. Coverage includes journals published in Great Britain, Ireland, Canada, Australia, New Zealand and the United States. Indexing is basically by author and subject. Other research features are its references to Cases, Statutes and Book Reviews.

The Index to Legal Periodicals is considered so important in legal research that the American Bar Association and the Association of American Law Schools require that it be available in the libraries of Law Schools accredited by them. *The Index to Legal Periodicals* is now published monthly, except in September, with a bound cumulation each year.

The *Index to Legal Periodicals* has increased its periodical coverage from 394 titles in 1979 to just over 600 titles in 1988. It is also made editorial revisions in subject headings, subheadings and cross references. The most specific subject heading is used whenever possible. With the exception of national surveys, annual surveys of the law of a jurisdiction or a court are indexed under the name of the jurisdiction. Annual surveys of the decisions of the higher federal courts are indexed under the name of the particular court. "See also" references, for example, are now displayed immediately after subject headings. The list of subject headings and cross references used in indexing will be found in each annual cumulative volume. It also offers more cross-references and increased indexing to book reviews and statutes. Entries for foreign periodicals list the publisher, the holder of North American distribution rights and the subscription price.

In addition, Author entries now include full bibliographic citations, eliminating the need for double look-up, as was true previously. The Table of Cases section which appears in each issue now lists cases alphabetically by defendants' names as well as plaintiffs' names. Subject headings are now subdivided by topical headings and geographic headings. All periodical citations in the *Index for Legal Periodicals* now conform to *A Uniform System of Citation,* 13th edition, published by the Harvard Law Review association. There is no doubt that these editorial changes and the expanded journal coverage enhance the quality of legal indexing and bibliographic reporting available to the legal profession.

Its Editorial Advisory Committee has also reviewed the policy of the *Index to Legal Periodicals* to index only those periodicals which "regularly publish legal articles of high quality and permanent reference value." This policy was established originally many years ago, by the *Index to Legal Periodicals* with the advice and approval of the American Association of Law Libraries. At that time, the American Association of Law Libraries sponsored the *Index to Legal Periodicals.* Actually this policy reflected a sophisticated decision that the research requirements of legal scholars and researchers demand that they should not waste time sorting through references of local gossip, clutter and other non-scholarly material found in certain legal periodicals and legal newspapers.

A conflict on this editorial policy as well as in other matters, between the H. W. Wilson Co., publishers of the *Index to Legal Periodicals,* and the American Association of Law Libraries, eventually led, in 1980, to the publication of a competing Index entitled the *Current Law Index*, (CLI). The CLI indexes all articles and incidental commentaries in about 750 legal periodicals, both scholarly and non-scholarly, including newspapers. As a result, the CLI's advertising "proudly" notes that it indexes more periodicals than the *Index to Le-*

gal Periodicals does. After considerable review of this situation, the Editorial Advisory Committee to the *Index to Legal Periodicals* strongly supported the publisher's policy concluding that the introduction into legal periodical index services of many non-scholarly legal publications unnecessarily compounds the difficulties of legal scholars seeking references to authoritative information and documentation.

The November 1983 issue of the *Index to Legal Periodicals* bears a notice to its subscribers which has important implications for legal research in periodical literature. "Beginning with this issue," it reads, "*Index to Legal Periodicals,* is being produced by the H. W. Wilson Company's computerized bibliographic systems." The Wilson Company has developed a computerized bibliographic system to support the editorial and manufacturing process involved in creating not only the *Index to Legal Periodicals,* but also the other twenty-six book and periodical indexes, catalogues and reference books that it publishes. These other periodical indexes cover material on a variety of subjects, of interdisciplinary interest to legal researchers, including the sciences, arts and humanities.

Since 1960, the Wilson Company has been supporting an ongoing project to automate the production of its many indexes and related publications. The first publication to be produced using the automated system was the October 1982 issue of *Cumulative Book Index, Business Periodicals Index* and *Readers Guide to Periodical Literature*. Starting in 1983, the other indexes are being automated, and the *Index to Legal Periodicals* was automated with the November 1983 issue. The system, called BEACON, supports data entry and revision of records through the use of an on-line screen-edit program called SCREED. As brought out by its developer, Davis B. McCarn, who had previously been involved in the design of the MEDLARS system at the National Library of Medicine, this system will be able to develop an on-line inquiry system to allow Wilson participation in the emerging national bibliographic network. (See Davis B. McCarn and Grace H. McCarn, "Beacon: H. W. Wilson's Computerized Information System," *Information Technology and Libraries,* June 1983.) Using a modified subsystem software entitled ELHILL developed by the National Library of Medicine, users will be able to search and retrieve information selectively from the H. W. Wilson Company's data base.

As a result of this research and development, the many Wilson indexes, including of course the *Index to Legal Periodicals* became available as an on-line computer retrieval system early in 1986. It thus joins a multitude of other data bases available to researchers by computers. Although, it is joining many other on-line literature-citing data bases which can be of use in legal research, still it is uniquely different. These other data bases are generally used independently of the other data bases. There are data bases, to mention a few, in accounting, (*The Accountants Index*, prepared by the American Institute of Certified Public Accountants, available through the SDC Search Service Business (The Harvard Business Review is available on line in full text through DIALOG Information Services (DIALOG); Government (The Congressional Information Service CIS, indexes and abstracts Congressional publication through DIALOG and SDC; the Government Printing Office (GPO) monthly catalogue lists publications of U. S. Government Agencies through BRS, Dialog and SDC); Labor (The International Labor Organization's doc File, abstracts and journals pertaining to labor published throughout the world, available through SDC). There are similar on-line services for medical information available through DIALOG and BIOSIS, such as MEDLINE and EXCERPTA MEDIA, which index thousands of medical journals published throughout the world; the News of the Day is captured through DIALOG.

Indexes to legal periodical literature are presently on line through the *Legal Resource Index* [InfoTrac] (accessible through DIALOG and the Social Science Citation Index is available through BRS and DIALOG).

Of course, this is only a mere sampling of on-line bibliographical citation services. There are full text files, such as business and financial information available from the Dow Jones News Service which will provide references not only to bibliographic citation to articles from the Wall Street Journal, Barrons and the Down Jones News Service, but also to the full text of the articles cited.

CHAPTER 15B

Periodical Literature Via Computer Searching

The following material comprises a new Chapter 15B for Legal Research and Law Library Management. *It is intended as supplemental material to the Main Text.*

[1]—Introduction to WILSONLINE

It is now possible to sit down at one's personal computer and dial in the contents of *Index to Legal Periodicals* as well as other periodical indexes, together with the *Cumulative Book Index*, which is a record of books published in English on all subjects, by issuing a few simple commands to one's machine. The source: WILSONLINE, the online access to the indexes published by H.W. Wilson Company—creator of the *Reader's Guide* and numerous other indexes.

For example, given the problem of finding everything written on the RIGHT OF PRIVACY—books and articles, both legal and nonlegal — there is no other single source that can accomplish this feat. Simply type in the expression, PRIVACY, RIGHT OF, and the result is a long list of articles. Numerous book titles are also included in the printout.

A total of eight indexes can be searched at a single command; eight others with a second command and the remaining three by a third command. The coverage: 2,900 periodicals. The likelihood of needing periodicals in more than eight branches of learning for a single problem is remote.

[a]—The Library's Contents. In addition to *Index to Legal Periodicals*, with its hundreds law reviews and journals that are now indexed on-line, *Reader's Guide to Periodical Literature* (182 periodicals), and *Cumulative Book Index*, WILSONLINE includes *Applied Science and Technology* (335 journals), *Art Index* (200 journals), *Business Periodicals Index* (304 journals), and *Social Sciences Index* (300 journals), together with other periodical indexes and related data bases in such fields as biography, biology, general sciences and even one devoted to book reviews on all subjects.

[b]—How WILSONLINE Works. Anyone familiar with LEXIS or WESTLAW will find WILSONLINE a simple-to-use data base. It can be mastered in less than a day. Access is obtained by subject, title, author, date or a combination of those factors. For example, the command "Find PRIVACY, RIGHT TO and from 1983 to 1986" will produce a list of books and articles on that subject during the period named. An accompanying printer can reproduce the list at the touch of a key.

Unique to this database is a thesaurus that has been developed primarily for that index. It expands on the indexing terms used in the index by grouping around major terms those words that either expand on the meaining of a term, limit its meaning, or are its synonyms. In addition, numerous cross references guide the reader from the term he may think of first to the term that WILSONLINE actually uses. One of the serious problems that LEXIS and WESTLAW must still solve is the choice of the precise word: if the judge writes *homicide* and the user thinks of *murder*, the user may miss the very case he needs. WILSONLINE expects to complete its legal thesaurus—the first full version—during 1986 and welcomes suggestions for its improvement and expansion.

With this thesaurus, it is making major strides in solving the choice-of-indexing-term dilemma for periodical article searching. It will be published as a separate, printed booklet and should prove useful both as a computer guide and in searching the printed version of *Index to Legal Periodicals* as well.

[c]—Machinery Required. This service is currently available and can be accessed through one's personal computer and through other computer systems in use in offices and libraries throughout the country. A modem would be needed to reach WILSONLINE with a PC (personal computer). It will shortly become available on all WESTLAW terminals.

[d]—The Cost. Charges to subscribers to the printed *Index to Legal Periodicals* range from $35 an hour of connect-time on the *computerized* index (for *Reader's Guide*) up to $55 an hour (for the legal and business periodical indexes). Simultaneous searches of more than a single database are billed as if they were searched separately. Other variations in the billing system are spelled out on a WILSONLINE rate schedule obtainable by calling [1-800-462-6060] in New York State and [1-800-367-6770] elsewhere.

[2]—Introduction to InfoTrac

InfoTrac is a computerized reference tool produced by Information Access Company in Belmont, California. It includes databases in various fields of learning with LegalTrac as its legal periodical and newspaper data base.

Its terminal keyboard operates in a fashion similar to WILSONLINE. The system uses Library of Congress subject headings with a few of its own additions. LegalTrac searches under both subject and author and can locate and print bibliographic references at great speed. A test search for selected newspaper articles published over a period of five years turned up twenty-one pertinent references in just under two minutes. This included both searching and printing time.

This data base covers approximately 750 publications, including law reviews, bar journals and seven legal newspapers, of which the *New York Law Journal* is one. The contents of this data base are also issued in hard copy form in *Current Law Index*. It appears in eight monthly, three quarterly numbers and a single annual cumulation, starting in January 1980.

A related service, accessible on the same terminal, is the Company's *Government Publications Index*. It is a computerized index to the *Monthly Catalog of United States Government Publications*. It can be searched by author, subject and by issuing agency. It is updated monthly and coverage begins in 1978.

[3]—A Plea for Coordination

There are now many hundreds of computerized data bases on all subjects that are available to lawyers. They cover law, business, finance, medicine and other scientific subjects and virtually every other branch of learning. Some are in full text, others in digest form and still others, like WILSONLINE, are indexes to other services.

Would it be too much to ask of LEXIS and WESTLAW, the leaders in this industry, to offer users a screened view of everything that is available, including the wares of competitors? What an advantage to see at a glance (1) a list of databases in each branch of knowledge; (2) the names of the supplying services; (3) the scope of each database—what it includes and for what period of time; and (4) the cost of its use!

CHAPTER 17

The Challenge of the Transnational Enterprise to Legal Research and Information Gathering

The following material comprises an addition to Chapter 17 of Legal Research and Law Library Management. *It is intended to be read in conjunction with the material in the Main Text.*

In reviewing the problems of research and collection development in international law the question "what is meant by international law?" has to be addressed.

Professor Edward Gordon has aptly described the context in which legal research in international law must be considered.[1] The phrases "international legal materials" and "international law" he notes, are not "synonymous." International legal materials "refers rather loosely to whatever materials an 'international lawyer' or scholar may find pertinent to his/her work. Even the phrase 'international lawyer' is imprecise. Most practising lawyers use the term to refer to lawyers specializing in transnational business problems, usually corporate and tax law but sometimes involving estates and trusts, criminal matters, and even immigration and naturalization . . . . Traditionalists would hardly regard these practitioners as 'international lawyers' for the simple reason that the legal norms these practitioners usually deal with are national—multinational perhaps, but still national—rather than 'international law' in the strictest or strictly traditional sense."

---

[1] Gordon, "Acquiring International Legal Materials," 72 L. Lib. J. 476, 477 (1979).

In essence, Professor Gordon's thinking reflects the changing role of public and private international law and how both practitioners and academics are being affected by this changing role.

Generally, public international law reflects the body of laws between and among sovereign states that govern relations with each other, such as rules of warfare and interstate relations in times of peace. In addition, it now encompasses economic, social, cultural and trade relations between countries and their nationals. These new developments are increasingly being codified in subject areas such as international trade, criminal law, admiralty, law of the sea, aviation law, immigration and naturalization and human rights.

International law, however, takes on an even more significant role for practitioners in the field known as private international law or, as popularly known in the United States, conflict of laws. Here we are concerned with the effect of different national laws on a specific international transaction. In this context, the rights and obligations of private persons come into question when a dispute arises over an international transaction involving the law of more than one country. In matters such as business, taxation, products liability, torts and property, and in this context, the questions arise as to which country's court obtains jurisdiction and which laws are to be applied to resolve the issue or issues that come into play. These ever-increasing problems in areas of international trade, involving choice of law, can no longer be described merely as being a subject of private international law. Rather, as the well known international jurist and professor, Philip Jessup, has suggested, a more relevant description would be "transnational law." Others have called it "multinational law."

Consider, for example, the role of an American lawyer in providing legal advice to a client involved in a transaction affected by rules of international law as well as the national laws of more than one foreign state. Obviously, there is a need to acquire an understanding of the national laws which may affect the international transaction. In addition, that lawyer will also have to look to international economic law found basically in primary sources such as treaties and conventions, statutes, decisions of courts and tribunals, both national, international and institutional, and in secondary materials such as commentaries, treatises and periodical literature.

Then again public international law as understood in its more classic sense (such as pertains to the use of the sea and air space, immunity of states, nationality of individuals and corporations, international responsibility of states and international claims, and agreements) may, on occasion, also be of concern to the lawyer negotiating an international business transaction. Public international law, with its effect on international transactions, can be highly relevant to the negotiating parties. For example, the United Nations Charter of Economic Rights promulgates principles affecting the peaceful settlement of disputes, the equal sovereignty of states and international cooperation for development. Chapter II of the United Nations Charter specifies the economic rights and duties of states, some of which obviously will affect international commerce. Consider, for example, such issues as sovereignty over natural resources, the right of association, the meaning of juridical equality, the transfer of technology and the prohibition of the use of economic, political or other measurers as sanctions.

Lawyers are also concerned with how European Common Market law affects antitrust and control of unfair competition, licensing, mergers, product liability and consumer protection. Most international business planning cannot avoid the effect of European private commercial transaction law. In this context, forms of international contracts, including sale of goods, loans, joint ventures, measure of damages, letters of credit, rights of commercial agents and tax conventions must also be considered. Similarly, international commercial arbitration is playing an important role in the settlement of controversies in international trade.

It would appear that for purposes of legal analysis and research, the law pertaining to international trade is reflected first in the national law of the countries where the multinational transactions take place (such as commercial law, conflict of laws, business organizations law, etc.). Then, national governmental regulations imposed on the transaction by customs, tariffs, tax laws, import controls, products liability, etc. must be researched. Finally, at the international and regional levels, applicable treaties and conventions must also be studied.

How should law libraries meet the thrust of these developments in providing reference service to their users? How much should they acquire of international, foreign and comparative legal materials, considering the exigencies of their budget and the overall research needs of those researchers? Although "transnational" and "multinational" are comparatively recent terms of art covering a wide range of what are essentially international business transactions, still they reflect a felt need of the legal profession for research support. Law librarians now recognize that these materials have become a necessary part of a law library collection—a far cry from the days when foreign law books were generally regarded as luxuries in a law library.[2] If they are to be treated as essential, what should be their size and contents in a particular law library? A mere scanning of current bibliographies is convincing evidence of the publication explosion that has taken place in this subject area. Note for example the tremendous output of official publications alone which as Professor Albert H. Garretson described "has taxed the ingenuity of law librarians and excited the groans of the laborer in the increasingly tangled jungle."[3]

It is in the medium-sized and small libraries where the need to provide reference service in foreign law and international law is recognized, that the limitations of budget and even space create the real difficulty in establishing a proper collection development policy. Here the experts generally agree, the collection should be limited to basic materials as a first step.

What is meant by a basic collection in international and foreign and comparative law? Here the answer lies in the purpose of the collection. In turn, the purpose of the collection will depend on the type of library. A practitioner's library should stress practical material, such as books on foreign corporations or tax law. Obviously, a specialized library such as one on copyright law, or taxation, or international trade will limit its foreign literature to those particular fields of interest. A university library must meet the thrust of its teaching program as well as its institutional research interest and research specialization of its faculty.

---

[2] See Thorne, "Foreign Law Books in American Libraries," 28 L. Lib. J. 173 (1935).

[3] See 12 J. Leg. Ed. 312.

Most law firm libraries tend to avoid acquiring international law materials unless the need is strongly justified. They would rather borrow and photocopy materials in other libraries collecting these materials. At the same time, lawyers aware of the significance of these materials in their research, are beginning to add foreign law specialists to their office staff. They recognize that having a good basic collection in this area, while insufficient to address professionally the resolution of a specific case in the office, still is essential for quick reference, for background and for preliminary review. It should also be noted that these types of legal materials are of even greater use to the private practitioner since they are of the type that the average library will not lend, because they cannot be spared.

Lily Roberts, then with the University of Michigan Law Library, noted in 1960 that American libraries are interested in foreign law only insofar as it is of interest to Americans.[4] This means, she added, that comparative law should be stressed—for comparative law is the bridge that leads the American lawyer to understand the methods and techniques of the foreign jurist. For similar reasons, conflict of laws must be emphasized for it establishes first contact with foreign law and in fact decides whether and what foreign law applies. The United States lawyer concerned with a client's problem in the international law arena will in the main consult a foreign lawyer for detailed information on specific aspects of the foreign law involved. Books providing general orientation and introduction to foreign legal systems are a useful beginning, but scarcely all that is required.

The greatest problem for United States lawyers concerned with foreign law is the language gap. Few American lawyers know foreign languages. Librarians should stress in their collection development policy the acquisition of foreign legal information and documentation in English.

Of great value would be translations into English of primary source materials such as constitutions, codes, laws and even some of the standard text books. Given the need for the text of foreign laws in English, there are far too few translations of specific

---

[4] See 53 L. Lib. J. 379 (1960).

codes. True—there are some of the French and German Civil Codes, for example, but these are isolated and not part of a comprehensive total context. Rothman, BNA, Matthew Bender, Oceana and other publishers have published some of these translations. Oceana is committed to a comprehensive program of published translations in English of the commercial business and trade laws of major trading nations, and has published digests in English of the commercial laws of the world. Both projects are organized on a country by country basis. Oceana seeks to provide a selection of the most important legislation in each of the jurisdictions covered pertaining to day to day commercial operations by corporations and other entities involved in overseas trade investment and establishment problems. These English translations of texts of laws should be part of every basic foreign law collection.

There are numerous books in English about foreign law which are also of value as part of the basic collection. A number of Anglo-American periodicals feature articles on foreign law as well. These are noted in the *Index to Legal Periodicals.*

Primary sources of foreign law are too often available only in publications in the original language. Obviously, it will be impractical for the average American law library to collect material in languages such as Russian and Arabic. The language difficulties, much too often, are insurmountable. It is gratifying to note that Oceana is publishing the English translations of Russian legal materials and those of Arabic states.

Fortunately, French, Spanish and German are languages that can be handled by a number of law librarians and many users of foreign legal materials. Hence development of the library collection in foreign law in those areas is feasible. In considering Western civil law countries' legal materials for acquisition, the experts recommend that French law is most important. The Code Napoleon has served as a model for the civil code of the nations of half the Western part of continental Europe, much of the Middle East, as well as Louisiana, Quebec and Latin American countries. Next to French, concentration should be on German codes. These too have been influential in many other countries whose codes have been modeled on them, such as Japan, Switzerland and Turkey. It has also been noted that local interests might stress the laws of specific countries. For example, libraries in New Mexico, Texas, Florida and California will emphasize Mexican and Latin American law.

When a law library decides to invest in the development of a civil law collection, after the codes—then what? The formal sources of law in the civil law system, after the constitution and the codes, are legislation affecting the codes, court decisions and doctrinal writings including periodical literature. Although the chief sources of civil law are to be found in the codes, it should be noted that codified law is amplified, restricted or modified by newly enacted legislation, judicial precedents and the opinions of commentators and text book writers.

There are five basic codes in the civil law system. These are the civil code, commercial and penal codes and the codes of civil procedure and criminal procedure. There are other codes, of course, in areas such as taxation, but these five are the important ones. They are continually being published in new editions. A good rule of thumb in this context is to follow the practice of a number of university law libraries and buy a new edition of the code about every three to five years.

Court decisions in civil law countries play a relatively secondary role, and actually are not precedents in the sense of common law decisions. However, opinions of legal writers are given great weight as authority by the courts. In Sweden, for example, opinions of eminent law professors can be submitted to the courts as authoritative statements of the law. After referring to the code, foreign lawyers consult these leading treatises or commentaries. It has been recommended that a smaller library has more to gain by purchasing these treatises rather than the expensive court reports for civil law countries.

Note that a great number of foreign legal periodicals are listed in the *Index to Foreign Legal Periodicals.* They are important for current developments. This is one area where selective acquisition should be the policy. The maintenance of a foreign legal periodical collection could be a continuing drain on the library's financial resources. Specialization should be the guiding rule here. A law library with an interest in copyright law should pick out some of the leading foreign copyright periodicals, while an insurance law library should concentrate on leading foreign insurance law periodicals.

As the acquisition of specific foreign law materials geared to international trade and business swells we create in effect a collection of transnational (or multinational) law materials. Publishers here aim at creating country-by-country coverage of legislation, regulations and related documentation in specific subject matter areas. Antitrust and restraint of business, for example, or product liability, or investment laws, or securities regulation are typical of the subject matter coverage. Oceana has developed perhaps the most extensive grouping of transnational services, followed by Matthew Bender and Clark Boardman. Predominantly these publications are issued in a loose-leaf format so that they may be readily updated.

It is also recommended that where English language publications are not available on foreign legal systems, it is helpful to acquire books in French, Spanish or German. Several highly specialized practitioner libraries collect original language material when their firms have internal translation capability.

It is essential for any foreign law collection to feature dictionaries, lists of abbreviations and foreign legal bibliographies. It is also important to keep a list of foreign law publishers and dealers and a record of foreign legal experts and translators in one's home city.

Basic to an international law collection are United States treaty law and the *United Nations Treaty Series*. In international law, treaties and other international agreements take the place of legislation. They have been aptly described them as "international legislation."

Another source of international law is "state practice." This reflects the statements of the position taken by governments on legal and diplomatic questions. These statements appear in diplomatic correspondence, in government documents, in judicial decisions by national and international courts and in opinions of Attorneys General or in the United Kingdom, Law Officers to the Foreign Office. As part of this process, acquisition should be made of the official records and documentation of the United States, Great Britain, United Nations and the international agencies, as well as those of the European Economic Community. The decisions of the International Court of Justice and of the Court of Justice of the European Communities are published regularly and are worthwhile additions to a basic collection. The National Court reports on international law should appear in the Court reporting of the nation concerned, but there are specialized collections of

American, British, Commonwealth, French and German international law decisions. Law reviews are helpful for this purpose. Leading treatises on international law are also important for research purposes in the field.

Vaclav Mostecky, then International Law Librarian at Harvard Law School, summed up the process of answering questions on foreign law substance in seven steps which suggest what the contents of a basic international and foreign and comparative law collection should be.[5]

1) Consult an English language treatise on the subject.

2) If the answer is not found, use a foreign language treatise on the subject and follow its footnotes to laws and court decisions.

3) Recent articles in periodicals may be of assistance in a similar way.

4) Search through the indexes to codes, commentaries to codes, or indexes to legislation when available. (Treaties are another valuable source.)

5) For some countries such as France, consult looseleaf services to legislation, digests and repertories. They will refer to both laws and court decisions.

6) When a pertinent section of the code or law is found, search official gazettes up to the present time for amendments or change in legislation.

7) Consult related treatises and compilations of laws of the country.

Of course, Mostecky wrote before the current vast proliferation of international law, international trade and foreign law materials in English. At that time, it was common to distinguish between public international law involving sovereignties, and private international law, involving individuals or entities of different countries. While the distinction remains valid, the interrelationship between the two in day-to-day international commerce and business is constantly reasserted.

Miles O. Price, then Law Librarian of Columbia Law School, had much experience in developing the foreign law collection of

---

[5] Mostecky, "Reference Service in Foreign Law," 55 L. Lib. J. 386 (1962).

Columbia. He had occasion in 1947 to set forth his thoughts on building a foreign law collection.[6] His advice is still good today:

> ". . . We cannot cover the ground thoroughly, but have to make up our minds what fundamental and secondary materials we shall acquire from each foreign country. You have to have a policy and stick to it. You must decide for each country whether you are going to get everything, laws, codes, commentaries, reports, periodicals, etc., nationally and for the provinces . . . You need a long range buying policy, because it is usually impossible to pick up back issues of this material with the facility with which it can be done in the United States."

---

[6] See 40 L. Lib. J. 170 (1947).

CHAPTER 17A

International Commercial Law Materials

The following material comprises a new Chapter 17A for Legal Research and Law Library Management. *It is intended as supplemental material to the Main Text.*

American publishers are responding to the need of practitioners in the United States for materials on international business and commercial law.

One of the pioneer publishers in the field is Oceana Publications of Dobbs Ferry, N.Y. It publishes a series of looseleaf collections of the principal commercial, business and trade laws of the major trading nations and regions of the world under the title *Commercial Business and Trade Laws-Text of Laws-Translated into English*. With a view to providing help for those who are concerned with international business transactions, the intention is to publish a selection of the most important legislation in each of the jurisdictions covered that is likely to be encountered in day to day commercial operations by corporations and other entities involved in overseas trade, investment and establishment problems. For this reason emphasis is placed on the provision of legislative texts, often in an original translation, in their current form with revisions and amendments.

The texts are accompanied by a brief commentary on the materials presented. An introduction gives a synoptical survey of the sources of commercial law in the jurisdiction concerned. In certain cases, notably in China and Iran, the materials thus made available are published for the first time in the English language.

Oceana has selected 64 major trading nations as its first priority in the publishing program and has classified them under the following groups: China and Northeast Asia; Asian and the Pacific, Asian sub-continent; Middle East and North Africa, North America and the Caribbean, Central America and South America, European Economic Community and European Free Trade Association.

Oceana also publishes, in English, a *Digest of Commercial Laws of the World* jointly with the National Association of Credit Managers. The digest, in looseleaf format contains abstracts of commercial laws only, and does not deal with such matters as import and export regulations, foreign exchange regulations, taxes and similar subjects. In this context, it is worthwhile to note the Bureau of national Affairs' *International Trade Reporter's U.S. Import Weekly, U.S. Export Weekly* and *Export Shipping Manual*. The *Export Shipping Manual* provides access to foreign import regulations and U.S. export controls for nearly 200 countries. The *U.S. Import Weekly* offers timely notification of significant developments, research materials and full text of statutes, regulations and judicial and administrative decisions on U.S. Import laws, as does the BNA *U.S. Export Weekly* for the export trade field.

Oceana also publishes works on Transnational Transactions such as *Antitrust and Restrictive Business Practices: International, Regional and National Regulations* by Julius J. Marke and Najeeb Samie; *East-West Trade: A Sourcebook on the International Relations of Socialist Countries and their Legal Aspects* by D.A. Loeber; *East-West Trade: COMECON Law; American Soviet Trade,* by T.W. Hoya; *The International Arbitral Process: Public and Private,* by J. Gillis Wetter; *International Tax Treaties of All Nations,* by W.H. Diamond and B. Diamond; *Investment Insurance in International Law* by Theodor Meron; *Multinational Corporations Law,* by K.R. Simmonds, and *Transnational Contracts: Applicable Laws and Settlements of Disputes (A Study of Conflict Avoidance),* by George R. Delaume.

For more than 108 years West Publishing Co. has been providing the bench and bar with the primary sources and finding tools for research in United States law. West announced that it is engaged in the publication of an *International Legal Library* which will stress transnational commercial law, covering extensively original sources, commentaries and annotations in competition law and antitrust, investment laws, contracts, sales, and doing business in general.

Some of the publications to appear in the *International Legal Library* have already been announced by West. They are: *Competition Law in West Europe and the U.S.A.*, a ten volume looseleaf set, cooperatively published with Kluwer of the Netherlands, a European legal publisher. In essence, this set is an encyclopedia of the competition and antitrust laws of the United States, Western Europe and the European Common Market, which will be updated monthly. Experienced lawyers for each of the countries covered and the European Common Market, under the general editor, E.J. Gijlstra, provide the antitrust laws of each Western European Country as well as texts of relevant legislation of the Common Market and the European Coal and Steel Community, regulations and policy statements of regulating agencies, and commentaries on case law and legislation.

International Business Series-Legal Aspects of Doing Business Throughout the World. Projected to be published in eight volumes with annual pocket supplementation and edited generally by Dennis Campbell, Director; European Programs of the McGeorge School of Law, this series will provide commentary and direction on doing business in the various jurisdictions of the world. Each volume will be written by practising lawyers and will cover the present political, social and economic climate for foreign business and investment in the area involved. A brief introduction to the legal system of each country, suggestions about the appropriate forms of business organizations available for the foreign investor, as well as regulation permit requirements, tax and labor aspects will also be provided. Volume 1, entitled *Legal Aspects of Doing Business in Europe* has already been published. The succeeding seven volumes to be published will be entitled: *Legal Aspects of Doing Business in Asia and the Pacific; Legal Aspects of Doing Business in Latin America; Legal Aspects of Doing Business in Africa; Legal Aspects of Doing Business in North America;* and *Legal Aspects of Doing Business in Eastern Europe and the Soviet Union*.

West has already issued its *West's Multi-Lingual Law and Commercial Dictionary*, a two-volume work which contains more than 14,000 entries. Each English word listed is completely defined with references to court citations where applicable followed by the equivalent foreign word or phrase in German, French, Spanish and Italian. It is so arranged that a user, whose primary language is German, French, Spanish or Italian will be able to locate the English equivalent under its separate title. Users with a knowledge lof English will have immediate access to all other equivalent foreign words and phrases.

Matthew Bender's International Catalogue also reveals a real commitment of its International Division to meet the thrust of the growing need of practitioners for authoritative materials in the field of international commercial business and trade laws. Its International Business Series features a number of looseleaf works on doing business in certain countries and areas. In its *Law of the European Economic Community,* authored by Hans Smit and Peter Herzog, in six volumes, which is updated as needed, comprehensive coverage is provided of relevant legal details of the EEC as established by the Treaty of Rome. Each article of the Treaty is reprinted in its entirety, followed by an explanation of its meaning, legal effect and implementation. A list of pertinent community enactments, court cases, a bibliography and an overview for each major subdividion of the Treaty are also provided. Community policies on trade, labor, and antitrust along with explanations of the EEC's organizational structure, the role of the Court of Justice and community relations with East and West are brought out. Other publications which should be noted in this context are: *Doing Business in Japan* by Z. Kitagawa (9 volumes, looseleaf); *Doing Business in Canada,* (2 volumes, looseleaf); *Review Law* by D. G. Willougby (2 volumes, looseleaf); *Business Transactions in Germany* (4 volumes, looseleaf); *Doing Business in Brazil* (1 volume, looseleaf); and *Doing Business in Mexico* (2 volumes, looseleaf). All these publications are updated regularly.

Matthew Bender has two reference works on Competition Law which are well-known. *World Law of Competition,* by Von Kalinowski in 11 looseleaf volumes, which is updated regularly provides analyses of the antitrust regulations of 15 major countries in the United States and Western Europe. Its *EEC Competition Law Reporter* in six bound volumes and one looseleaf, current reporter, provides materials relevant to EEC Competition law translated into English. Bender also co-publishes with Beck of Munich, Germany, a *Dictionary of Legal, Commercial and Political Terms-English/German* in one volume. This is a reference tool which contains German translations of 60,000 legal, economic and political terms, including British and American usages that have no German equivalents.

Matthew Bender also features looseleaf treatises on *Japanese International Taxation; Tax Havens of the World* by W.H. Diamond and D.B. Diamond; and *Tax-Free Trade Zones of the World* by the same authors. In the field of Intellectual Property, Bender publishes *World*

Patent Law and Policy, by Baxter and Sinnott (2 volumes, looseleaf); a *European Patents Handbook* 9 volumes looseleaf) and a *World Trademark Law and Practice* by E. Horowitz (4 volumes, looseleaf).

Mathew Bender also publishes *The International Economic Law Series,* 2nd Edition, edited by Professor Andreas Lowenfeld. Volume 1 is on *International Private Trade,* volume 2, *International Private Investment,* volume 3, *Trade Control for Political Ends,* volume 4, *The International Monetary System,* volume 5, *Tax Aspects of International Transactions,* by David Tillinghast, and volume 6, *Public Controls of International Trade.*

Another publisher with a marked interest in international legal materials is Clark, Boardman. Its *International Business and Law Series* features a number of reference sources in the field. The *Law of Transnational Business Transactions* will provide current treatment of major legal aspects of those transactions and is designed specifically for practitioners. It analyzes and examines the practical implications involved in establishing a U.S. client abroad or helping a foreign client transact business in the U.S. The *Law and Practice of International Finance* provides reference sources to the laws which can affect a contract in financing an international transaction.

Particularly worthy of note is this publisher's *Licensing in Foreign and Domestic Operations* which not only covers the licensing of all standard industrial property rights throughout the world but also includes patent, trademark, copyright and licensing laws of various countries around the world. It also covers commercial arbitrations and overseas investment factors. A related volume on *Forms* contains a selection of over 1500 pages of licensing agreements. The company also publishes a number of books on licensing: *A Manual on Licensing Procedures; Forms and Agreements on Intellectual Property and International Licensing; Licensing Law Handbook;* and *The Law and Business of Licensing.* Its works on *Patents Throughout the World* and *Trademarks Throughout the World,* provide digests of the laws of 200 countries and their territorial subdivisions and colonies in those areas.

Obviously there are other publishers and other publications in the field. Their omission should not be interpreted as a reflection on their value to the researcher.

CHAPTER 22A

The Compact Research Center

The following material comprises a new Chapter 22A for Legal Research and Law Library Management. *It is intended as supplemental material to the Main Text.*

Great lawyers have many talents: the power to analyze and synthesize ideas; negotiating abilities; debating and even acting skills. Rarely is legal research one of their talents. Most lawyers fear and hate it. Many have to be dragged kicking and screaming into the library. Once there all they see are walls of reporters, codes, digests, encyclopedias with no entry key. Yet their work generates endless questions that require quick and accurate answers.

Why not create a compact research center in the form of a five-foot shelf of books? It would answer routine questions on the spot and serve as a guide in resolving the complex ones. For those who maintain a professionally managed library, it would complement that library. In it would be placed four types of books:

A. Directories, for example, that identify other lawyers and firms; that locate county seats or court clerks and in general answer the current "who," "what," "where" and "when" kinds of questions about people, companies and other institutions;

B. Bibliographies. Checklists and Periodical Indexes that show what books and articles have been written on specific subjects;

C. Legal Research and Library Management manuals that explain how to use that wall of books in the library, how to plan the best and most economical use of library space and even how to move a library; and

D. General Reference Works, including almanacs, handbooks, quotation collections and road atlases.

Set out below are some books recommended for a lawyer's five-foot shelf of books. Unless restraint is exercised it will quickly grow to ten feet. The list is selective, not all-inclusive. Others might select fewer or more or different or bigger books. It is offered as a checklist of suggestions. It should be tailored to each lawyer's particular needs.

As time passes, the desktop computer will begin to replace many of those books. Right now it has the capacity, for example, to store directory information or lists of all the books and memoranda of law in one's library. Moreover it can display them by subject or in any required form. Until that is done the five-foot reference shelf will continue to prove its worth.

A. Directories

Martindale-Hubbell Law Directory and Digests, Summit, N.J., Martindale-Hubbell, Inc. With new volumes issued annually, the Martindale-Hubbell set is probably the most useful single reference tool in any law office. Its current edition has seven volumes the first six of which contain a directory of lawyers in the United States, arranged alphabetically by state and then city, which includes the District of Columbia and Puerto Rico (that appears following Pennsylvania and before Rhode Island), and foreign countries, alphabetically by country.

The seventh volume contains a series of digests of state, United States and foreign country laws and the full text of uniform and model acts.

Examination of any of the first six volumes will show the common features of all the directory volumes—the ones that make *Martindale* indispensable in any office.

1. Inside the front cover is a guide to the rating system used for legal ability of lawyers: a. very high; b. high; c. fair. In addition the symbol "v" is used to mean a very high rating with respect to ethical standards, professional reliability and diligence. These are not empty signposts. The ratings have won acceptance throughout the profession.

2. Corporate legal departments included in the directory are listed by company at prefatory pages in the last volume.

3. A list of colleges, universities and independent law schools is also included. Canadian and foreign schools follow the U.S. list. Each institution is assigned a number. For example, Columbia is 178, Harvard 309, Penn 659 and Yale 976.

4. Preceding the lawyers' directory for each state is the name of the state capital followed by a list of counties and county seats.

5. The balance of each of the directory volumes is divided into two main divisions:

First, a geographical section containing as complete a list of lawyers in each city as the publishers can collect. For each lawyer, there is listed a birth date, date of admission to practice, the code number of his or her college and law school, the state in which admitted, the rating and firm or company affiliation, if any. The firm affiliation appears last and contains the full or major portion of the first name of the firm, e.g., Morg. followed only by the initials of the other names in the firm: L for Lewis and B for Bockius.

Second, a biographical section containing directories of individual firms, showing for each member fairly detailed biographical information and for some firms, particularly in medium-sized and smaller cities, a representative list of clients.

Examination of the seventh volume shows a digest of the laws of each state, of Puerto Rico and the Virgin Islands; Canada and of its ten provinces separately; of U.S. Patent, Trademark and Copyright laws and of the law generally for fifty-two other leading countries of the world. Ireland and Northern Ireland are treated separately.

The digest for New York was drafted by the firm of Rogers & Wells, that for Pennsylvania by the Ballard, Spahr firm in Philadelphia. They are arranged alphabetically by major topics, e.g., "Commercial Law," "Corporations," "Deeds." Every digest statement—almost every sentence—cites to a specific numbered provision in the state's code or in the court rules. The digests also contain model forms and a statement of prescribed fees. This volume also contains the full text of the Uniform Commercial Code, the Uniform Probate Code and other uniform and model acts. It provides too some information on United States, state, Puerto Rican and Virgin Island courts.

Recommended as the first and, if necessary, the only law office purchase.

Directory of Law Libraries, Chicago, American Ass'n. of Law

Libraries. With new editions published biennially, this volume provides a list of law libraries arranged alphabetically by state and then city for the United States; by province and then city for Canada and by country and then city for foreign libraries. It contains an alphabetical list of active, life (mostly retired) and associate (most publishing house) members. Under each library is a librarian's name, address and phone number, and a rough classification of the size of the collection in volumes. The 1980 edition gives specific collection size statistics not contained in subsequent issues. Instead collections are classified in one of four size groups.

Classified Telephone Directories. The "yellow pages" is one of the least appreciated of reference books. Next to Martindale-Hubbell, it should be the most heavily used directory in the library. In larger cities, the classified phone book has numerous special features of value to lawyers. In Manhattan, in New York City, for example, the "yellow pages" includes:

1. Local Zip Code map;
2. Subway and bus routes;
3. A formula for locating the nearest cross street to addresses on all north-south avenues in Manhattan;
4. Special listings of interest to lawyers;
    a. Appraisers;
    b. Associations—including trade associations;
    c. Book Dealers;
    d. Government Offices—City, State, U.S. and Foreign Representatives;
    e. Lawyers—This listing is often more current than the one in *Martindale*;
    f. Political Organizations;
    g. Social Service Organizations;
    h. A 250-year calendar.

The United States Government Manual, Washington, D.C., Government Printing Office (Office of the Federal Register, National Archives and Records Service, General Service Administration). This official handbook of the federal government is published every other year. It provides information on the agencies of the legislative, judicial and executive branches of government, including names of officials, addresses, phone numbers, functions of each agency, statutory authority for it to operate and lists of leading publications.

Most important, set out in bold face type for each agency is the name of an office, an address and telephone number where additional information about the agency and its rules can be obtained.

For example, being unable to find the FCC's rules for "Loud Commercials" on radio and television in either C.F.R. or Federal Register indexes, a call was placed to the phone number for the agency listed in the *Governmental Manual*. Help was offered by an actual person (not a mere recording) who knew immediately that these were guidelines, not rules, and who cited two publications where they were set out and willingly mailed a copy of those guidelines the same afternoon.

In addition, there are a series of tables and appendices that provide information about the leading multilateral and bilateral organizations in which the United States participates, a list of abolished and transferred agencies and functions mentioned in the body of the manual together with a fairly detailed subject index.

State and City Directories. Some states and larger cities issue directories of value to lawyers. New York City, for example, issues the *Official Directory of the City of New York* every other year. This is a directory of all New York City agencies, giving for each its official name, address, telephone numbers, chief officers, a statement of functions and for many agencies a reference to the law under which it operates. The listing for the Law Department, headed by the Corporation Counsel, is divided alphabetically in accordance with functions from administrative law to worker's compensation. The City's legal problems are complex, enormous and growing. This Directory tells who handles which kinds of problems and how to reach the appropriate lawyer.

A fascinating feature of the directory is the section headed "Licenses, Permits, Certificates—Where to Apply" which lists some 1,500 kinds of activities that the City of New York regulates. Also included is the name of the agency that supervises each activity. Some examples: antique dealers, architects, homemade wines, water heaters, working papers.

There is an alphabetical list of agencies at the front and a list of all city officials at the back. To my knowledge no city in the United States issues a more useful annual directory than this one.

If that were not enough, the book, popularly known as "The Little Green Book" also provides information about offices of county, court, New York State, federal and international agencies in the City.

There is also the *Medical Directory of New York State,* published by the Medical Society of the State of New York in Lake Success. The *Directory* lists New York physicians showing their educational background and qualifications or specialties. Also included is information about hospitals in the state.

B. Bibliographies, Indexes

Recommended Law Books. ABA. Business Law Libraries Committee of the Section of Corporation, Banking and Business Law (Chicago, ABA, 1986). A practitioner's source for leading treatises and other publications on law and related subjects. Its most important feature is the annotations, written by a specialist, about many of the books listed.

Law Books in Print. Dobbs Ferry, Glanville, five volumes. An author, title, subject and publisher catalog. Kept current by a quarterly and annual supplement: *Law Books Published.*

Books in Print, New York, R. R. Bowker. A multi-volume set issued annually, these volumes list currently available books in all fields by author, title and subject matter. There is a separate set for books currently available in paperback.

After exhausting *Law Books in Print* and *Recommended Law Books,* the title one may need on any subject (except Law in which this series is fairly weak) is likely to be found in one of these catalogs. Because of their relatively high cost, it may be sensible to buy a set of these books every other year or two, or to consult them at one's local book store. It should be remembered that the "yellow pages" for all cities lists dealers in both new and out-of-print books.

Environmental Law: A Guide to Information Sources, Compiled by Mortimer D. Schwartz, Detroit, Gale, 1977. An annotated guide in three parts: 1. The Legal Process; 2. Political Controls; and 3. Conservation of Resources. This guide is illustrative of the kinds of subject guides that Gale issues. Others cover accounting, business law and real estate sources.

Index to Legal Periodicals. Bronx, N.Y., H. W. Wilson, Monthly with periodic cumulations. The standard index to law reviews and legal periodicals with entries under authors and subjects. There is a separate case table and book review section in each issue. A new competitor is Current Law Index, published in Menlo Park, California by Information Access Corp.

C. Legal Research

In addition to the volume you are now reading, which also contains chapters on law library management, four books are recommended as refresher or reference texts on legal research.

Legal Research in a Nutshell. 4th ed. by Morris L. Cohen, St. Paul, West, 1985. Presents the main facts in simple-to-understand language. Answers a surprisingly broad number of questions basic to research in case, statute and regulatory law.

How to Find the Law. 8th ed. Morris L. Cohen and Robert Berring, St. Paul, West, 1983. A collection of essays on the main phases of legal research.

Effective Legal Research. 4th ed. by Shirley M. Bysiewicz (Based on Price and Bitner), Boston, Little, Brown, 1979. The scholar's sourcebook, carefully and thoroughly edited.

Fundamentals of Legal Research. by J. Myron Jacobstein and Roy M. Mersky, 2d ed. Mineola, Foundation Press, 1981. A basic manual for law students modernized from Pollack's well-known guide.

D. General Reference Works

Included in this group are books that will answer a high proportion of the factual questions that lawyers ask. It is divided into three main parts: (1) Legal Information Handbooks; (2) Dictionaries, Style Manuals and Quotation Books; and (3) Legal Newspapers.

1. Legal Information Handbooks.

The Lawyer's Almanac, New York, Law & Business—Harcourt, Brace Jovanovich, 1982.

Subtitled, "A Cornucopia of Information about Law, Lawyers and the Profession, this handbook has six main divisions only a few features from which are listed below to illustrate the varied kinds of facts that the book contains.

I. The Legal Profession: Lists of large law firms, data on leading corporate legal departments, lawyers' compensation, career opportunities in federal government, approved law schools, bar admission requirements in the various states, lits of legal periodicals and newspapers throughout the country, bar association officers, staff members and committees.

II. The Judiciary: The federal bench, the state benches with jurisdictional and fee facts, litigation statistics.

III. Government Departments and Agencies: For the federal government, abbreviated lists of what appears in massive detail in the *U.S. Government Manual.* For state governments, some facts about the operation and rules of the various legislatures, a table showing state review of administrative regulations (reprinted from *The Book of the States,* 1980-81 published by Council of State Governments in Lexington, Kentucky) and a list of leading state agencies and agency officials; a state by state chart (with a separate entry for the City of New York) that shows where to write for birth, death, marriage and divorce records.

IV. Statutory Summaries and Checklists: Summaries of statutory facts, state by state, showing age of majority, rights of women, marriage and divorce laws, consumer laws, usury and bad check laws among many others. For example: employment, motor vehicles and natural resources. Also included are tables that show the adoption of uniform laws by the various states of the United States.

V. Text of Selected Statutes and Codes: Privacy Act of 1974, Government in the Sunshine Act, Titles in the United States Code and Agencies appearing in C.F.R.

VI. Commonly Used Abbreviations: Court reports, government agencies (with their acronyms) and abbreviations of periodicals.

The Law Librarian's Professional Desk Reference and Diary. Compiled by Arlene J. Stern, N.Y., Infosources Publishing. A law librarian's sourcebook that collects current information about federal, state and other agencies, each with names and telephone numbers of officers. In addition, it includes the following kinds of facts:

I. *Legislative:* Popular names of public laws together with references to major bills enacted and house and senate reports filed; "Hotline" telephone numbers in each state for learning the status of bills; a list of current state codes and their publishers;

II. *Library and School Information:* A directory of suppliers and law book publishers; a directory of Government Printing Office book stores in twenty-seven cities; a list of law schools in the United States and Canada; lists of periodicals indexed in both the *Index to Legal Periodicals and Current Law Index* with subscription information for each publication.

III. *General:* Consumer Price Index figures for Urban Wage Earners (U.S. City Averages) monthly from January 1949, a United States time zone map with telephone area code numbers for major cities or regions of the country.

Subject Compilations of State Laws compiled by Lynn Foster and Carol Boast, Westport, Greenwood Press, 1981. This extensive and annotated bibliography was developed at the University of Illinois School of Law Library from answers to the question, "What are all the states' laws on—?" It covers the twenty-year period from 1960 to 1979 and includes a few hundred subjects ranging from abortion to workmen's compensation. There are separate chapters on "Doing" and on "Locating a Subject Compilation of State Laws." Each entry has a short informative annotation. The arrangement is alphabetical by subject with numerous cross references. It contains an author index and a directory of publishers. Altogether a fine contribution that can save lawyers and librarians many hundreds of hours in research.

2. Dictionaries, Style Manuals and Quotation Books.

Black's Law Dictionary, St. Paul, West.

Ballantine's Law Dictionary, Rochester, Lawyer's Cooperative Publishing Co.

Webster. The latest Merriam-Webster edition of their *Collegiate* and *New International Dictionary* in the third and second editions. All three are exceptionally useful. The second edition of the "New International" is available through out-of-print sources.

Roget's Thesaurus of English Words and Phrases. New York, St. Martin's Press. Available in numerous editions. There should not be a law office that does not have one or more copies of *Roget.*

A Uniform System of Citations, Cambridge, The Harvard Law Review Association.

Modern Legal Usage. New York, Oxford University Press, 1988.

A Manual of Style. Revised. Chicago, Univ. of Chicago Press. A personal favorite among style books. Also useful is any recent edition of the *Government Style Manual* issued by the Government Printing Office.

Familiar Quotations (John Bartlett). Edited by Emily Morison Beck, Boston, Little, Brown. Probably the best and most comprehensive collection of quotations in English. Some offices still find concordances to the Bible and to Shakespeare useful. *Strong's Exhaustive Concordance of the Bible* has been re-issued many times since 1894 and is still in print. Bartlett's *New and Complete Concordance . . . to Shakespeare* was also issued in 1894 and was reprinted by St. Martin's Press in 1953.

3. Legal Newspapers.

News reporting that years ago would have brought disciplinary action against lawyers by bar groups or the courts is now commonplace and acceptable.

The Lincoln Steffens or Louella Parsons branch of reporting belongs to *The American Lawyer*, a monthly. *The National Law Journal*, a weekly, is factual without being flamboyant. The *New York Law Journal,* issued weekdays, remains a straight-forward newspaper of court information and court reports, legal news and feature columns.

CHAPTER 22B

Background Reading for Lawyers

Senator Albert J. Beveridge, the great biographer of John Marshall, writing around 1905, gave young lawyers advice on what to read. That advice remains valid today. In his article *The Young Lawyer and His Beginnings,* which was reprinted in Arthur T. Vanderbuilt's *Studying Law* (1945), he counselled them:

"*Do not confine yourself to law books*. A man who does so is like the farmer who persists in planting the same soil with the same crop: exhaustion, barrenness, and unprofitableness are the results in each case. Read generously, widely. It is impossible for a man to be a great lawyer, so far as the learning of his profession is concerned who has not saturated himself with the *Bible*. He may be a great practitioner, but not a great lawyer. It illuminates all our law and is the source of much of it. There is no more curious and fascinating study than a comparison of the ordinances of the Hebrews with what we think our modern statutes.

"Read deeply in science. Read widely the *great* novelists. They are scientists of human nature and you are dealing with human nature in your profession. Read profoundly in history. A comprehensive knowledge of history is absolutely indispensable to an understanding of our Constitution. . . .[1]

---

[1] A thought echoed by the late Chief Justice Arthur T. Vanderbilt in his *Report on Prelegal Education* presented to the Section of Legal Education and Admissions to the Bar of the American Bar Association on September 12, 1944.

"I have never known a judge or a practitioner or a law professor who deserved to be called great, who was not well versed in the best of English and American literature especially the Bible and Shakespeare. Victor Hugo once wrote, 'England has

"I am told that the leader of the American Bar has a standing order with his booksellers to send him every new book of approved merit in all the departments of literature. The result is that when he comes before the court his mind is fresh and sparkling with clear ideas and varied knowledge poured into his brain from every mountain-peak of inspiration in all the world of human thought. He brings to the service of his client not only a study of his case and an understanding of the grand science of the law, but the vivifying, vitalizing power of all the great minds on all the realms of intellect."

In this context, law schools have long recognized the need to recommend extracurricular reading to their students. Many of them actually prepare such lists to meet the thrust of Senator Beveridge's thoughts on what lawyers should read. Obviously these lists reflect the personal tastes of their compilers and hence vary considerably in subject coverage, selected titles and comprehensiveness. What would be an "ideal" reading list has never been fully accepted. The main difficulty is the lack of knowledge on the part of the compiler of the sophistication and background of the people for whom the list is prepared. It has been suggested, for example, that not every law student is qualified to read with advantage books such as *The Common Law* by Justice Holmes and even *The Bramble Bush* by Llewellyn.

With respect to a recommended reading list for future lawyers, there

---

two books, one which she made, and one which made her: Shakespeare and the Bible.' For centuries the influence of these two books here was as great as in the mother country. Great literature widens and deepens our knowledge of human nature. It stimulates the imagination and the emotions and so enlarges and enriches life. In an age preoccupied with society and social problems it safeguards the individual; for literature like all the arts, is concerned with the emotions and the emotions are always personal. This, great literature does for all men, but it especially serves the lawyer. The lawyer's life is spent in solving problems. He is in some danger of becoming a thinking machine . . . The lawyer living and working with people, cannot afford to become intellectually lopsided. The mind requires the balance that is afforded by the cultivation of the emotions and the sense of beauty through the best in the field of art in the broadest sense of the term . . . Moreover, the lawyer is likely to see the pathological side of life. He needs literature to heal him, to restore his balance, to give him perspective, which is one of the characteristics that distinguishes the great lawyer from an ordinary attorney. And by example it constantly aids and enriches his power of expression. No wonder, then, that the language and literature of England and America stand first on the list of recommended studies."

is the *Deans' List of Recommended Reading for Prelaw and Law Students*, containing 694 titles, classified under 58 subjects, such as administration of justice, advocacy, biography, fiction, legal history, and jurisprudence.

The *Deans' List* was well received. One reviewer suggested that as some people would already have read some of the recommended books that the list itself could serve as a convenient standard for comparison and selection of books to be read. Professor Arthur J. Keeffe, reviewing it in the American Bar Association Journal, suggested that it could be of value to "lawyers called upon to advise youngsters [and oldsters] as to what to read about the law." Keeffe added that "Deans and professors are a queer breed and the suggestions for readings range from the Bible and creative thinking to sex and forensic English. . . .

In case you don't believe they've gone about as far as they can go in Kansas City, we should add [that a committee of Kansas City Law School] suggests students read *Gargantua* and *Pantagruel* by Francois Rabelais written 'around 1533 to 1567.' [The] annotation . . . states: 'Earthy, gay and prodigous eaters and drinkers dominate the story.'" Incidentally, about thirty-two deans recommended Beveridge's *Life of John Marshall*, and one dean recommended the play, *The Winslow Boy* by Terrence Rattigan. Other books on the "Hit List" were *The Bramble Bush* by Llewellen, Holmes' book on *The Common Law*, Cardozo's little book on *The Nature of the Judicial Process*, Pound's *Spirit of the Common Law*, Pepper, *Philadephia Lawyer*, Pusey, *Charles Evans Hughes*, Seagle, *Men of Law from Hammurabi to Holmes*, Swisher, on *Chief Justice Taney*, Mason, *Brandeis, A Free Man's Life*, Bowen, *Yankee From Olympus, Justice Holmes and his Family*, Cozzens, *The Just and the Unjust*, Partridge, *Country Lawyer*, Frank, *Law and the Modern Mind*, and practically every dean recommended that the *Bible* be read.

Also recommended were Aristotle's *Politics*, Plato's *Dialogues and Republic*, Cicero's *Delegibus*, Dickens, *Bleak House*, *Great Expectations*, and the *Pickwick Papers*, Melville's *Billy Budd*, Elmer Rice's *Counsellor-at-Law*, Anthony Trollope's *Orley Farm*, Robert Penn Warren's *All the Kings Men* and Herman Wouk's, *The Caine Mutiney Court Martial*.

Both of Edmond Cahn's provocative books on jurisprudence, the *Sense of Injustice* and the *Moral Decision*, were recommended as were *Jurisprudence in Action, A Pleader's Anthology* published by The Association of the Bar of the City of New York, Berle's *The Modern Corporation and Private Property,* Boorstin's, *The Mysterious Science of the Law,* Cain's, *Legal Philosophy From Plato to Hegel,* Morris Cohen's, *Law and The Social Order,* Fuller, *The Law in Quest of Itself,* Gray's, *The Nature and Sources of the Law,* Henry Maine's *Ancient Law,* Roscoe Pound's *The Formative Era of American Law,* as well as his *Introduction to the Philosophy of Law,* Max Radin's, *The Law and Mr. Smith,* Reuschlein's *Jurisprudence, Its American Prophets* and that most comprehensive and thorough survey of the important theories of or about law by Julius Stone, entitled, *The Province and Function of Law.*

On the scope and depth of the recommendations made, one reviewer noted that "A comparison of the opinions held by the various deans is challenging. Would one not expect that the routine law factory would present a down-to-earth reading list and the culturally enlightened school (by repute) one which would aim at the education of the well-rounded personality? But from the very start, such a playful comparison appeared to turn into a play with dynamite. Suffice it to say that some regional law schools compare rather favorably with their national big brothers. It is gratifying, to say the least, to find that a regional law school has enriched this bibliography with its student reading recommendations of Shakespeare, Horace, Martial, Juvenal, Balzac, Twain and the Greek classics!"[2]

As twenty-six years have elapsed since the first edition of the *Deans' List of Recommended Reading for Prelaw and Law Students*, a new edition has been prepared. Professor Marke and Professor Edward J. Bander, Law Librarian of Suffolk University Law School, are its editors. The publisher: Oceana Publications. The 2d edition is in both paperback and hard covers. The list has been broadened and the number of subjects under which books are classified is almost 100. As in the first edition, every title has been annotated with a description of the book and the reason for its choice. An obvious conclusion to be drawn is that a lawyer should be well read in all the intellectual disciplines. Dean David Sargent of Suffolk University Law School in his Introduction to the new edition quotes Sir Walter Scott to the effect that "a lawyer without history or literature is a mechanic, a mere working mason.

---

[2] Mueller, 26 U. Dan. City L. Rev. 59 (1958).

If he possesses some knowledge of these, he may venture to call himself an architect," but the message is clear. The education of a law student and lawyer is never complete."

As the editors evaluated the Deans' recommendations for the second and first editions they realized as stated in the Preface to the second Edition:

> "If a Hall of Fame for the legal profession is ever established, the *Deans' List of Recommended Reading for Prelaw and Law Students* will be a prime source for candidates. Here are all the hallowed names of men and women who have contributed to law as known in our Western civilization. From thinkers as early as Plato to those as contemporary as Grant Gilmore, the list of names that appears in the *Deans' List* includes all the immortals. As one reads from Aristotle to Peter Zenger, one is also aware that the *Deans' List* is not limited to lawyer-authors. There is a galaxy of names connected with other disciplines—Charles Dickens with literature, John Stuart Mill with political theory, E. Adamson Hoebel with anthropology, and so on.

Some of the newer books recommended for the second edition were: John Frank's *American Law: The Case for Radical Reform,* Robert Keeton's *Venturing to do Justice,* and Walter Gellhorn's *When Americans Complain; Governmental Grievance Procedures.*

Under Biography, Dean Acheson's *Morning and Noon* was added, as were Catherine Drinker Bowen's *Francis Bacon; The Temper of a Man*, Gerald T. Dunne's *Hugo Black and the Judicial Revolution,* Kevin Tierney's *Darrow, a Biography,* William O. Douglas' *The Court Years, 1939–75, Felix Frankfurter Reminisces, Recorded in talks with Harlan B. Phillips, Samuel Johnson* by W. Jackson Bate, *Justice Joseph Story and the Rise of the Supreme Court* by Gerald T. Dunne and a few books on Earl Warren, including his *Memoirs* and *Super Chief: Earl Warren and His Supreme Court* by Bernard Schwartz.

Under Constitutional History and Law were added Bowen's *Miracle at Philadelphia; The Story of the Constitutional Convention, May to September, 1787,* Hugo Bedau's *The Courts, The Constitution, and Capital Punishment,* Alexander Bickel's *The Morality of Consent,* Morris Ernst's *The Great Reversals, Tales of the Supreme Court,* Fred Graham's *The Self-Inflicted Wound* and Tribe's *American Constitutional Law.*

Under Legal History were added John Baker's *Introduction to English Legal History,* Lawrence Friedman's *History of American Law,* Grant Gilmore's *The Ages of American Law,* John Honnold's *The Life of the Law: Readings on the Growth of Legal Institutions,* Morton Horowitz' *The Transformation of American Law, 1780-1860,* and I am pleased to note, my own *Vignettes of Legal History,* both First and Second Series.

Reflecting developing interests in law, new subjects added were Communications, Creative Thinking, Foreign Affairs, Forensic English, Preventive Law, Psychology and Law, and Women. John Selden in his *Table Talk,* published in 1689, some years after his death in 1654, suggested that "in quoting of Books, quote such authors as are usually read; others you may read for your own satisfaction, but not name them."

The *Deans' List* should prove of value, acting as Emerson's "charitable soul" in naming those books "which have been bridges or ships to carry [the neophyte] safely over dark morasses and barren oceans into the heart of sacred cities, into palaces and temples."

CHAPTER 22C

Business Information Sources and Services

The following material comprises a new Chapter 22C for Legal Research and Law Library Management. *It is intended as supplemental material to the Main Text.*

The successful researcher knows which institutions and individuals are likely to help the most. The writers believe that international banks excel in the range of their information sources. Many years ago around Christmas, one of the writers drove across the island of Puerto Rico, arriving in downtown Mayaguez at lunchtime. Seeing no restaurant among the gaily decorated shops—his command of Spanish was too limited to ask a policia or peaton—he asked for advice at the main branch of the First National City Bank, as it was then called. "Go to Bolo's," said a friendly banker on the platform, "You will like it."

Although he was there to offer financial advice, he was equally courteous and accurate in volunteering culinary help.

Lawyers are huge consumers of information—more frequently on the financial and economic than on the culinary side. But there is no limit to the scope of the help that bankers can provide. This chapter reviews business information sources and services. Much of it is based on advice from banking institutions.

Lawyers and law librarians have a choice of gathering their own facts or of employing a banking or other research service to do it for them. This chapter may help them decide when to work on their own and when to seek help.

Bank and Business School Advice

The writers recently asked some fifty librarians, half of them in major banks across the country and half in graduate schools of business, for their advice. At the time, the University of Pennsylvania Law

School was planning to build a book collection for its newly established Institute for Law and Economics.

The basic aim was to establish a library for an economic "Rand Corporation of the East"—where combined and complex legal and economic problems could be explored and resolved. Members of the Institute's Advisory Board and Wharton School faculty members also offered suggestions.

Like the banker in Mayaguez, the correspondents were generous with their information and specific in their advice. Set out below are their answers given in response to two questions: What sources do you consult in building your own collection and in learning what has been written on any subject?

Sources and Services

The lists are presented in five main parts: business and financial bibliographies; serial guides to books; periodical and pamphlet indexes and periodical lists; government publications; and databases.

1. Business and Financial Bibliographies

- Baker Library. Business Reference Sources: an Annotated Guide for Harvard Business School Students. Compiled by Lorna M. Daniels. Rev. ed. Boston, Baker Library, Graduate School of Business, Harvard University, 1979, 133 pp. See comment under Daniels, *Business Information Sources* below.
- Baker Library. Core Collection: An Author and Subject Guide. Boston, Baker Library, Harvard University, Graduate School of Business Annual.

  "Index to the 4000 books in Baker Library's Reading room collection, with emphasis on recent titles. . . ." $15.
- Baker Library, Mini-Lists. Annual revisions. Boston, Baker Library.

  "Each list of two to six pages suggests where to look first for information, and is normally updated once a year." There are seventeen lists in the series, including "Basic Investment Sources," "Where to Find Information about Companies" and "Sources of Information on Foreign Countries." Basic and informative. $.60 each, $3 minimum, $9 set.

- Daniels, Lorna M. Business Information Sources. Rev. ed. Berkeley, California, University of California Press, 1986. Unquestionably the most authoritative, informative and comprehensive guide published. Now seven years old and in need of revision. Particularly important for its annotations that are not found in the compact *Business Reference Sources*
- Melnyk, Peter. Economics: Bibliographic Guide to Reference Books and Information Sources. Littleton, Colo. Libraries Unlimited, 1971. 263 pp. Includes 1,500 reference titles in many languages. Annotated.
- Schlessinger, Bernard S., ed. The Basic Business Library: Core Resources. Phoenix, Ariz., Oryx Press, 1982. $32.50. "Over 150 Basic business resources are included, with full bibliographic data, prices and descriptions. The 232 page volume also contains a bibliography with abstracts of recent literature on business reference. . . ." American Libraries, Nov. 1983 at 684. Note particularly the entries under "Economics" which embraces accounting, business, finance and banking in this guide.

Reference should also be made to the economics and related entries in two general Bowker publications: *Subject Guide to Books in Print* and *Paperbacks in Print*. Both are issued annually and purport to cover most trade publications in English. Similarly in law, *Law Books in Print,* together with its annual supplements, is an essential tool. It is issued by Gianville in Dobbs Ferry, N.Y.

2. Serial Guides to Books

- Choice. Monthly (July and August are combined). Chicago, Association of College and Research Libraries, Division of American Library Association. Current. $85 a year. Contains short, authoritative reviews, covering all fields of knowledge, including economics. Includes about 500 reviews an issue. There are separate consultants for each issue—almost as many as there are reviews. "Choice is a monthly book and non-print selection journal." It was recommended by several of the fifty librarians who responded to our survey as well as by one lawyer-economist.

- Harvard University, Graduate School of Business. Recent Additions to Baker Library. Monthly and cumulated annually. Boston, Harvard Graduate School of Business. Current, $14 a year. Arranged under seventeen subjects from "Accounting and Control" to "Reference Highlights." Includes "Industry Studies" and "International Business." *Highly recommended.*
- Journal of Economic Literature. Quarterly. Nashville, Tenn. American Economic Association. Current. $100 a year. One economist-lawyer rated this the best single source for acquisitions purposes. But because of the long time-lag between publication and review, he also recommended *Choice* as a "first screen."
- Library Journal. Semimothly. Business Books of the Year issued in March. Chicago, ALA, Current. Lists the best of the past year's crop, in the editor's opinions, with short annotations that describe the purpose and contents of each. In contrast to the reviews offered by *Choice,* the annotations are relatively spare. All the same, an extremely useful guide to the latest works. The November 1, 1983 issue contains a classified list of forth-coming scientific, technical, medical and business books scheduled for release between November, 1983 and March, 1984.
- University of Pennsylvania. Wharton School. Lippincott Library. Publications Catalogued. Monthly. Philadelphia, Lippincott Library. Current. An alphabetical list of new publication by author, with an addendum of reference publications.
- University of Virginia. Darden School. New Books: Recent Additions to the Darden School Library. Monthly. Each issue is presented in thirty-seven parts from "Accounting and Control" to "Writing and Public Speaking." Includes Industry Studies and works on legal aspects of business that are generally found in law libraries.

3. Periodicals and Pamphlet Indexes and Periodical Lists

- Business Periodicals Index. Monthly, Quarterly and other cumulations. Bronx, N.Y., H.W. Wilson Co. Current. A subject index to business articles and guides to business book reviews published in the leading business periodicals.

- Business Publications Index and Abstracts. Monthly with annual cumulations. Detroit, Gale. Current. (Subject-author citations—$250 a year; Monthly Abstracts—$250 a year; Annual Cumulations—$250 each. "Fast subject and author indexing and abstracts of articles in over 700 periodicals."
- P.A.I.S. Bulletin. Semimonthly, with Cumulations. N.Y., Public Affairs Service. Current. The publisher's comment reads: "A selective subject list of the latest books, pamphlets, government publications, reports of public and private organizations, and periodical articles relating to economic and social conditions."

  Available on line through DIALOG. Lockheed Information File No. 49 and on BRS (Bibliographic Retrieval Services).
- Wall Street Journal Index. Monthly and Annual. N.Y., Dow Jones and Co., Inc. Current. Compiled from the final (4-star) Eastern edition and presented in two parts: corporate news and general news.
- Baker Library. Current Periodical Publications in Baker Library. Annual. Boston, Baker Library $26. Arranged by title, subject and geographical region. "Includes 6,500 active serial titles: magazines, journals, bulletins, statistical annuals, yearbooks, proceedings of conferences, directories, government annual reports and looseleaf services."

4. Government Publications

- Monthly Catalog of the Superintendent of Documents. Washington, D.C., Government Printing Office. Current. Monthly with annual indexes and ten year cumulated indexes. A subject guide to United States Government documents including congressional hearings, reports and studies and agency reports and studies on all phases of business. financial and related matters.

Her Majesty's Stationers Offices in London and Ottawa, and the Australian Government Publishing Service in Canberra issue similar catalogs that cover British, Canadian and Australian publications.

Virtually indispensable to finding Congressional hearings, reports, committee prints and documents are the various CIS (Congressional Information Service) indexes. Most law libraries are subscribers.

The major studies of the Library of Congress' Legislative Reference Service/Congressional Research Service have just been collected on microfilm by University Publications of America. They comprise many hundreds of studies drafted for Congressional committees and individual legislators and cover the years 1916-1974. Price $850. Supplements covering approximately two-year periods from 1975 through February 1982 are available at about $50 a reel. There are seventeen reels in the basic collection and sixty-two reels in the supplements.

A useful new guide to U.S. Government publications is *Locating U.S. Government Information: A Guide to Sources* by Edward Herman. Buffalo, Hein, 1983.

5. Databases

There are literally hundreds of databases available through various computer services. They are more numerous than the cable television outlets listed in the daily newspapers. A good overview of them—keyed to lawyers' interests—is found in Chapter 25 of the main text and in this Cumulative Supplement.

Four systems are worth noting here: Lexis and its companion Nexis, Westlaw and RLIN.

- *Lexis*. For economic data, has three special libraries: Securities, Trade Regulation, and Taxation. Of particular current interest in the Securities library is its Commodity Futures Trading Commission collection of decisions and orders set out in full text from the inception of this agency. It may prove to be the most active field of regulation and litigation during the next two decades.
- *Nexis*. This is a news and business information service that provides *The New York Times* in full text since June 1, 1980 and abstracts of articles in some sixty business publications, including newspapers, magazines, wire services, newsletters and a few government documents. A recent addition is its accounting library that includes (a) annual reports selected by the AICPA from among companies whose stock is listed on the

New York Stock Exchange and the American Stock Exchange or which is traded in the over-the-counter markets, (b) extracts from proxy statements and (c) various AICPA publications.

- *Westlaw*. Comparable to Lexis. Westlaw is beginning to add economics-oriented databases such as the CFTC decisions and orders. It already includes a tax library and some additional federal regulatory material.
- *RLIN* (Research Libraries Information Network). This service maintains a catalog record of the holdings of major university, law school and research libraries across the country. Its members are enabled to determine via computer two important kinds of facts: What publications exist on any subject and which libraries own them. The New York Public Library, Association of the Bar of the City of New York, Harvard, Yale, Columbia, Pennsylvania, Michigan and Stanford are among its members, as are the law school libraries of the universities mentioned here. *RLIN* is useful to lawyers because member institutions lend to one another for the benefit of their readers. An obscure industry study in the library at the University of California in Berkeley, for example, may be the only comprehensive source of information about that industry. Without *RLIN* it could easily escape notice.

Business Resources In-House

How far should even the largest law office libraries go in building business collections? Their libraries and librarians should be able to answer two basic questions: (1) What publications exist on any business subject or, indeed, in any branch of knowledge; and (2) Where can those publications be borrowed, purchased or consulted?

The sources, services and databases cited in this chapter help answer the first of these questions.

In addition, law libraries should be flexible. They should support law firm or legal department practice directly. If new litigation or corporate acquisition matters require new kinds of information—for example, "everything on silver trading," then the library should be able to respond immediately. The judgment whether to buy or borrow is an individual office matter. But nothing should stand in the way of collecting the information or locating the sources.

CHAPTER 22D

Leisure-Time Reading for Lawyers: A Review of Satire

The following material comprises a new Chapter 22D for Legal Research and Law Library Management. *It is intended as supplemental material to the Main Text.*

> *I don't care a straw for your newspaper articles, my constituents don't know how to read, but they can't help seeing them damned pictures.*
> —William March "Boss" Tweed's comment about Nast's political cartoons.

[1]—Introduction

Out-of-print booksellers always have field days in attempting to fill the demand by lawyers for works of satire, including caricature. However, as a result of court papers filed in the case of *Flynt v. Falwell*, the satire market should boom. The first set of papers is an *amicus* brief filed in the Supreme Court of the United States on June 15, 1987 (No. 86-1278) on behalf of the Association of American Editorial Cartoonists, the Authors League of America, Inc. and Mark Russell, the well-known television comedian.[1] The second is the

[1] On the brief for the *amici curiae* are Roslyn A. Mazer, George Kaufmann and Martin Kimel of the firm of Dickstein, Shapiro & Morin in the District of Columbia. The firm's librarian, Frances Durako, played a significant part in compiling the list of authorities.

opinion of Judge Wilkinson, dissenting from the denial of rehearing *en banc* in the same matter.[2]

Under the headline, "Here's a Switch: A Court Brief That Doesn't Put You to Sleep," the *Wall Street Journal* highlighted a few of the brief's legal and literary features.[3] Its literary and artistic riches are the brief's main interest here.[4]

In a nutshell, the Reverend Jerry Falwell sued the publishers of an advertisement parody for libel, invasion of privacy and intentional infliction of emotional distress. Even though the plaintiff lost on the first two counts, he won an award of $200,000 for emotional distress. The issue on appeal: Can a nonlibelous publication constitute grounds for a public figure's claim for emotional distress? The Fourth Circuit held, "Yes". The *amici* defendants argue, "No". Judge Wilkinson in his dissent urged a rehearing.

The resulting *amicus* brief is a windfall bibliography in the field of satire that stresses political caricature down the ages. If satirists show extreme malice—as they have always done to get their points across—they may lose their first amendment rights. This chapter provides supplemental references to form Any Intelligent Citizen's Guide to Leisure-Time Reading. That savagery and malice predominate over gentle criticism and irony will quickly become evident.

[2]—Satirical Anthologies

Johnson, Edgar, *A Treasury of Satire* (Simon & Schuster 1945). Included are critical evaluations and generous extracts from the writings of Aesop, Aeschylus, Euripldes, Horace, Ovid, Juvenal, Lucian, Chaucer, Rabelais, Cervantes, Shakespeare (*Henry IV* and *Hamlet*), Donne, Jonson and Moliere, (The dissenting opinion in *Flynt v. Falwell* singled out *Tartuffe* to illustrate Moliere's "natural urge to bring down self-appointed moralists.")[5]

Beerbohm, Max, *Catalogue of the Caricatures of Max Beerbohm*, compiled by Rupert Hart-Davis (Macmillan 1972).

---

[2] Flynt v. Falwell, 805 F.2d 484 (4th Cir. 1986). Prior report: 797 F.2d 1270 (4th Cir. 1986).

[3] *Wall Street Journal*, June 18, 1987, by staff reporter Naomi S. Travers.

[4] The *amicus* brief, N. 1 *supra*, at 20-30.

[5] *Flynt v. Falwell*, N. 2 *supra*, 805 F.2d at 487.

Brokaw, Tom, *The Gang of Eight: America's Best Political Cartoonists Pick Their Best Work* (Faber & Faber, 1985).

Brown, Ashley and Kimmey, eds., *Satire: An Anthology* (Harper & Row 1978).

Editors of FPA, *A Cartoon History of U.S. Foreign Policy, 1776-1976*. (Foreign Policy Ass'n 1976).

Furlong, Norman, ed. *English Satire, An Anthology* [reprint of 1946 ed]. (Arden Library 1977).

Kernan, Alvin B., ed. *Moden Satire* (Harcourt, Brace 1962).

Lucie-Smith, Edward, ed., *The Penguin Book of Satirical Verse* (Penguin 1967).

Westin, ed. *Getting Angry Six Times a Week: A Portfolio of Political Cartoons* (Beacon Press 1979).

[3]—Biographical Writings

Behrman, S. N., *A Portrait of Max* (Random House 1960). Contains a lively collection of Max Beerbohm's caricatures, both literary and political. Included: Sidney Webb, George Bernard Shaw, Queen Victoria and the Prince of Wales (later Edward the Seventh) and the Honorable Arthur James Balfour.

Buchwald, Art, *Down the Seine and Up the Potomac* (Putnam's 1977). Buchwald's work urged a class action to be brought by himself, Bill Mauldin and others for "grievous professional injury and public humiliation" because, unlike other journalists, they were left off President Nixon's "enemies list".

Buchwald, Art, *You Can Fool All of the People All of the Time*. (Fawcett 1986).

Hill, Draper M., *Mr. Gilray, the Caricaturist* (Phaidon Press).

Keller, Morton, *The Art and Politics of Thomas Nast* (Oxford University Press 1968). Probably America's most influential caricaturist. Nast's detestation for crooks (Tweed and his "Ring") and humbug (Greeley for allowing presidential ambition to soften his behavior toward Tweed) shows in every line of his savage drawings.

Keogh, *This Is Nixon* (G.P. Putnam's Sons 1956).

Mack, Maynard. *Alexander Pope, A Life* (W.W. Norton, 1986).

Murrell, A. "Nast, Gladiator of the Political Pencil," The American Scholar (Autumn 1936).

Rosenheim, Jr., *Swift and the Satirist's Art* (University of Chicago Press 1963).

Schorer, *Sinclair Lewis, An American Life* (University of Minnesota Press 1963).

Vinson, J. Chal., *Thomas Nast, Political Cartoonist* (University of Georgia Press 1967).

[4]—Encyclopedia Articles

Note: The references to articles in the *Encyclopedia Britannica*, 15th edition, are always to the "Macropaedia" portion of the set, except for "Parody" which appears in the shorter "Micropaedia."

Caricature by Marion H. Spielmann in Encyclopedia Britannica (hereafter EB), 11th edition (1910), Vol. 5 at 331–336.

Caricature, Cartoon and Comic Strip by David M. Kunzle and Winslow Ames in EB, 15th edition, Vol. 3 at 909–922.

Daumier in EB, 11th edition, Vol. 7 at 849.

Daumier in EB by Jean Adhemar in EB 15th edition, Vol. 5 at 515–517.

Parody in EB, 11th edition, Vol. 20 at 860.

Parody in EB, 15th ed, Vol. 7 at 768.

Satire by Richard Garnett in EB, 11th edition, Vol. 24 at 228-229.

Satire by Robert C. Elliott in EB, 15th edition, Vol. 16 at 268-272.

[5]—History and Analysis of Satire

Dickinson, H. T., *Caricature and the Constitution [English], 1760-1832* (Chadwyck-Healey 1986).

Frye, Northrup, *Anatomy of Criticism* (Princeton University Press 1971).

Geipel, John, *The Cartoon, A Short History of Graphic Comedy and Satire* (A. S. Barnes & Co. 1972).

Granger, Bruce Ingham, *Political Satire in the American Revolution, 1763-1783* (Cornell University Press 1960).

Hess, Stephen and Kaplan, Milton, *The Ungentlemanly Art—A History of American Political Cartoons*, Rev. ed. (Macmillan, 1975). [Profusely illustrated—oversize].

Highet, Gilbert, *The Anatomy of Satire* (Princeton University Press 1962).

Jack, James, *Augustan Satire: Intention and Idiom in English Poetry, 1660-1750* (Clarendon Press 1952).

Johnson, Edgar, "Hate in Aldous Huxley". University Review, Vol. 6 No. 4 (June 1940).

Johnson, J., *The Lines Are Drawn: American Life Since the First World War, as Reflected in the Pulitzer Prize Cartoons* (J. B. Lippincott, 1958).

Lock, F. P., *The politics of Gulliver's Travels* (Oxford University Press 1980).

Long, "The Political Cartoon: Journalism's Strongest Weapon," *The Quill* (Nov. 1962).

Lucie-Smith, Edward, *The Art of Caricature* (Cornell University Press 1981). [An illustrated history].

Press, Charles, *The Political Cartoon* (Fairleigh Dickinson University 1981).

Roth, Philip, *Reading Myself and Others* (Farrar, Straus & Giroux 1975).

Smith, "The Rise and Fall of the Political Cartoon," The Saturday Review, May 29, 1954.

Sullivan, Mark, *Our Times, 1900-1925* (Scribner's, 1939) (6 Vols.). A political and social history, with hundreds of contemporary illustrations, including the leading caricatures and cartoons of the period.

Sutherland, William Owen, *The Art of the Satirist* (University of Texas Press 1965).

Walker, *English Satire and Satirists* (Octagon Books 1965).

Wardroper, John, *Kings, Lords and Wicked Libellers: Satire and Protest, 1760-1837* (Murray 1973).

[6]—Law Review Articles

Franklin and Bussell, "The Plaintiff's Burden in Defamation: Awareness and Falsity," 25 Wm & Mary L. Rev. 825 (1984).

Givelber, "The Right to Minimum Social Decency and the Limits of Evenhandedness: Intentional Infliction of Emotional Distress by Outrageous Conduct," 82 Colum. L. Rev. 42 (1982).

Magruder, "Mental and Emotional Disturbance in the Law of Torts," 49 Harv. L. Rev. 1033 (1936).

Mead, "Suing Media for Emotional Distress: A Multi-Method Analysis of Tort Law Evolution," 23 Washburn L. J. 24 (1983).

[7]—Legal Treatises and Digests

Gatley on Libel and Slander (7th ed.), by Sir Robert McEwen and Philip Lewis, (London, Sweet & Maxwell 1974). See particularly Sections 33 and 34 on "Ridicule", 35 on "Caricatures" and 40 on "Words Injuring Feelings",

Halsbury's Laws of England, Vol. 28, Sec. 11 (Libel and Slander) (Butterworths 1979).

Hooper, David, *Public Scandal, Odium and Contempt, An Investigation of Recent Libel Cases* (Sacker & Warburg, 1984).

Keaton, W. P., *Prosser and Keaton on the Law of Torts*, 54-55 (5th ed. 1984)

Restatement (Second) of Torts, Section 46 and comment b (1965).

CHAPTER 22E

Law Library Information Reports

The following material comprises a new Chapter 22E for Legal Research and Law Library Management. *It is intended as supplemental material to the Main Text.*

A specialized series of mongraphs is directed to law librarians. It is titled *Law Library Information Reports* and is published by Glanville Publishers, Dobbs Ferry, New York. It features reports prepared by experienced professionals in the field. It is designed to provide constructive information which law librarians and administrative personnel can apply in making professional and sophisticated judgments on issues and problems affecting the law library.

The subjects treated are not readily found in law library literature—certainly not with the organization, depth, and comprehensiveness reflected in the reports.

Among the reports issued is *Insuring the Law Library: Fire and Disaster Risk Management*, by Professor Bernard D. Reams, Jr. Law Librarian of Washington University in St. Louis and Professor Erwin C. Serrency, Director of the Law Library, University of Georgia, provides information concerning financial protection against possible devastation of the law library facilities and its contents.

Methods of insuring books and library materials are discussed as well as how to establish the monetary value of the library's contents. It also concentrates on approaches to fire risk, fire prevention and water emergencies. Factors for preventing losses and insurance coverage considerations are reviewed in that context. The importance of the shelf list and the need for periodic inventory are also brought out in establishing the value of the loss incurred by fire and water damage.

It is interesting to note that there are various causes other than fire which subject books and libraries to water damage. Flooding, broken pipes or other mechanical failure for example. There are a number of precautions that can be taken to prevent and curtail water damage, including:

—Keeping electric pumps on hand and knowing where they are so that they can be obtained promptly.

—Avoiding electrocution hazards of control panels (and any electrical approaches) in wet areas.

—Considering the possibility of water damage in planning the layout and mechanical equipment of the library.

—Knowing in advance where freezers can be obtained on short notice for emergency storage of wet books.

—Designating (in advance) as salvage officers any staff members with experience in recovery of wet materials.

—Having a written plan.

—Locating sources of supply for portable dehumidifiers.

—Knowing the effects of any salvage materials and control measures needed.

—Educating the staff in details of the plan.

There are many other practical actions that can be taken for preventing losses, such as arranging that the air circulation system be shut down quickly in an emergency to avoid the spread of smoke and fire, and individually fusing all fluorescent ballasts to avoid operation failures and the quick ignition of nearby combustible materials, dripping pitch, or explosives of the ballast case.

Insurance coverage, in the final analysis, is the most economical disaster coverage option. In this context, it is important to agree in writing with the insurance company on the values the library has assigned to books, equipment, supplies and buildings. If this is not established in advance, the insurance company can demand an inventory of lost items after the loss occurs, an extremely difficult list to produce. Policies should also cover books and other property loaned to the library. Rare books should be itemized as well as valuable art objects and unusually expensive items. If the library has a sprinkler system make sure it is protected against any loss incurred if the sprinklers are activated when there is no fire. The policy should also contain a self-inflation rate.

Another useful member of this series *Rare Books For Law Li-*

braries, was prepared by Thomas H. Reynolds of the University of California Law Library, at Berkeley, for the guidance of law librarians seeking information pertaining to the acquisition, arrangement, maintenance and preservation of rare law books and related materials. This monograph addresses the need for information in those areas because most law librarians lack the expertise and knowledge to acquire and service rare books. Law Librarians usually come into their responsibilities with no experience and little familiarity with rare books, and yet they deal with them, willing or not, quite often. It is for such an audience, the non-expert entrusted with rare materials, that this report was written.

Noting the various definitions of a "rare" book, the author observes that a book is rare only if it is sought after and it has some interest for more than a few collectors or institutions. It must be out-of-print. Passage of time and the number of copies printed are always significant. Beyond those basics, the historical and intellectual impact of the work, its provenance, its fame, number of editions, place in the development of typography and the physical book's intrinsic value as a beautiful object are always relevant in this context. Thus, although *Blackstone's Commentaries* are rare in early printings, the first edition was an eighteenth century best seller and there are still hundreds of copies in existence. That is why one of the first criteria for rarity is the size of the original edition. How many are still existence is important because of the vicissitudes of fire, flood, destruction and actual use. The 16th century justice of the peace manuals, for example, were issued in relatively large numbers, but they were literally used to the point of disintegration and few have survived intact.

Professor Betty Taylor, Director of the Law Library of the University of Florida and Professor Henke of Hastings College of Law are the authors of another *Law Library Report* entitled *Budgeting for the Law School Library*. It provides information on the preparation of budgets for the law school library in light of the standards for accreditation established by the American Bar Association and the Association of American Law Schools. It notes the influence of professional accrediting agencies on law library budgeting and discloses the methods of allocations and the responsibilities of the librarian as a fiscal manager.

Law Library Fund Raising: A Primer by Gerald C. Crane, then Assistant Dean, External Relations, New York University School of

Law, advises how the law librarian and the law school administrator can raise funds for the development of the law library by taking advantage of the fund raising resources of the academic institution of which it is a part. It also describes the strategies, methodologies and techniques of fund raising pertinent to libraries in general and how they can be applied by the law librarian independently.

Law librarians have traditionally concentrated on collection development, staff services and physical growth of library quarters. A number of them are beginning to play a more active role in seeking non-institutional funds in support of those functions. This is so because even though an educational institution may have a fund-raising department, it probably is overwhelmed with work and lacks the staff to service sufficiently the total needs of a school or university. It follows that the law librarian and law school administrator, as a matter of course, will increasingly have to participate in seeking funds from sources outside the institution. Crane stresses that fund-raising techniques are comparatively easy to master once the professional language is understood—and then proceeds to demonstrate it.

Crane's report is divided into three parts. The first section, entitled "Resources," deals with the supportive fund-raising services that are probably available at an academic institution. The second section, entitled "Strategies," deals with fund-raising methods and techniques which can be applied to law library fund raising. The third section entitled "Materials," provides illustrative materials which can be readapted for library fund-raising use, and are presented to stimulate ideas.

The first issue to appear in the *Law Library Interpretation Reports* series was entitled *What Law School Administrators Should Know about the ABA/AALS Law Library Inspection Process*. Authored by Professor Roy M. Mersky, Director of the Law Library of the University of Texas and Professor Julius Marke, it advises law school librarians on how to meet the thrust of the inspection requirements and standards imposed by the American Bar Association and the Association of American Law Schools. It alerts them and other law school administrators on how the accreditation team evaluates the law library's collection and operations and how they can formulate a plan of action that will respond successfully to the qualitative and quantitative demands of the ABA and AALS.

In addition to providing the do's and don'ts of accreditation, it describes the accrediting agencies, the law school inspection process, the law school questionnaire/self study and the on-site inspection.

Of great interest is the Report by Catherine A. Pennington, Associate Law Librarian, St. John's University School of Law entitled: *Microcomputer Software Selections for the Law Library Part One: General Business Software*. It provides a down to earth account on the use of software in law libraries and is written both for the neophyte and the more experienced users of personal computers. Some of her practical hints on hardware include:

—"Stick to well known, well tested brands of computers for which software is obtainable from a lot of different companies."

—"Make sure that your system can expand to meet changing needs."

—"Buy twice as much memory as you think you will ever need. You will use it."

—"If you have a hard disk (and you should) and more than 10 MB (Megabytes) of storage make sure you have an easy to use back-up system and USE IT FREQUENTLY."

—"If you have a hard disk, use an external modem. Modems, like the disks, generate a lot of heat. More than one user has 'crashed' the system, with subsequent loss of data, due to temperature build up."

Some basic software rules include:

—"Do not purchase software during the first six months of release. Let others 'debug' the program without you."

—"Use general business software whenever possible. Adding the words "law" or "library" to a software package typically doubles the price. If you can adapt *SuperCalc*, *dBase*, *Lotus*, or *Framework* to meet your needs, you will save yourself lots of money. . . ."

—"Do not use a programmer. Someone has probably already invented the system you need to use and it will cost you a lot less to buy off the shelf than to reinvent. If what you want to do is not available for the micro yet, it probably means that a P.C. is too small for that function at this time."

The monograph covers word processing, spreadsheets, databases, management and graphics, communications, educational software, project management and outline processing software, utility programs, and planning for the future. Helpful bibliographies, forms and a glossary are also provided.

CHAPTER 25

Technical Data Available With On-Line Searches

The following comprises amended material for Chapter 25 of Legal Research and Law Library Management. *It is intended as replacement material to the Main Text. On page 271, substitute the following for the last four paragraphs on the page:*

There are innumerable on-line bibliographic search services which lawyers can profitably utilize when they seek interdisciplinary information. Following are descriptions of a few of the better known ones: *The Information Bank, NEXIS,* (SDC) *Systems Development Search Service, DIALOG* and (BRS) *Bibliographic Retrieval Service.*

The Mead Corporation and the New York Times Company have entered into an agreement under which Mead Data Central, a division of Mead, has been granted an exclusive license to distribute the databases now produced by the *New York Times Information Service.* These databases are now available as part of the NEXIS Library at no additional charge.

The New York Times On-Line—contains the complete articles from the Times since June 1, 1980.

The New York Times Information Bank—contains more than two million abstracts of articles that have appeared in the Times and some sixty other publications since January 1969.

Deadline Data on World Affairs—contains geopolitical information on the countries of the world, the fifty states, the Canadian provinces and territories and major international organizations.

Advertising and Marketing Intelligence (AMI)—a database created by the Times Company in association with J. Walter Thompson, which contains approximately 125,000 abstracts from some sixty trade and specialized publications and newsletters since September 1979.

LEXIS and WESTLAW are leading computer-assisted legal research services, serving subscribers in the United States and the United Kingdom. LEXIS features another on-line database service, known as NEXIS, which now includes the full text of national and international newspapers, wire services, magazines, newsletters and government publications. The following is a representative list of publications contained in the NEXIS database.

General and Business News
—The Washington Post
—Newsweek
—U.S. News and World Reports
—Business Week
—AP, UPI, Reuters

Specific Industry Publications
—The American Banker
—The 0.1 and Gas Journal

International Sources
—The Economist
—The BBC Summary of World Broadcasts
—The English language wires of Japanese and Chinese News Agencies

In addition BNA has signed an agreement with Mead Data Central to offer a number of its information services in electronic form via Mead's LEXIS and NEXIS information retrieval systems, including:

—Antitrust and Trade Regulation Report
—Daily Labor Report
—United States Law Week
—Government Employee Relations Report
—Environmental Reporter
—Securities Regulation and Law Report
—Patent, Trademark & Copyright Journal

The following material comprises an addition to Chapter 25 of* Legal Research and Law Library Management. *It is intended to be read in conjunction with the Material in the Main Text.

It is interesting to note, that on-line accessible databases are not only continuing to proliferate, but are also having an increasing impact on the services and operations of all types of libraries. The Cuadra Associates' *Directory of On-line Databases,* has reported that as of Spring 1982, there were over 1,000 databases, an increase of over 25% since 1981.

Library Journal features a column on ONLINE DATABASES, which reports on the many developments in every aspect of the use of on-line databases in libraries. The February 1, 1983 *Library Journal* issue features the first monthly *Library Journal* column on databases for reference use. Its purpose is to provide information about databases to the librarian who would like to stay current. It concentrates on the reference use of databases and emphasizes commercially available databases. It also includes a list of sources for catching up and keeping up with databases and on-line searching in the library. Listed are selected recent sources (in most cases 1980 or later) that provide basic information on online searching and sources for keeping up with the on-line database field. This listing is herewith reprinted with the permission of the author, Carol Tenopir, and the *Library Journal.*

Introductory Textbooks

The following offer basic introductory overviews of on-line searching, keyed to the needs of neophytes in the field. They all cover policy, planning, and issues on on-line searching as well as introductions to techniques of searching. They also provide information on databases.

Chen, Ching-chih and Susanna Schweizer. *Online Bibliographic Searching: A Learning Manual.* Neal-Schuman, 1981.

Fenichel, Carol Hansen and Thomas H. Hogan. *Online Searching: A Primer.* Marlton, N.J.: Learned Information, 1981.

Hartner, Elizabeth P. *An Introduction to Automated Literature Searching.* Dekker, 1981.

Henry, W. M., J. A. Leigh, L. A. Tedd and P. W. Williams. *Online Searching: An Introduction.* London: Butterworths, 1980.

Meadow, Charles and Pauline Cochrane. *Basics of Online Searching*. Wiley, 1981.

Other Useful Monographs

Some recent general works on databases and other aspects of on-line searching in libraries:

Hoover, Ryan E., et al. *The Library and Information Manager's Guide to Online Services*. White Plains, N.Y.: Knowledge Industry Publications, 1980.

Hoover, Ryan E. *Online Search Strategies*. Knowledge Industry Publications, 1982.

Katz, Bill, ed. *Reference and Online Services Handbook: Guidelines, Policies and Procedures for Libraries*. Neal-Schuman, 1982.

Keenan, S. K. *How to Go Online—Guidelines for the Establishment of Online Services in Public Libraries*. London: British Library Research and Development Dept., 1980. (Report No. 5533).

Kent, Allen and Thomas J. Galvin, eds. *The Online Revolution in Libraries. Proceedings of the 1977 Conference in Pittsburgh*. Neal-Schuman, 1978.

Online Bibliographic Search Services. SPEC Kit 76. Washington, D.C.: Systems and Procedures Exchange Center, Office of Management and Studies, Assn. of Research Libraries, July 1981.

Journal Articles

Many articles have appeared in periodicals on databases and on-line searching in libraries. The following articles, selected from those published in the last three years, were found to be especially useful.

Adams, Arthur L. "Planning Search Strategies for Maximum Retrieval from Bibliographic Databases," *Online Review*, December 1979, p. 373-79.

Bourne, Charles P. "Online Systems: History, Technology and Economics," *Journal of the American Society for Information Science*, May 1980, p. 155-60.

Harper, L. G. "A Comparative Review of BRS, DIALOG and ORBIT," *Reference Services Review,* January—March 1981, p. 39-50.

Hawkins, Donald T. and C. P. Brown. "What is an Online Search?," *Online,* January 1980, p. 12-18.

Keenan, S. K., N. Moore and A. Oulton. "Online Information Services in Public Libraries," *Journal of Librarianship,* January 1981, p. 9-24.

Lamb, Connie. "Searching in Academia—Nearly 50 Libraries Tell What They're Doing," *Online,* April 1981, p. 78-81.

McClure, Charles R. "A Planning Primer for Online Reference Service in a Public Library," *Online,* April 1980, p. 57-56.

Nitecki, Danuta A. "Reviewing Online Resources," *RQ,* Summer 1981, p. 335-6.

Roberts, S. K. "Online Information Retrieval: Promise and Problems," *Byte,* December 1981, p. 452-61.

Weiss, S. "Online Bibliographic Services: A Comparison," *Special Libraries,* October 1981, P. 379-80.

Bibliographies

Many useful articles can be found in the following bibliographies.

Hawkins, Donald T. *Outline Information Retrieval Bibliography, 1964-1979.* Medford, N.J.: Learned Information, 1980. (Bibliography and first three updates published in March issues of *Online Review* 1977-1979.)

Hawkins, Donald T. "Online Retrieval Bibliography, Fourth Update," *Online Review,* April 1981, p. 139-82.

Hawkins, Donald T. "Online Retrieval Bibliography, Fifth Update," *Online Review,* April 1982, p. 147-208.

Pugh, W. Jean and Stephanie C. John. "A Bibliography of Database and Search System Comparisons," *Online,* September 1982, p. 41-55.

Shroder, Emelie J., ed. "Online Reference Service—How to Begin: A Selected Bibliography," *RQ,* Fall 1982, p. 70-75.

Keeping Up

Librarians who are experienced searchers still need to spend several hours each week on keeping up with new databases, techniques and issues. The following are the most important sources for keeping up:

Periodicals

Database: The Magazine of Database Reference and Review. Weston, Conn.: Online, Inc., 1978. (11 Tanery La., Weston, CT 06883.) Four issues per year.

IDP Report: Information and Data Base Publishing Report. White Plains, N.Y.: Knowledge Industry Publications, 1980. (2 Corporate Park Dr., White Plains, NY 10604.) Biweekly.

Information Intelligence Online Hotline. Phoenix, Ariz.: Information Intelligence, Inc., 1982. 24 issues per year hard copy or daily editions available online through the publisher.

"Messages from MARS" in *RASD Update.* Machine Assisted Reference Service Section, Reference and Adult Services Division, American Library Assn., 50 East Huron St., Chicago, IL 60611. Six times per year.

Monitor. Learned Information, Ltd. (Besselsleigh Rd., Abingdon, England.) Monthly.

Online: The Magazine of Online Information Systems. Weston, Conn.: Online, Inc., 1977. (11 Tannery La., Weston, CT, 06883.) Six issues per year.

Online Chronicle. Weston, Conn.: Online, Inc. Available online via DIALOG (file 170). Updated twice a month.

Online Database Report. New York: LINK Resources. (215 Park Ave. South, New York, NY 10003.) Monthly.

Online Newsletter. Phoenix, Ariz.: Information Intelligence, Inc. (P.O. Box 3108, Phoenix, AZ 85046.) Ten issues per year.

Online Review. Medford, N.J. and Oxford, England: Learned Information. (143 Old Marlton Pike, Medford, NJ 08055.) Six issues per year.

RQ. Reference and Adult Services Division, ALA. Quarterly. Includes reviews of new databases in the "Sources" section.

Vendor Periodicals

BRS Bulletin. BRS, 1200 Rte. 7, Latham, NY 12110. Monthly newsletter, free with BRS account.

Chronolog. DIALOG Information Services, Inc., 3460 Hillview Ave., Palo Alto, CA 94304. Monthly newsletter, free with DIALOG account.

Inforum. The Information Bank of the New York Times Information Service, Suite 86035, One World Trade Center, New York, NY 10048. Monthly newsletter for Information Bank accounts.

Search Service News. System Development Corp., 2500 Colorado Ave., Santa Monica, CA 90406. Monthly newsletter, free with ORBIT account.

Directories

"Databases Online," *Online Review*, August 1982, p. 353-90.

Directory of Online Databases. Santa Monica, Calif.: Cuadra Associates. Quarterly.

Directory of Online Information Resources. Capital Systems Group Pr., Rockville, Md. New editions published regularly.

Kruzas, Anthony Thomas and John Schmittroth, Jr., eds. *Encyclopedia of Information Systems and Services*. 4th ed. Gale Research, 1981.

Williams, Martha E. *Computer-Readable Databases: A Directory and Data Sourcebook*. White Plains, N.Y.: Knowledge Industry Publications, 1982.

See also:

Smith, Linda C. "Data Base Directories: A Comparative Review," *Reference Services Review*, October/December 1980, p. 15-21.

Database Search Aids. Online Inc., 11 Tannery La., Weston, CT 06883. Search aids on several subjects. Shows copies of print versions of and printouts from online searches for data bases and compares them.

Professional Groups

Machine Assisted Reference Service Section (MARS), Reference and Adult Services Division, American Library Assn., 50 East Huron St., Chicago, IL 60611.

Online Section, Division of Information Technology, Special

Libraries Association, 235 Park Ave. South, New York, NY 10003.

Online Users Groups are located in many areas. For the groups near you see:

"Online User Group Directory," *Online,* January and July issues.

National Online Circuit (NOC) Coalition of online users groups. For further information contact: Rebecca A. Gonzalez, IIT Research Institute, 10 W. 35th St., Chicago, IL 60616.

Special Interest Groups on Computerized Retrieval Services and User Online Interaction, American Society for Information Science, 1010 Sixteenth St. NW, Washington, DC 20036.

Conferences

The national meetings of the American Library Association, Special Libraries Association and American Society for Information Science usually feature programs on online searching programs and problems. Their published proceedings are helpful in keeping one up-to-date on new developments. On-line vendors also hold annual meetings, national and regional. Information and notices about these meetings usually are published in the publications of the professional organizations listed above. Note too:

National Online Meeting. Yearly. Contact Thomas H. Hogan, National Online Meeting, c/o Learned Information, Inc., 143 Old Marlton Pike, Medford, N.J. 08055

Refer also to the published proceedings.

Online '83 ('84, etc.) Contact: Online Inc., 11 Tannery La., Weston, CT 06883

Database Learning Aids

Database manuals and vendors publications usually provide the best information about databases. There are also audiotraining kits produced by Data Courier, Inc. *Learn Inform,* Guide to

ABI/INFORM was published in 1981 and *Learn PNI* came out in 1982 (looseleaf manuals with accompanying audio cassettes). They combine introductory information with sample searches. *Learn Inform* and *Learn PNI* are available from Data Courier, 620 South Fifth Street, Louisville, KY 40302.

CHAPTER 25A

New Technology and Law Libraries

The following material comprises a new Chapter 25A for Legal Research and Law Library Management. *It is intended as supplemental material to the Main Text.*

A basic need in legal research today is accessibility to legal and law-related information and documentation, past and present. To achieve this objective, innovative programs reflecting the tremendous potential of the new technology are being developed with striking success. The traditional tools of research are giving way to the hardware of this new technology to such an extent, that it is believed the law library of the future could be unrecognizable to the researchers of today.

Researchers, professional librarians, lawyers and educators are already involved with the new techniques of electronic document-storage and computerized information retrieval systems and are gradually learning and adjusting to the exciting possibilities of miniaturization and remote transmission of data. How will the "paperless" library of the future affect law library management then? It is already obvious that even the planning of a law library today, in light of new technological developments, is becoming more and more challenging. Planners of new law libraries must decide whether tested traditional methods of library science should be replaced with untested substitutes, reflecting the new technology. For those who are in doubt, how long can they delay in meeting the thrust of this new technology in the interests of their users?

Before responding to these problems it will be helpful to give a law librarian's perception of how the law library could eventually serve its users. As seen at the Massachusetts Institute of Technology, the library will be the central facility of an information-transfer network that will extend throughout the entire law school and university community. Students and scholars will use this network to gain access to the law school's total information resources. Through touchtone telephones, teletypewriter keyboards, television-like displays and quickly made copies, the users of the system will communicate with each other as well as with the library; data just obtained from research of faculty, legal clinics and comments made by observers will be as easily available as the texts of books in the library or documents in the departmental files. The information traffic will be controlled by means of the law school's timed-shared computer utility, such as today's verbal communications are handled by the law school's telephone-exchange. Long distance service will connect the law school's information transfer network with sources and users elsewhere.

As seen by another observer, there is no technical obstacle in principle, and probably none of an economic kind either, why a legal researcher should not be able to dial a roll of microfilm in a London library, have some pages transmitted to him or her in New York City by telefacsimile, and pay for the service on his or her telephone bill.

In this context, it should be recognized that the attainable goal in library service must be guaranteed access to the library collection. This brings to mind the instructions given to John Randolph, Esquire, bound for England in 1732, from the President and Masters of the College of William and Mary: "As we do not live in an age of miracles," they reminded him, "it is not to be doubted that Indian scholars will want the help of many books to qualify them to become good pastors and teachers." Paraphrased, barring a miracle, it is not enough to know of a law book in existence to be useful, the law book must be in hand. Today, libraries provide access by lending the original document or the single copy of the book. Whoever seeks the same book or document thereafter, must wait until it is returned. That method is incompatible with the principle of guaranteed access. Transient or permanent access that does not preclude the concurrent access to the same documents by other users of the system will be accomplished by video disc, duplication of microform and visual displays on optical or electronic screens. For permanent access, full size paper copies will be provided, made directly from the original document or even produced at a distance by signals transmitted over electrical circuits.

Obviously, such a system raises questions as to the physical appearance and requirements for the law library, as well as seating accommodations for readers. Telefacsimile and computerized printouts make feasible the prospects of study terminals, located not only in the library, but in faculty offices, student dormitories, researchers' homes and elsewhere so that the stored resources of the library can be available twenty-four hours a day.

One copy of a book fed into an electronic data-base can service all simultaneous demands for it because the computer in essence assumes the role of a duplicating, rather than a circulating library, and as a result the integrity of the basic collection will be preserved. Even more significant, if by joining a network of other law libraries, the same process can be used to obtain access to the collections of these libraries, what should be the book selection policy of that library? What standards should be applied to a library's book collection holdings and development to determine whether it can meet the research requirements of its users?

Basic to this development is how the copyright law will be used to protect the rights of creators and owners of intellectual property being duplicated in that system and how statesmanlike the owners of copyrighted works will act in really effectuating the constitutional mandate that the copyright law's purpose is to promote the arts and sciences.

What role will the information explosion play in managerial decision making affecting law libraries? Certainly, it should change the traditional tools of research, because of the need to master tremendous masses of information in inter-related disciplines affecting law. As the necessary relevancy of economic, sociological, scientific and technical data in legal research is imposing new responsibilities on lawyers, the need to have access to such documentation and information is compounding the difficulties of legal research both in law school and in the practice of law. How to learn of the availability of these materials is a challenge by itself. The information explosion creates additional problems of identification and control. The New York Times has estimated that "the quantity of information generated in the past ten years alone will exceed the total from all of mankind's previous history. And the amount of available data continues to expand at a relentless, ever-increasing rate." Law librarians who have given any thought to the future development and organization of law libraries now believe that there is little time left to face the challenge of an increasing lack of book storage in libraries. The growth of law book collections in the last thirty years has taken on such proportions that Fremont Rider's prediction in 1944 that research libraries will eventually double in size almost every sixteen years is becoming more and more significant.

Law in the books has become a formidable storage problem and economic factor for law libraries. Administrators concerned with their maintenance and use must now take stock not only of how to cope with the increasing cost of book storage and the increasing lack of shelf space, but also with the obvious deterioration of older books and their replacement in more permanent form.

The use curve of most law books diminishes rapidly after periods of from ten to twenty years. This suggests the following solutions to reducing the stack space occupied by these books.

1) Storing them in a "depository" library situated at a distance varying from minutes to days away from the library proper. This solution entails not only the expense of renting the deposit space but also the cost of messenger service. There is little doubt that library service will suffer from such a solution, although it could be an effective space saver.

2) Highly extensive additions to the stack areas. This too is costly.

3) Compact shelving.

4) A new and enlarged library building.

5) The use of microform copies as substitutes for books already in the collection.

Miniaturization of library materials, in the form of micromaterials, must be considered in law libraries and especially in firm law libraries as part of a new concept of library management. Translated into terms of rental costs, the amounts involved become so significant that conversion of the hard copy volume into micromaterials should be recognized as a capital investment rather than as a book purchase.

For example, New York City law firms located in the business and financial areas are paying annual rentals as much as $50 a square foot. Construction costs have also risen dramatically to approximately $60 to $100 per square foot. Thus, in deciding whether to convert to micromaterials, library managers should not only consider the cost of replacing hard copies and the cost of rebinding them and the fact that the paper of many 19th century books is turning brittle and turning to dust, but also the actual costs involved in maintaining them on library shelves in light of the ever-pressing need to accommodate the many new publications libraries must acquire to service their users. Law books, when shelved, occupy on the average twelve to fifteen volumes per square foot; 4500 law books therefore occupy about 300 square feet, which at rentals of approximately $20 to $40 a square foot, could cost from $6,000 to $12,000 per year in rent alone, apart from the cost of the book.

Even the use of compact shelves is limited in many office buildings. A weight bearing floor of 250 pounds per square foot is needed to support compact shelving. Most modern buildings are constructed to withstand pressures averaging about seventy-five to 125 pounds per square foot.

Just as the storage of books in a law library has become a formidable challenge to librarians, law hidden in those books has become a formidable challenge to lawyers seeking legal authority. There was a time at the turn of the seventeenth century, when the English lawyer had to contend with only 5000 reported cases. Today, the American lawyer can consult millions of judicial opinions, increasing at an annual rate of approximately 50,000 published American appellate opinions alone. There is also a mass of federal and state legislation supplemented annually by hundreds of huge volumes of codes aggregating about 500,000 pages by themselves. Then there are the tens of thousands of pages of legal periodicals, government documents, administrative law and regulations, foreign law and international law, as well as topical looseleaf services. As noted, in the last three decades this challenge has been heightened by the increasing relevancy of economic, sociological and scientific data in legal research, so that the mere process of identifying, locating and referring to these materials confounds not only the practicing lawyer, but the legal scholar as well.

In addition to LEXIS and WESTLAW, online or interactive searching is the newest and most sophisticated way of locating information sought for a specific law-related subject. A great number of online search services in a wide range of disciplines have been introduced commercially for library and in-house use. Such searches are usually carried out by means of a comparatively inexpensive terminal located in a library or business office and can just as effectively be installed in a researcher's house. By this means, bibliographies and research related databases can be searched, containing millions of citations, abstracts or research summaries and the results can be reprinted within seconds.

These developments will be costly. The miniaturization of the library collection by microform and electronic database collections as a replacement for ever-expanding collections of law books in costly stack areas and deteriorating valuable research materials are more in the nature of a capital investment. Still, the costs could be prohibitive. Law firms will address the problem of costs as they meet the challenge of other rising costs in the practice of law. Law school libraries will turn to networking. The growth in volumes and cost of legal publications and the increasing labor costs of operating libraries have made it impossible for law libraries, even the best supported, to be self-sufficient. Cooperative programs will be necessary, such as coordination of acquisitions, shared cataloging, reciprocal borrowing and inter-library lending arrangements.

In New York City, the law libraries of the Association of the Bar of the City of New York, Columbia and New York University are working with an AD HOC Committee on library cooperation of the Association of the Bar and a preliminary plan for a regional law library network is now being reviewed by the interested parties. The planners recognize that automated library systems already developed have progressed to the point that a turnkey or modified turnkey system can meet the needs of a group of similar libraries, such as N.Y.U., Columbia and the Bar Association, in close proximity to one another. Document delivery will be simplified by the geographic proximity of the libraries. The study is now taking into consideration the implications of possible future participation by other large law libraries in the geographical area and the role of the bibliographic utility used for shared cataloging by the libraries: RLIN. The planners are interested in exploring the suitability of the various available turnkey systems not only for regional cooperation but also for the special needs of each library's functions, such as acquisitions, circulation, patron access catalog and remote searching, and this they plan to do without unduly compromising local needs and procedures in the libraries involved.

How will the physical features and services of the law library be affected by computer technology, microform technology and developments in communication? It is obvious that they have a significant role to play for storage, retrieval and exchange of information.

Are we really approaching the "paperless society"? Will the book become obsolete, its functions displaced by electronic circuitry? Will law libraries have the opportunity to elect to provide legal information in the traditional mode of printed materials or through the use of technology providing electronic or micrographic or other access to legal information? Just as the book has survived the competition resulting from radio, film and television, so it will survive the threats of the computer age. However, even assuming that the book will continue as a basic medium of communication, still the computer must eventually alter the traditional operation of libraries and their buildings. Any new library complex being designed today must meet the needs of the new technology.

An obvious problem library planners must address is the necessity and cost involved in providing sufficient space to house the flood of publications resulting from the information explosion and the publication explosion, as well as the bibliographical control necessary to obtain access to them. If, as quoted from Fremont Rider, academic and research libraries tend to double the size of their collections every sixteen to twenty years, then the conclusion of a mathematician, J.K. Kerny, has merit when he stated "the cost of building, of purchasing volumes, of cataloging and of servicing these gigantic libraries, could eventually ruin our richest universities." That will create sufficient problems by itself, but above all, how will the user obtain bibliographical control of that great mass of documentation?

There is more needed at the planning stage than to provide more materials, more buildings and more librarians. The concept of a library as merely a depository of books will necessarily have to give way to the concept of the library as an information transfer network. As one observer has noted, "the new technologies offer the hope of realizing this concept, and librarians above all welcome it. Through computer storage and retrieval, microforms, long distance transmission and the like, it may yet be possible to multiply the usability of every information unit to transcend the physical and geographic limitations of the library building and ultimately to make one's home or office, no matter where located, as fruitful a place for learning as the best public, academic or research libraries in major centers." There is little doubt that this prediction is the "wave of the future," but when it will become a reality is questionable. Library planners note that well-planned flexible buildings being erected today can serve for 100 years, and cost in construction around $80 to $100 per square foot in New York, with total project costs amounting to tremendous sums of money.

If the library of the future will depend on computer technology, microform technology and communications technology, to store, transmit and service the knowledge acquired by the library—through terminals, located at home or in service stations remote from the library building itself, where the information is stored—then, it has been asked, "is it imprudent, if not illogical, to plan costly structures to house non-existent books and their readers?" This is the dilemma faced by many administrators concerned with the expansion and development requirements of their libraries, and the answer obviously will depend on whether the new technology will become a substitute for traditional library service.

What are the library services the new technology will affect? Computers can alter the processing of materials and information in libraries. Many of the changes will take place behind the scenes—in the automation of the acquisitions and cataloging functions—but then will affect the public directly by the introduction throughout the library of a great number of terminals allowing the public (users) themselves to operate the computer terminal to locate a book or monograph. Known as the "on-line catalog," it arranges for the information now located in a library's public catalog to be stored in a computer (micro computer located somewhere in the library building) and will be accessible all over the library system through a network of public terminals with access to the same database. They are designed as "user friendly," which means that users can operate them without prior instructions. Users are given step-by-step instruction by the system, as they search the database. The screen presents the user with as many choices as possible and eventually will retrieve for the user by title, author, or subject, all the holdings of the library, as well as location by call number. The application of computers to library processes can be used to reduce and limit soaring costs of processing banks and the publication explosion. Online cataloging has become a part of the current library scene. Catalogs of all major research libraries will eventually be computerized. Completed are those at the University of California, Northwestern, Ohio State and the University of Delaware. The New York Public Library stopped filing cards many years ago, relying instead on a book catalog produced by computer tapes. All of their current cataloging is done in computer form rather than by separate cards filed in a public card catalog.

Another part of this development is taking place in university libraries that subscribe to computerized cataloging known as RLIN or OCLC. This allows a subscribing library to have accessibility by computer to the recent holdings of all the libraries in the system. A computer terminal located anywhere on the campus offers immediate access to bibliographic citations and location information of holdings in all libraries which have put their holdings online.

This system offers fringe benefits in the areas of acquisitions. There is also an automatic acquisition function which permits a library staff to keep track of materials from the time ordered until fully catalogued.

Another fringe benefit is the ability of the member libraries to share their resources. They can seek to avoid duplication of costly items and build on existing strengths, by notifying one another of impending major purchases and new serial subscriptions.

New technology will also allow for physical access to materials located in another library through the use of telefacsimile, which can transmit material from bound books over telephone lines. The libraries of Reno and Las Vegas campuses of the University of Nevada and the Davis campus of the University of California—also from Davis to Berkeley—have thus been linked already.

Circulation control can also be affected by computer programs. Computers will affect library services first in the area of housekeeping chores—order records and reports, fiscal control, circulation systems, bookkeeping records—which are the easiest to accomplish with obvious advantages. Then computers will affect cataloging and on-line operations.

LEXIS and WESTLAW types of services provide information retrieval through electronics with the added service of converting to machine readable form legal texts and periodical literature. An example of such program is the one instituted by LEXIS and the Matthew Bender Co., which will put online, through LEXIS, such books as Nimmer, *On Copyright,* and Collier, *On Bankruptcy.* The change to computer storage of full texts of secondary legal materials will take place with measured dispatch and, as described elsewhere, "will be evolutionary and not revolutionary." The next step would be retrospective conversion of texts to machine readable form. This is a long way down the road. It would appear therefore, that scholars and researchers will depend basically on books for the next thirty to forty years from now.

Facsimile transmissions of text over long distances can be of tremendous significance for legal research in libraries for it can obviate duplication, growth and rapid access problems.

Even with the great increase in the ability to receive information from remote sources—in private homes and elsewhere—outside the library buildings, it has been noted that "the present surge of students, to the library for concentrated, disciplined study, especially at times of academic pressure, is not likely to be rendered less by technology and will probably increase." The more that technology facilitates access to information, the more will information and libraries be used. This will tend to increase, not reduce, library workloads and the size of library facilities. Libraries planned today must be able to accommodate the hardware of the new technology for future use as well as the traditional book collection for continued use.

CHAPTER 31

Law Office Library Economics

The following comprises amended material for Chapter 31 of Legal Research and Law Library Management. *It is intended as replacement material to the Main Text. On page 335, substitute the following for the second paragraph under the heading Proposed Solution:*

Three works at least belong in the first category: *Collier on Bankruptcy, Moore's Federal Practice,* and *Rabkin & Johnson Current Legal Forms with Tax Analysis.* Individual practice needs may enlarge or contract the list and these titles are given as examples only. These works should be kept current.

CHAPTER 31A

Valuation of a Law Office Library

The following material comprises a new Chapter 31A for Legal Research and Law Library Management. *It is intended as supplemental material to the Main text.*

I. Introduction

There is ample precedent to support the view that the value of a law office library is both less than the value of the sum of its parts in one respect and greater in several others. For example, a run of *Federal Reporter* 2d series can be purchased for considerably less than the current per volume price times the number of volumes in the set. But in addition, skill and judgment are required to assemble a collection of law books. The time expended to select, locate, order, pay bills, stamp, affix book pockets and catalog that collection adds considerably to the library's value. Many people devote many hours over a period of years to this work. It should not be overlooked.

Nor does a library consist of publications alone. There are articles of furniture, shelving, computer terminals, microform reader-printers, copiers, cabinets, carpets and lighting fixtures. Each has a value.

This chapter discusses the appropriate standards for valuing the publications in a law library and the different purposes to which valuation may be applicable. It does not cover a library's furniture or fixtures.

II. Replacement Costs

In the absence of a statute or regulation, the most authoritative standard on the subject of valuation is the holding of a court of record. In New York, at least, such a standard was set in a Supreme Court case decided in September, 1980.[1]

Indeed, it is unusual to find a more sensible or realistic statement on law book valuation than was made in that case. A single practitioner ended a loose association with other lawyers, leaving behind his own law office library. The issues: who owned it, was it converted, and how much was it worth? The court held that, ". . . the market value of the converted books in this case is the cost of replacement by the plaintiff in the used book market and not the lower market at which the used book dealer would purchase the volumes. . . . Plaintiff is not in the used book business and would have to pay the higher cost in order to replace his library."[2]

The most practical way to apply this standard is to divide a law book collection into its major divisions or forms of publication, usually ten in number, as shown below.

Division of Law Collection

1. Court reports;
2. Statutes and Regulations;
3. Legal encyclopedias and digests;
4. Law Reviews and legal periodicals;
5. Shephard's Citations;
6. Treatises and Documents;
7. Looseleaf Services;
8. Newspapers;
9. Reference Works, including directories, indexes and dictionaries; and
10. Microform publications as a group.

The used-law-book market is an excellent source for purchasing or valuing publications in the first five divisions. That market

---

[1] Ashare v. Mirkin Barre, 106 Misc. 2d 866, 435 N.Y.S. 2d 438 (N.Y. Sup. 1980).

[2] *Id.,* 106 Misc. 2d at 867.

sometimes deals in publications in the other divisions, too, particularly in out-of-print treatises. Values for the remaining forms of publications can be obtained from the publishers.

1-5. The first five divisions. The replacement costs of court reports and the next four divisions of legal publications vary widely among dealers. The price per volume of a court report may be no higher than $3 if located among law school duplicates or in a retired lawyer's estate. But in the used book market, it may range from $6 to $9 or more a volume, and it will cost considerably more if purchased from the publishers.

Some recent examples: The New York Supreme Court[3] placed a value of $2,200 on a run of *New York Supplement,* both series, in its Sept. 29, 1980 opinion, but did not state the number of volumes held. A local New York dealer offered the first 432 volumes of NYS 2d for $2,900 in a list circulated in November 1981. Two years earlier another dealer offered the first 402 volumes of that series for $2,450. These offers average respectively $6.71 and $6.09 a volume. In each case to complete the set, all missing or later published volumes must be purchased from the publishers at their higher prices.

One should value statutes, encyclopedias, law reviews and Shephard's Citations similarly—according to their replacement costs in the used book market as shown on dealers' lists, and if not offered in that market, then at published prices.

Moreover, a lawyer should not have to scour the entire market and devote long periods of time away from his practice in order to arrive at a value. Otherwise, the cost of valuation itself would become a major factor in the value or replacement cost of the collection.

Advertisements in the classified columns of the *New York Law Journal* for the New York region, and in other legal newspapers and bar journals elsewhere, will help locate dealer or individual practitioner offerings.

An additional way is to obtain an impartial outside appraisal.

6. Treatises. Because a large proportion of legal treatises are currently published in looseleaf form, their value drops quickly

---

[3] See N. 1 *supra.*

depending on the extent to which they have been kept current. But whether in looseleaf form or issued with provision for pocket parts, one arrives at the value of any treatise by totaling the dealer's offering price and the publisher's cost of updating the set (so long as the total does not exceed the list price). For example, Cavitch, *Business Organization with Tax Planning* was offered by a used book dealer for $375. Its 1981 publisher's list price was $650. The 1979 supplements cost $313.50 as shown in the publisher's catalog. The second-hand set was a good buy and was worth $375 only if it had been kept current. In no case could it be worth more than $650.

For this reason, the best method of valuing a treatise that is still in print is to accept the publisher's list price. It is no secret to law book publishers that a second hand market exists. But their pricing of supplements effectively discourages any brisk trade in used treatises.

With respect to out-of-print texts, the second-hand dealers' catalogs are excellent guides. However, there are thousands of out-of-print titles, and the probability of locating a particular title in a dealer's list is statistically low. One should feel free therefore to use the following criteria in combination: the current usefulness of a particular book, its age, length, reputation of the writer and original list price, if known. Based on these factors, a range in values of anywhere from one to five cents a page is reasonable.

Exceptions may occur for books that are relatively rare, but still useful. For example, McCeleland & Fisher, *Corporate Mortgage Bond Indentures,* was issued by Callaghan at $15 in 1937. Yet practitioners have been willing to pay up to $75 for a copy of this one-volume work in recent years. Its scarcity, authority of the authors and continued usefulness dictate its relative high value.

7. Looseleaf Services. The value of a looseleaf service rests on its currency. Should the volumes of a set be scorched by fire or drenched by sprinklers or fire hoses, the new report letters keep piling up until the subscription expires. To some extent, publishers can maintain copies of their services filed to date in their offices. Commerce Clearing House, Inc. has always been willing to supply replacement volumes for a nominal charge. A damaged set is not worth the full subscription price unless it cannot be replaced for less.

Past year runs of looseleaf reporters may still have value. For example, the successive annual editions of *Standard Federal Tax Reporter* should follow the value set by the second-hand book market—to the extent that a market exists. Otherwise, the standards for unavailable out-of-print treatises, discussed above, are suitable. But any value for those reporters in excess of one cent a page would seem unwarranted.

8. Newspapers. Those offices in which newspapers are kept for a year or less can replace most of them at the rate set by the publishers. Typically, a newspaper publisher will sell back issues up to a few weeks in the past at the original newsstand price, and charge a rising premium on earlier issues, depending on their age. Microform replacements are also available for many newspapers.

9. Reference Works. The market in current, second-hand reference books is relatively thin. It is difficult, for example, to purchase the current edition of *Martindale-Hubbell Law Directory and Digest* anywhere but through the publisher and then at the list price. Sets of *Index to Legal Periodicals* and both *Black's Law Dictionary* and *Ballentine's Law Dictionary,* for example, appear on dealers' lists occasionally. But the frequency of resale is so low, especially for the *Index,* that the publisher's list price ordinarily determines the value.

10. Microforms. There is not yet any extensive market in second hand microforms—film or fiche. Publishers' list prices should therefore apply.

These various methods of valuation should be accepted for insurance purposes, and in connection with a merger or dissolution of a law practice. But they may not satisfy the requirements of the Internal Revenue Service in connection with the deduction on a tax return of the value of a gift of books to a law school or other "charitable" institution. The government might insist on setting the value at whatever the lawyer could realize from a sale by him to a dealer or any other purchaser, rather than the price that the book dealer would charge after adding on his profit.

Naturally, the condition of the publications is a factor in determining their value. A set of books with numerous underscored passages cannot be valued as high as a set in mint condition. What then is the answer to the question: "I know my *Shepard's United States Citations* volumes were heavily marked up and sprung from their bindings, but can't I value them at the publisher's new book price?'' Yes, if the insurance company will agree. Yes, if one's new partners will agree. But no, if those books have been donated to a charitable institution. In the first two instances, compromise is the general rule.

III. Selection and Acquisition Costs

With respect to runs of court reporters, it is generally accepted that the whole is worth less than the sum of its parts. But with respect to the hidden costs of selecting, acquiring, processing and cataloging a collection, the whole is worth far more.

1. Book Selection. It would seem eminently fair to quantify that portion of a lawyer's and librarian's time spent on building a law office book collection, and then to assign a value to that time over a period of several years. The judgment exercised in book selection is a factor of experience and special skills. It should not be underestimated.

2. Book Ordering and Processing. It is a relatively simple matter to determine the time spent and the salaries paid in connection with locating books, writing orders, paying bills and preparing publications for the shelves. True, some saving is effected by trying to replace an entire collection in a single year, compared to the cost of performing the same tasks piecemeal over several years. Therefore, a reduction of about fifty percent in book ordering and processing costs seems justified. But the expenditure of five dollars a volume is not far from actual costs on a day-to-day basis.

IV. Summary

The valuation of a law library should proceed in two main stages as outlined above:

1. The valuation of each of the ten major forms of publications in the collection; and

2. The estimate of the cost of professional and clerical efforts that were expended in assembling that collection.

CHAPTER 37A

Law Libraries at Crossroads—Cooperation or Curtailment

The following material comprises a new Chapter 37A for Legal Research and Law Library Management. *It is intended as supplemental material to the Main Text.*

"Librarians [especially law librarians] are a bunch of snits." So confided the night nurse to her newly-admitted patient, as she began her midnight rounds in the intensive care unit of Philadelphia's oldest hospital. The term "snit" combines the best-publicized attributes of a snake and a rat.

Coming out of the blue as it did, her revelation puzzled, but it did not surprise the patient. He had heard clients make even less flattering characterizations of their own lawyers. Still he wondered why she greeted him with it. It may, therefore, be useful to reflect on what law libraries and librarians will continue to face in the years to come. Theirs is more than a mere image problem. It may be that their existence, the very nature of libraries and the function of librarians are undergoing basic changes. If the addition of the single letter "a!" can change the term "snit" to read "saint," can librarians be far behind?

Making Cooperation Work

This chapter has the single theme: *Making cooperation work.* It has three sub themes: (A) Co-operation within one's own office; (B) Cooperation among law libraries, and (C) Co-operation between law libraries, and other fact-finding agencies. Librarians are in the forefront in all three efforts.

The central problems are apparent to everyone. Libraries occupy too much space. At $10-a-foot rent, the 3,000 square-foot library required an annual outlay of $30,000 a year only a few years ago. The same size library at $50 a foot costs $150,000. But it never stays the same size. Little is discarded and more is always being added. Instead of an annual over-all growth rate of five percent, libraries face a six percent increase.

The cost of new books, supplements to codes and treatises, subscriptions to services and legal periodicals is increasing by about ten percent a year. New computer and microform equipment—a necessity in most libraries—is expensive to purchase or rent and maintain.

Libraries are expensive to administer. They are a microcosm of the larger office. Staffs are bigger, the problems that they handle more complex. Professional assistance—with regular additional training—is a necessity. It is often recommended that a law-trained research coordinator be employed to direct research activities in large law offices. That idea is winning slow acceptance. As one instance, a major insurance company financed the law schooling of its own gifted librarian for that purpose.

A. Cooperation Within One's Office.

Librarians can best anticipate lawyers' needs and sharpen research services if information about current matters in the office are fully and promptly disclosed. In that way, the collection can be developed to meet current needs. It is incumbent on lawyers and librarians to exchange advice both on weeding and adding to the collection.

Candidates for weeding that strike anyone who enters an office library for the first time are runs of rarely consulted reporters (often identified by a uniform film of dust across the tops), law reviews older than twenty or twenty-five years (formerly regarded as sacrosanct by those with a fetish for complete runs of every set), superseded treatises and encyclopedias.

For works of intermediate usefulness, there remain the solutions of microform conversion, stack rearrangement, compact shelving or cellar storage. All four have their supporters among office planners. With collections constantly accumulating at their current end, it is wise not to let them hang on indefinitely at their ancient end.

The most important prerequisite for internal cooperation is the employment and continuing training of a librarian who possesses the attributes of the best lawyers: unflagging drive, flexibility, intelligence, imagination and availability.

B. Cooperation Among Law Libraries.

Sharing of resources is more of a necessity than ever before. The high cost of books and the high rent of space are reasons enough.

Inter-library borrowing of reporters missing or in use in one office and available in a nearby one is the most common form of borrowing. The compilation of union lists enormously simplifies the location of needed publications. These lists show, for example, the holdings in various offices of legal periodicals, looseleaf services, legislative histories and foreign country publications. The lists themselves are, of course, the result of cooperative efforts of the participating libraries and librarians.

The reputation of a firm or its librarian as a good "loan risk" frequently determines whether borrowing privileges will be extended at all. "Sorry, we can't seem to find it ourselves," is a frequent response to the librarian who—having lost one book—tries to borrow another. Non-cooperation has speedy penalties.

With the advent of computer networks, it has become possible for office libraries to pool information about any of their holdings—book, document or microform.

Cooperative book purchasing arrangements have been accomplished informally among a small number of libraries. This offers room for considerable savings. For example, each of five libraries in one building can share the cost and use of the codes of the fifty states of the United States. Each might purchase, for example, nine different codes and all acquire those for New Jersey, New York, Connecticut, Massachusetts and California.

A little-heralded form of cooperation is the exchange of information between the veteran librarian in one office and novice in another. Also worth pointing out are the seminars sponsored by

LLAGNY (the Law Library Association of Greater New York) and by AALL (The American Association of Law Libraries). The newsletters issued by both organizations contain announcements of forthcoming sessions.

Finally, there are the major institutional libraries—those maintained by associations, such as The Association of the Bar of the City of New York, New York County Lawyers' Association and the New York Law Institute, all in New York, and those maintained by the various law schools. It would be virtually impossible to practice law successfully in New York without their cooperation.

C. Cooperation Between Law Libraries and Other Fact-Finding Agencies.

"The practice of law is changing. It is more fact-oriented, more business-oriented." This idea was expressed by a law office librarian in a Wall Street firm. No doubt it will be increasingly apparent in the coming years.

In consequence, librarians must reach out to help lawyers satisfy their need for facts. The intellectual resources of large cities make possible the kind of law practiced there. New York has a large number of distinguished universities and specialized educational centers. The leading foundations and numerous professional and technical associations maintain headquarters in the City. Its libraries, as shown in the Special Library Association *Directory,* represent virtually every branch of learning and business endeavor. New York remains the publishing center of the country. The City is home to the major trade associations and trade papers ranging from atomic energy to the wool trade. The United Nations secretariat is still located in New York and it is surrounded by a cluster of foreign consulates and foreign trading organizations.

The law librarians who know their way through this maze of information sources are among the most valuable in the profession. Rarer are the librarians who combine this knowledge with the ability to win and keep the cooperation of a host of those agencies—nonlegal in nature—whose sponsors owe little to law offices. This work requires diplomacy of a high order.

Changing Face of Fact-Gathering

Three new factors are changing the face of fact-gathering.

(1) *Reduced Services.* Reliable old sources are disappearing or are curtailing services. Government agencies, such as the SEC, have been forced to retrench. Regional offices are being curtailed. Many of the foundations and associations are also cutting back services.

Twenty years ago a telephone call to the *New York Herald Tribune* was all that was needed to obtain a reference to any story published in that newspaper during this century and virtually up to the latest day's edition. *The New York Times* provided similar free information. The *Tribune* itself is now long gone and the *Times* telephone index service long discontinued.

(2) *Accelerated Information Growth.* The sheer volume of useful information available to lawyers and the time required to digest and absorb it are beyond the capacity of any one office.

(3) *Computer Services.* Several hundred separate computer data banks are in daily use in many offices. They collect data on a host of subjects—business, financial, medical, political. If facts or ideas can be expressed in words, numbers or symbols, a computer can collect the information, store it, rearrange it in any sequence and deliver it on demand—for a fee.

As a result of these three factors, librarians have begun to employ specialized commercial services outside the office to do a portion of their searching and fact collection. Few office librarians can cope with all this work by themselves any longer. The services charge a fee that can reasonably be passed on to clients.

The field is now wide open for the most resourceful librarians themselves to enter this branch of commerce. In San Francisco, one law office has been marketing its routine librarian services to other lawyers for a fee. It is realistic that librarians should be able to market their *non-routine* information skills, particularly business information skills, to law offices for a similar fee.

CHAPTER 37B

Turning the Office Library into a Profit Center

The following material comprises a new Chapter 37B for Legal Research and Law Library Management. *It is intended as supplemental material to the Main Text.*

> *"Lawyer productivity in our firm—the number of hours billed to clients—advanced each month for the past five years. Suddenly last month it declined by a whopping 10 percent. Also last month, our library was closed for reconstruction. I can ascribe our billing decline to only one thing: the closing of our library."*—Managing Partner of a Large Law Firm in the South.

This is the most recent concrete evidence to come to light that links law firm profitability directly to library services. How concrete is the evidence? Upwards of $125,000 was lost because this library was closed for a single month. At a modest 1,500 hours a year, the typical lawyer in that firm billed 125 hours monthly, and probably more, to make up for vacations. But in the month in question, the average dipped to 112½ hours. That represented a loss of 1,250 hours to this 100-lawyer firm. Given an equally modest $100 an hour average billing rate, the loss totalled $125,000.

That libraries make a positive contribution to profits has long been clear to librarians. But few office managers and administrators show it on their balance sheets.

[1]—Raising Productivity

Superior librarians increase lawyer productivity in four main ways:

(1) They run a "tight ship" in which missing books are kept to a minimum, outside borrowing services are performed with imagination and speed, and the book collection is maintained at a broad enough level to permit lawyers to complete most of their research on the premises;

(2) They provide directional, informational and instructional services of a high order, enabling lawyers to find or learn what they need with no wasted motions;

(3) They relieve lawyers of fact-gathering and many legal research activities that they, as librarians, can frequently do faster and more efficiently; and

(4) They help raise the quality of the firm's work by showing lawyers new ways of solving legal problems—particularly through the use of recently established computer data bases.

In the illustrations that follow, the value of these services to a single lawyer in a single year is estimated at $12,500. To a 100-lawyer firm: $1,250,000. That the southern firm's loss was approximately the same when its library was closed is persuasive that this estimate is on target.

The first group of examples relates to library activities that help lawyers *avoid wasting time*, the second group to services that help them *make more effective use of their time*, and the third group to *librarian services that can appropriately be billed to clients*.

[a]—Eliminating Wasted Time.

[*i*]—*Missing Books*. In many offices lawyers are forced to waste their own time chasing up and down corridors for books not signed out. Or they comb through piles of books reserved on tables or in carrels in the hope of finding reporters that should be on the shelves. Or they waste time responding to demands for books that they returned weeks earlier or never had in the first place. The problem is cut to a minimum in sharply run libraries. What is this service worth in dollars? In a 100-lawyer office, a single hour wasted this way each week by each lawyer is worth $10,000 for the books not found and not used at all. The waste caused by inferior work is even more costly.

[*ii*]—*Trips to Other Libraries*. In recent years the migration of downtown firms to the midtown or other areas in large cities, such as New York, has been heavy.[1] The New York midtown firms are scattered between Sixth Avenue and Third Avenue and from Fortieth to Fifty-ninth Streets in Manhattan. Their population center clusters around Forty-ninth Street and Park Avenue. It takes about one hour to start from one's desk on an upper floor of any of these midtown buildings and travel by subway to the New York Law Institute—one of the country's oldest and best stocked association law libraries. The return trip requires a second hour, desk to desk. The journey to the Bar Association library on West Forty-fourth Street takes at least half an hour for uptown lawyers, a full hour for those remaining in the Wall Street area.

Librarians help eliminate a number of these journeys by enlarging the office collections, by drawing more heavily on other outside resources and by expanding their messenger services. Sometimes the addition of a run or two of regional reporters or of a few more state codes or of heavily used treatises will eliminate the need for many of those outside trips.

What is the value of this kind of service? In the 100-person firm, assume that an average of only half an hour is saved each week. This is a conservative estimate when one remembers that the round trip between uptown and downtown is likely to take two hours. Total saved: fifty hours or $5,000 a week.

In other cities the time lost in traveling may be somewhat less. In Los Angeles the County Library maintains a motor cycle delivery service that covers the city and its suburbs. But good as that is, it is no substitute for a well-stocked library.

Effective circulation controls and book acquisition and borrowing practices together can save the large firm upwards of $15,000 a week So much for mere "housekeeping" and management functions in a law library. What about reference assistance?

[b]—Reference Services. The answers to the questions "Where is it?" or "What do we have on a subject?" or "What exists?" repre-

---

[1] "Law Libraries on the Move in Midtown Manhattan." New York Law Journal, Dec. 16, 1980, page 4.

sent the most basic librarian services. "Did the Supreme Court grant 'cert' or schedule arguments in a particular case?" "Has H.R. 1 been reported by either house?" "Were hearings held?" "How fast can I see them?" "What has the FDA done about that new sugar substitute—I can't remember its name?" "Where are the FCC guides about 'loud commercials?'" Left to himself, the typical lawyer will spend three to four times as long as will an experienced reference librarian before finding answers to these questions.

At an average saving of only one-half hour per lawyer each week, the value of library reference services in the same firm is $5,000 for fifty hours.

[c]—Research Services. Librarians perform numerous services for the express benefit of individual clients.[2] Whether or not a direct charge is made for those services, the firm gains the time that lawyers would otherwise have spent in doing the same work. Moreover, lawyers hesitate to charge in full and frequently to make any charge for fact-gathering activities.

For example in litigation, a librarian can be expected to marshal the pertinent facts about potential expert witnesses: what they wrote; how they testified in similar actions in the past; who their clients have been; which congressional committees they appeared before.

In corporate and commercial matters, the librarian can relieve lawyers of the need to search for background information about an industry or company. The well-run office library maintains a basic collection of business directories and the librarian has access to a broad range of computer data bases with which few lawyers are familiar.

These and similar tasks could hardly be completed by most lawyers in large firms in less than half an hour a week each. The saving: fifty hours or $5,000.

In summary, the elimination of wasted lawyer efforts (i and ii above) in the 100-attorney office can be expected to average one and one-half hours or more per week. Reference and research services can save lawyers upwards of one hour each in the same period. Total value of two and one-half hours for 100 lawyers: $25,000 weekly and $1,250,000 a year.

---

[2] See Chapter 37 in the main text.

How realistic are these estimates? The experience of the southern firm bears them out. The experience of other major firms, however, is that they have yet to use cost accounting methods to prove them one way or the other. This knowledge is worth gathering. Once amassed it will help to confirm the library as an actual and not merely a potential income-producing center.

[2]—Billing for Library Services

It is not too many years ago that little support could be found for billing clients for librarian reference and research services. However, cost pressures of maintaining a library have forced a complete reversal of the former attitude. Two librarian help wanted ads are revealing of the concern of law firms in charging clients for library services:

> "DIRECTOR OF LIBRARIES: . . . national law firm . . . has an immediate opening . . . one of the three largest west coast law firms, with . . . over 1,200 employees, a library staff of ten, with ten paraprofessionals, and an annual budget of over $1,500,000. We are seeking an innovative librarian/manager who can provide expanded services to the firm's practice, *while appropriately recovering costs. . . .*"[3]
>
> "RESEARCH SPECIALIST: . . . 325-attorney firm. . . . Its research specialists provide sophisticated research support using state of the art technology and extensive book collections. *They generate revenue sufficient to produce a profit margin on the cost of all library staff. . . .*"[4]

[3]—Reference and Research Work

The collection, sifting and analyzing of information needed by clients is a service that they are willing to pay for and cannot get more economically anywhere else. In most instances, client requests are made to partners or associates in the first instance and passed on to

---

[3] See the Newsletter of the American Ass'n of Law Libraries (April 1988).
[4] *Id.*, Special Issue of January 1988.

the librarian. The examples given here of speech writing, supplying legislative histories, and document identification barely touch on the scope and variety of research inquiries that come into a busy law office.

[a]—Speech Writing. It is not unusual for law librarians do research for the firm's clients who are preparing to deliver a speech. Speech writing inquiries help explain why law offices keep collections of quotations, as well as copies of the Bible, the works of Shakespeare and other writers. On occasion, the collections of such works in law libraries surpass comparable collections in well stocked public and college libraries.

Research for speeches can go beyond the search for an appropriate quotation or even a legal point. In one instance, the incoming president of a Texas conglomerate asked the firm representing the company, not for an entire speech, but only for a joke about Texans that he could use in his address. He wanted to poke fun at his fellow Texans for their boastfulness that everything is bigger and better in Texas than it is anywhere else. The library staff came up with the following line which, incidently, was apparently well received by the listening audience:

> "Down here in Texas, you can't make up your minds whether to boast that you have the largest or the smallest midgets."

[b]—Legislative Histories. Describing how a law librarian can be of service to a paying client needing a legislative history can best be illustrated by the example in which a merger-minded client approached his legal advisers to obtain for him exactly what the draftsmen of the Clayton Act and their fellow congressmen had in mind when they drafted and debated Section 7 of the 1914 bill. The law firm had retained all the pertinent reports and the *Congressional Record* volumes for that year, but a peculiar fact about the bill's history complicated the research. The bill had been renumbered at various times, and what eventually became Section 7 was designated Section 6 at one time and Section 8 at another. Even the congressmen debating the bill were confused.

The firm's law librarian solved the problem by compiling a Clayton Act history that contained as an introduction a numerical time table that resembled in appearance an elevator starter's board. It showed for each applicable month in 1914, the "ups" and "downs" in what is now Section 7 until the bill was signed into law.

[c]—Document Identification. An illustration of how a law library's ability to identify documents can be of value to clients goes back several years. At one point during the well known dispute between Senator Joseph McCarthy and CBS political commentator Edward R. Murrow, the Senator insisted on equal television time to reply to Murrow's criticism. Agreement was reached to give McCarthy a half hour of prime television time on the condition his remarks were filmed and submitted a week in advance.

In examining the film submitted by McCarthy, the people at CBS noted that the Senator flashed on the screen a number of unidentified documents that he claimed proved his contention of corruption and communist infiltration into the government. Photostatic blowups of the frames containing the documents were sent to the lawyers for CBS for identification. In turn, they were given to the law firm's librarian.

Although the Senator's hands obscured most of the front covers of each document, part of a title, a fragment of a government seal, or a portion of a date remained visible. Noting that the seals looked "funny" in that they did not resemble the Great Seal of the United States, the librarian collected copies of the seals of those states that maintained committees comparable to the House Un-American Activities Committee. Within a few hours, he connected the non-federal documents to the appropriate states. With the assistance of the New York Public Library's Economic Division, he was able to identify all of the state documents among the ones McCarthy used as illustrations.

The librarian then compared the portions of titles and dates on the remaining documents with similar dates on the covers of similar congressional reports, committee prints, and transcripts of hearings. One by one, each document was identified well in advance of Murrow's rebuttal program.

[4]—Billing Rates and the Extent of Library Income

In order to obtain information on how a law firm's library works as a profit center, four firms consented to disclose a few facts about their library billing practices, but each kept confidential the full picture. Nevertheless, some interesting deductions can be made even from the limited information these firms were willing to supply.

Firm A disclosed that their billing rates ranged from $60 to $100 an hour for library services for clients. The chief librarian, for example, spends two hours on research and earns $200 for the firm. The time for a messenger who spends an hour-and-a-half getting the results into the hands of the client is billed at $60 an hour, earning another $90 for the firm. These amounts add up to make the library a valuable profit center.

Firm B supplied less information, but did disclose that that their monthly library billing averaged $18,000, coming to $216,000 per year.

Firm C would not disclose specific billing rates, but the librarian did indicate that the library billing rates were lower than Firm A's, but they billed substantially more than Firm B, close to $500,000 each year. Some of the firm reference librarians billed as much as six hours a day.

Firm D declined to submit any billing rates, but did supply a record of weekly lawyer requests for an entire month. The 2,384 requests for a single month ranged from simple copying of documents to fairly intense legal research. Among the items listed were 762 requests for computer retrieval, 644 requests for reference work, and 300 requests for specific items of research.

Assuming that only half these requests were billable, that comes to almost 1,200 billable tasks. If the searches required only half an hour per request, that is still almost 600 billable hours. At an average rate of $75 an hour, the monthly income comes to $45,000, or $540,000 per year.

[5]—Law Schools

The Biddle Law School Library at the University of Pennsylvania has introduced two programs that extend law school library services to the private bar. One program provides a service of lending and delivering law books to an attorney's office for a fee of $25 per item plus messenger charges. An annual access card, which permits use of the library, is available at an annual charge of $200. These cards are free to the school's alumni and non-profit organizations. For a $500 annual fee, an access-plus card is issued which permits borrowing of books in addition to access to the library. The program also includes a subscription plan with annual fees ranging from $600 for firms or legal departments of thirty lawyers or less to $1,600 for larger organizations of seventy-five or more lawyers.

The second program is an expanded photo copying service with a basic charge of forty cents per page plus delivery costs. A unique feature of this service is that requests can be made twenty-four hours a day, seven days a week. After regular library hours, telephone requests are recorded and handled as soon as the library opens. Because Biddle is a repository of the administrative codes of all states, and has an enormous collection of foreign materials, calls are received and encouraged from outside of Pennsylvania.

CHAPTER 37C

Law Librarians: Value and Compensation

The following material comprises a new Chapter 37C for Legal Research and Law Library Management. *It is intended as supplemental material to the Main Text.*

Today's starting salaries for associates in the leading firms, including housing grants and bonuses, average $65,000 a year—more than quadruple the 1968 amount. Going back still further to 1950, lawyers "struggled along" on $3,600. There has been an eighteen-fold increase since then.

The pay of *veteran* librarians in the same firms matched or slightly exceeded *beginning* lawyer compensation early in the four-decade period. For example, $3,600 was on the low side for librarians in 1950. But today $65,000 is very much on the high side, with a bare handful of librarians in New York area firms earning that amount after ten or twenty years in their profession. Most earn far less. Moreover, the gap between lawyer and librarian salaries widens sharply by the associate's third or fourth year following law school graduation.

Members of the legal and library professions differ in the kinds and quantities of services they perform. Lawyer services are easier to evaluate and far simpler to measure. The firms have no handy benchmark against which to gauge librarian services. But there are dozens of associates to compare one with another. Moreover, a librarian is expected to bill very few hours a year. A lawyer's future may very well hang on his ability to bill very many hours a year.

A typical associate can be expected to perform upwards of 1,800 hours of billable services to clients in a single year.[1] That is a finite amount. According to a 1982 survey—rates have since risen—the

---

[1] Compiled from data appearing in the National Law Journal *Directory of the Legal Profession*. N.Y., Law Publishing Co., 1984. It shows for a few representative firms,

lowest hourly rate at which major firms billed those services was $71.[2] This applied mainly to first-year lawyers. At a conservative $100-an-hour average for experienced and novice associates combined, a typical Wall Street lawyer—not a partner—could then be expected to bring in approximately $180,000 a year to the firm. In addition, each associate was and still is expected to keep abreast of developments in his field, attend seminars, and even perform some *pro bono* work.

It is no surprise that the 365-day calendar year shrinks to 227 work days for most firm employees—lawyers excepted—when weekends, four-week vacations and eight holidays a year are subtracted. Attendance at conventions, workshops and seminars may further deplete the working year, as do two or three almost inevitable "sick days," leaving about 220 days a year for actual work. The associates reach their 1,800 average of billable hours by giving up evenings or weekends to work at the office. A number of librarians also work exceptionally long hours. But only a few match the associates' weekly schedule.

Given their shrunken 220-day working year, librarians have a tough public relations job to persuade management of their true value to a firm. Nevertheless, librarians can prove their value on two specific fronts. The first is in the traditional way in which the best librarians have always excelled, that is, by building and maintaining a fine book collection, by assisting lawyers in its use through constant and innovative service, and by making available the intellectual resources of the city, the country or the world. This front needs no additional comment here.

The second front is in mastering, using and teaching lawyers to use the resources of the computer. This is the librarian's "growth industry." It is the source of the librarian's, and in many ways, the firm's advancement. Few people in any firm are computer experts. The computer offers a librarian the opportunity to match an associate's 1,800 hours of billable time—in a far shorter work week.

---

first, the number of billable hours actually worked by their associates in 1982 and *second*, the suggested number of hours to be billed. The lead firm in productivity was Wachtell, Lipton, Rosen & Katz in New York, whose associates averaged 2,200 hours in 1982. No firm admitted to a policy requiring that many hours. The average for the twenty firms for which 1982 data was supplied came to 1,812 hours.

[2]*American Lawyer Guide to Leading Firms, 1983-84*. American Law Publishing Corp., 1983.

An article in the *New Jersey Law Journal*[3] listed some twenty ways in which laywers in small and medium-sized firms in New Jersey are applying computers to their litigation, real estate and estate problems. The legal journals, law reviews and legal newspapers are filled with additional imaginative proposals.

The librarian who would become a more valuable employee and be compensated for it need master only three things:

(1) Everything that can be learned about existing and forthcoming software, that is, the programs that retrieve facts or organize data;

(2) Everything that can be learned about the hardware, the machines that run the system; and

(3) Everything that is needed to train lawyers to operate the machines and use the programs to advantage.

A sensible first step is to establish a file of current books and articles in the field, together with a list of available programs (with their attributes) and catalogs of existing data bases and computer machinery.

A second step is to survey current course offerings in library schools and in graduate schools of business and engineering and to enroll in courses that appear to be useful.

Third is the gradual application of computer methods to library management and to the firm's legal and non-legal research.

Finally, set forth below are illustrative computer and other services once available through Citicorp library, all of them developed by Mrs. Jean Strohofer when she was their librarian. They are the kinds of services that law firm libraries can perform for themselves or employ an outside agency to supply:

(1) On-line searches of some 300 data-bases available through ADP, Control Data, Datasolve, Dialog, Investext, Nexis and NYTIS;

(2) All SEC filings since 1978;

(3) Statistical information collected by the Bank from commercial data assembled by the United Nations, the European Economic

---

[3]English, "A Terminal on Every Desk?—Computers in New Jersey Law Firms", 114 N.J.L.J. 1 (Nov. 8, 1984) (Index page 477). Curiously, there is no mention of librarians in any of the illustrations given in the article.

Community, the International Monetary Fund and other international agencies;

(4) The contents of some 1,500 business, financial and consumer publications to which the Bank subscribes, with access to some 8,000 additional periodicals.

During Mrs. Strohofer's tenure at the Bank, nearly all the resources of the Citicorp library, both on-line and those in hard-copy form, were made available for a user's fee—making this the first true profit center among New York libraries.

When law firm librarians combine this level of service with their own law-based resources, their librarians will find the $300-a-day salary barrier easier to pierce and even surpass. A library's best public relations program is a combination of sustained and spectacular *service*—with emphasis on the final word.

CHAPTER 37D

Law Librarian Burnout

The following material comprises a new Chapter 37D for Legal Research and Law Library Management. *It is intended as supplemental material to the Main Text.*

> "Dick Vermeil burned himself out *as coach of the Eagles. . . . His sense of responsibility was overwhelming him. 'I worked time to death and it killed me.'*" [1]
>
> *"The winning of Super Bowl XI secured for Madden such fame as a football coach can expect. But it wasn't until a year or two after he retired at the end of the 1978 season—at 42, ulcerated and afflicted by what was then not called burnout—that his fame began to compound itself into celebrity."* [2]

[1]—Introduction

One might expect psychological burnout to afflict victory-haunted football coaches and partnership-aspiring associates, or even rainmaking partners—but law librarians? Never!

The facts are otherwise. The literature on the subject is impressive and growing. Veneese Nelson in her article "Burnout: A Reality for Librarians?"[3] cites twelve other writings on the subject, all but two published in the 1980s.

One of these articles concerned corporate librarians.[4] Most of the

---

[1] Smith, "A New Life," Sports Illustrated, p. 11 (March 28, 1983).

[2] "John Madden, Mr. Big," Los Angeles Times Magazine, pp 2-3 (Jan. 25, 1987).

[3] Nelson, "Burnout: A Reality for Librarians?," 79 L. Lib. J. 267 (1987)

[4] Smith and Nielsen, "Burnout: A Survey of Corporate Librarians," 75 Special Libraries 221 (1984).

others included law office librarians in their surveys. However, none limited its study to the private law library scene.

Law firm and corporate legal department librarians nevertheless face special problems. Identifying burnout and curing it is not always an easy task.

[2]—Burnout: Definitions and Symptoms

A few definitions of "burnout" have been offered. For example:

> "Physical or emotional exhaustion, esp. as a result of long-term stress."[5]
>
> "To fail, wear out or become exhausted by reason of excessive demands on energy, strength or resources."[6]
>
> "[T]o burn oneself out; to exhaust one's strength (by overexertion).[7]

Unlike the typical first or second year associate, the office librarian is a long-term employee who is not trying to "make partner." He or she is not running for head of a union or competing for quarterback or tight end. The librarian is simply trying to perform a job that has no counterpart in the firm. It is a unique position—the organization and delivery of information services.

Yet the librarian is caught up in a network of stress, caused in part by the determination, singlemindedness and ambition of associates, in another part by the lack of those same characteristics in young, nonpermanent library staff members, and in a third part by the remoteness of partners, administrators and office managers. The symptoms of burnout vary widely, but the result is inevitable—poor, even grudging, service.

An adversary relationship has grown up between lawyers and paralegal assistants on one side and library staff members on the other. Symptoms among librarians include irritability and remoteness, fre-

---

[5] *Webster's II New Riverside Universal Dictionary* (Riverside Pub. Co. [Houghton, Miffin] 1984).

[6] *Webster's Third New International Dictionary of the English Language Unabridged* (G & C Merriam Co. 1981).

[7] *Oxford English Dictionary*, Supplement (A to G. Oxford [England] 1972).

quent tardiness, unexplained absences, and illness of various sorts, including headaches and colds.

[3]—Causes of Burnout

There appear to be three main causes of burnout among private law librarians and their assistants.

[a]—Workload. The increase in the lawyer and paralegal population in firms and corporations without an equivalent expansion in library staff size is a significant cause of librarian burnout. Staff workloads have increased in some cases to close to the breaking point. However, rather than let themselves break, many staff members just do not do the work. They lose, bury or ignore lawyer requests. They shirk the work, leaving a few conscientious staff members with doubled responsibilities. These latter staff members are the real burnout candidates.

The staffing of law office libraries is amazingly uneven. One leading firm employs a library staff member for each seven and one-half lawyers. Included are eight professional librarians. Other well-known firms have a ratio of only one library staff member to nearly thirty lawyers. One world class corporation employs a single full time librarian with a limited amount of part time help for more than 100 lawyers. Very little service, particularly sophisticated research assistance, can be expected or given in such a situation.

[b]—Inadequate Management. The shift in lines of authority from managing or library partners to offfice administrators is a major cause of librarian burnout. One corporate law department administrator, for example, has his hand on every facet of legal and library activity in his company. This particular administrator is trained in the law and is unusually sensitive to the needs of his people. However, few administrators grasp the vital importance of the interplay between lawyers' research and the services of sophisticated librarians.

To many administrators, the librarian is just another department head, albeit a unique and important one. The result is occasional job freezes while legal staffs explode; harsh and often unnecessary budget squeezes that please a few partners but hamper the firm's work; and apparent indifference to library staff space requirements or working conditions.

These matters are usually resolved knowledgeably and quickly whenever a library partner or managing partner remains the policy link between the library and the firm. One major firm achieved a novel solution by promoting its law librarian to the post of administrator.

[c]—Failure to Recognize the Value of the Librarian. The failure of management to learn, appreciate and acknowledge the unique research abilities that the best librarians bring to their work is another cause of librarian burnout. The compilation of legislative histories, knowledge of the intricacies of the federal regulatory system, the full use of electronic research services, and familiarity with the flood of non-legal databases, are all matters in which the best librarians excel and in which few lawyers are their peers.

The most galling feature of this cause of librarian burnout, at least in the eyes of librarians, is management's failure to acknowledge, publicly and regularly, the real worth of the librarian. Curiously, low compensation is only a contributing factor and not a main cause of librarian burnout. It is unusual for librarians to question the disparity between fourth and fifth-year associates' salaries and those of twenty-year veteran law librarians. Few librarians enter the profession for the money, but they do protest the stress of the workplace, the inability to gain and hold the ear of knowledgeable partners, and the failure of management to acknowlege superior ability and performance.

[4]—The Cure for Burnout

In many offices, the partners have removed themselves so far from management details that they are often unaware of the rumblings of discontent in the ranks. On one side, the partnership-seeking associates are afraid to complain of poor library service. On the other hand the librarians have little opportunity to be heard.

It is up to administrators or managing partners to ascertain if the conditions causing librarian burnout, as outlined here, exist and to eliminate the causes. The librarian should be a strong ally of each partner and associate, and not their antagonist. Every firm deserves a service oriented library, but not all firms achieve it.

It is amazing how quickly the wall between lawyer and librarian can be removed. Some suggestions:

(1) Set a library-staff ratio low enough to get the work done, preferably no higher than one librarian to every twenty lawyers. It is up to office management to provide a sensible work load. But the librarian should inform management when that work load is exceeded—when burnout is imminent.

(2) Determine the functions the librarian and the library staff should be performing.

(3) Ackowledge superior library service when it is delivered, but do not hesitate to complain when it is withheld.

(4) Re-establish the lines of authority between partner and librarian.

Applying these four suggestions can cause confrontation to be replaced with cooperation. This is no "Pollyanna" nostrum. It is a realistic way of curing burnout and achieving a service oriented library.

CHAPTER 37E

Changing Role of Law Office Librarians

The following material comprises a new Chapter 37E for Legal Research and Law Library Management. *It is intended as supplemental material to the Main Text.*

Private law librarianship has undergone some significant changes as a profession since the late 1970s. Marie G. Wallace, a librarian at O'Melveny & Myers in Los Angeles, sums up these changes in a useful handbook published by The Practicing Law Institute as a supplement to a program it held on Private Law Librarians in October-November 1986.[1]

Ms. Wallace pointed out, for example, that the program title "Private Law Librarians" focused on librarians rather than libraries: "reflecting the trend toward what Naisbitt describes in *Megatrends* as the high tech/high touch society." In addition, Ms. Wallace noted the following significant changes:

(1) Reference activities of private law librarians include extensive use of non-legal materials and interdisciplinary databases.

(2) Whether LEXIS or WESTLAW is better is not relevant today. Instead, what is relevant is how to use both systems to their best advantage.

(3) Microcomputers are now an accepted tool and have changed the procedures for many technical processes.

(4) Many firms participate in or use bibliographic utilities. A con-

---

[1] *Private Law Librarians* (1986), Marie G. Wallace and Teresa E. Wrenn, co-chairpersons, N.Y. Practicing Law Institute (Commercial Law and Practice, Course Handbook Series, Number 396).

comitant of this development is the proliferation of library software packages.

(5) Managerial skills are as important as technical skills.

(6) There is a growing and large body of new professional literature encompassing computers, software, legal reference services, data bases, data base use, loose-leaves and newsletters, and treatises.

(7) More private law firms are opening new branches requiring extensions of library service to the firm members practicing there. They are also relocating to new buildings or merging with other firms, thus requiring a reorganization and replanning of library service.

(8) Not only is productivity of the library operation being examined, but budgets are becoming common.

(9) It has become acceptable for a librarian to charge research time.

(10) The allegiance of many private law librarians has shifted from the firm to professional and private concerns, resulting in a great deal of job-changing. There are more employment options available to the librarians.

(11) There is a growing and large cadre of private law librarians in other fields or with new titles, such as consultants, contractors, information brokers, publishers, database designers, programmers and film makers, reflecting the "gold collar worker" syndrome described by Robert Kelley in *Gold Collar Worker*.

(12) Professional indoctrination has moved beyond the traditional methods. For example, there is now a videotape on how to manage a law library distributed by the American Bar Association. In this context, it should be noted that skills are now expected of private law librarians such as knowing how to engage in computer assisted legal research and use other on-line technology.

(13) In the past, law librarians primarily tended to move to academic law librarianship primarily. Now, they are being attracted to other types of law libraries, particularly to private law libraries.

(14) There are twice as many private law libraries as there are law school libraries and firm staffs have grown.

Despite these changes, the traditional aspects of private law librarianship remain characteristic of the professional. Most lawyers seem not to understand what librarians do nor how they do it. For the most part, librarians are still seen within the framework of books rather than information. However, a former ABA Journal editor and publisher has suggested a new name for the profession, "informarians." Private law librarians still find it necessary to teach legal research as a major part of their jobs because legal research continues to be inadequately taught in law school. Lawyers see books and databases "as an either or choice rather than as complementary systems."

Ms. Wallace also noted that law book publishers, unlike electronic publishers, do not offer good customer service. It is questionable whether academic law librarians would fully agree with this appraisal. Much too often the customer service provided by electronic publishers to academic law librarians could be greatly improved. Perhaps the private law firm libraries are better served by them because their subscriptions and service fees are much higher than those paid by the academic law libraries.

Other findings characteristic of the profession are that business managers of law firms still do not understand the librarian's function and the operation of the library and that microformats are a begrudging substitute for space. The same law book publishers who dominated the field ten years ago dominate it today. Many firms still do not have professionally trained librarians, and when they hire people, they usually lack appropriate education or experience. In this context, there continues to be no training or hiring pool for library clerical staff.

As previously indicated, "Private law Librarians, 1986" was published as a course handbook to accompany a Practicing Law Institute program given on private law librarians. Its bibliographies particularly are well selected.

The following chapters, among others, in the handbook should prove useful not only for neophytes in the field, but also for the more experienced.

Job Description Guidelines for Attorneys and Office Managers by Marie G. Wallace. Cautioning that "no job description is forever" and that it should be updated and reviewed on a regular basis, this chapter recommends that the job description for the law librarian contain (1) job identification; (2) job summary; (3) job duties; (4) qualifications; (5) job specifications; and (6) evaluation standards. The information which should be set forth in each category is spelled out in a sample job description.

Roberta's Rules of Reference by Roberta Leskowitz. This chapter explains how the librarian through interview and, sometimes, instinct, can translate what the patron asks for into what the patron actually wants. The advice given is practical, for example, "If you can't give them what they want, give them what you've got." While such information may not be exactly on point, it may prove to be analogous. Other practical advice includes: "You don't have to understand the subject to find the answer," you can know what books the answers are in without knowing what is in the books; an explanation of how to get by with "a little help" from friends.

The chapter on *Reference Services in the Large Law Firm Library* by Jill Sidford, adds another dimension to this branch of work as does *Reference as a Public Relations Tool* by Mary Ann Donaldson.

The effect of the new technology on private law library service is brought out in a number of chapters on computers in the law library.

An enlightening presentation is given by Catherine A. Pennington on *Microcomputers in the Law Library: Hardware Selection*, which addressed the problem of how to select hardware and software compatible with that used by the law firm. Pennington identifies hardware options for the private law library using IBM-PC compatible equipment, the Apple MacIntosh, Wang micro- and mini-based systems and the Barrister Office Systems.

As Pennington notes, law libraries basically use computers for three types of activities: (1) general business functions (accounting, word processing and on-line access to data bases); (2) library management functions (cataloging, acquisitions, serials control, and routing); and (3) research functions (access to Lexis and Westlaw, litigation support and management of in-house generated documents). Pennington advises that by analyzing a library's existing manual activities and systems, as well as desired functions, a fairly accurate picture of hardware and software functions can be developed. Shen then gives case studies illustrating how this analysis works in making hardware decisions. By answering a library functions questionnaire she has devised, it can be determined whether the library is ripe for automation. After a given set of questions on a topic (e.g., accounting, consultations and the like) is completed, the point given to each answer can be added up and compared to a guide. The guide recommends the use of hardware and systems that should be considered to support the function or services involved. For example, it indicates whether a good manual system of accounting is sufficient or should be replaced by a spread sheet program or an integrated data base manager. Even the more experienced in the field can learn something from these exercises.

In this context, too, Helen P. Burwell's *Using a Library Systems Package in the Law Firm Library* provides good advice on why a turnkey application for law firm library automation should be chosen; and why the library files such as acquisitions., cataloging, serials and circulation should be automated. In addition, the chapter discusses what are the right questions to be addressed to vendors of library software services and with respect to other law firm applications for information management software. The chapter on *Software for Law Firm Applications* by Bobbie Johnson is also helpful on these subjects.

Other helpful and basic information highlighted in the handbook includes:

(1) *Library Orientation Programs*, by Teresa Wrenn

(2) *Technical Services in Law Firms: Some Policy Considerations*, by Margaret Landahl

(3) *Space Planning for Law Librarians*, by Lawrence Cheeseman

(4) *Branches and Twigs, or How to Survive from Expansion*, by Catherine C. Palmer

(5) *Management Communications and Public Relations: The Art of the Possible*, by Jean P. O'Grady

(6) *The Law Firm Library Budget: A Systematic Approach*, by Gitelle Seer

(7) *Budgeting for the Corporate Law Library*, by Eleanor A. Sabo

(8) *Evaluation of a Law Firm Library*, by Marie G. Wallace

CHAPTER 39A

Suggested Solutions to the Library Space Dilemma

The following comprises a new Chapter 39A for Legal Research and Law Library Management. *It is intended as supplemental material to the Main text.*

According to Oliver Wendell Holmes:

> "If all the law libraries burnt to the ground every ten years little would be lost. The reason: the judges repeat themselves so frequently that the best *old* principles always reappear in the *new* reports."[1]

The question, however, is whether this Holmesian view is true in the modern world.[2]

Introduction

It doesn't take a consultant to tell hard-pressed lawyers and librarians that their book shelves are bulging. Yet the eminent

---

[1] This is a paraphrase of what Holmes actually wrote.

[2] See The Path of the Law, the address delivered at the dedication of the new hall of Boston University School of Law, Jan 8, 1897 and published in Collected Legal Papers at 169 (N.Y., Harcourt Brace, 1921). Also reprinted in 10 Harv. L. Rev. 457.

> "It is a great mistake to be frightened by the ever increasing number of reports. The reports of a given jurisdiction in the course of a generation take up pretty much the whole body of the law and restate it from the present point of view. We could reconstruct the corpus from them if all that went before were burned."

jurist quoted above missed the mark. Neither fire nor water will relieve overcrowded book shelves. Practical solutions are needed. What books should be discarded, what books should be saved, what form they should be kept in, are the subjects demanding decision.

Eight solutions to library space problems are set out under "Recommendations" below in descending order of preference. The purpose is to *save* rather than *destroy* the best that remains of the libraries that lawyers have built. The twin aims: (1) to promote the greatest convenience for those who conduct legal research or manage libraries and (2) to keep down the cost of book storage and delivery of library services.

Newness is no guarantee of judicial wisdom. Nor has the existing judiciary a corner on great writing. When firm A and B throw out the same sets of reports because firm C has them and C throws them out in the belief that A and B are keeping them is to describe a circular dilemma all too common. Hence the value of slowing the discard race.

Past Weeding

In many offices the choice of which books to throw out has been based only partly on what can best be spared. Condition or appearance of the books, even their placement on the shelves (in the way of progress, for example) or simply whim have often outweighed usefulness. At an annual storage cost of two dollars a volume and upwards, there is a great incentive to weed law office book collections. Obvious candidates include the first series of the regional reporters, the *Century* and *Decennial Digests*, the side or nominative reporters, and the nineteenth and early twentieth century session laws. Less obvious candidates include early law reviews and older treatises.

Sets of books most frequently discarded from libraries in New York include:

New York side reports (those identified by reporters' names);
Regional reporters, first series;
Federal Reporter;
Federal Cases;
New York State session laws; and Federal Register (1936 to the current year).

In one case a major New York firm threw out both the first series of the *New York Supplement* and *New York Reports* to make room for more recent reports, thereby destroying both versions of the State's highest court reports.

One drawback to the weeding process is that these books must remain available somewhere. If all firms discard them, and if a local bar association law library decides to store them (for space saving reasons) in out-of-the-way places (usually in cellars or off-site), then outright weeding may prove expensive and unwise.

Meanwhile, the federal and state courts rely hundreds of times each year on the holdings in cases decided fifty, one hundred or more years ago. These "ancient" cases turn up as citations in modern decisions in opinions covering diverse questions of law, including criminal law,[3] evidence,[4] negligence,[5] and patent law.[6] Numerous old English cases are still cited by today's American courts.[7]

Assuredly many of the old cases are the more eloquent and the better reasoned. But the sheer bulk of the new has shaken our conviction in the merit of the old.

---

[3] See, for example, People v. Diaz, 51 N.Y. 2d 841, 433 N.Y.S. 2d 751, 413 N.E. 2d 1166 (1980), citing People v. Rice, 159 N.Y. 400, 54 N.E. 48 (1899).

[4] See, for example, Daviero v. Johnson, 441 N.Y.S. 2d 895 (N.Y. Sup. 1981), citing: Horowitz v. Hamburg-American Packet Co., 14 App. Div. 631, 43 N.Y.S. 1156 (1897); Reardon v. Third Ave., R.R. Co., 24 App. Div. 164, 48 N.Y.S. 1005 (1897); Buel v. New York Central R. Co., 31 N.Y. 314 (1865); Filler v. N.Y. Central R. Co., 49 N.Y. 42 (1872).

See also, People v. Conyers 52 N.Y. 2d 454, 438 N.Y.S. 2d 741, 420 N.E. 2d 933. (1981), citing People v. Rutigliano, 261 N.Y. 103, 107, 184 N.E. 689 (1933), and People v. Molineux, 168 N.Y. 264, 61 N.E. 286 (1901).

[5] Akins v. Glens Falls City School Dist., 53 N.Y. 2d 325, 441 N.Y.S. 2d 644, 424 N.E. 2d 531 (1981), citing Murphy v. Steeplechase Amusement Co., 250 N.Y. 479, 166 N.E. 173 (1929). *Murphy* discusses the history of the New York Code of Civil Procedure enacted in 1876 and derived from the collection of Revised Acts of 1801, which itself was "substantially a transcription of the English statute of 29 Car. II. c. 3. Section 16." 166 N.E. at 176. The twenty-ninth year of the reign of King Charles II was 1677, since the fiction is preserved in England that he began his rule from the moment of the beheading of his father and that the interregnum between 1649 and 1661 did not occur. Thus a 304-year old English statute still holds interest for New York lawyers in 1981.

[6] Diamond v. Chakrabarty, 447 U.S. 303, 100 S. Ct. 2204, 65 L. Ed. 2d 144 (1980) citing Hartranft v. Wlegmann, 121 U.S. 609, 165, 7 S. Ct. 1240, 30 L. Ed. 1012 (1887).

[7] Wilson v. State of Florida, 363 So. 2d 1146 (Fla. App. 1978), citing English cases from as far back as 1628.

Overcrowded Libraries

American courts are sensitive to the plight of those who must use the myriad of volumes that their opinions create. The statements quoted below testify to that. But sensitivity in some has not led to restraint by all.

"Judge MacMahon was mindful that more time might improve the fullness of [his] Memorandum but wisely refrained from adding to the volumes which already overtax the space or our law libraries. . ."[8]

"The facts which are the background of this particular piece of litigation have been stated so many times that we shall not waste . . . law library shelf space by a long recital of them."[9]

"We find no one of the appeals to have merit, nor to present problems that justify in themselves, the space in law libraries that this opinion will take."[10]

". . . until a valid reason for voting to grant one of these petitions is put forward, I shall continue to vote to deny. In the interest of conserving scarce law library space, I shall not repeat this explanation every time I cast such a vote."[11]

"Our reports are, by reason of the volume of our case load, taxing the legal library space available to bench and bar alike. Thus we eschew whenever possible long discussions of settled principles with supporting discussions."[12]

"We shall have to quote extensively from the record and thus extend the length of this opinion despite our realization of library space limitations to accommodate our reports."[13]

In one case, a contempt order was issued against the Board of Commissioners of Mahoning County, Ohio for its failure to "provide the Mahoning Law Library with sufficient floor space

---

[8] REA Holding Corp. v. Sowerwine, 558 F. 2d 1127 (2d Cir. 1977).

[9] Singer v. A. Hollander & Son, Inc., 202 F. 2d 55 (3d Cir. 1953).

[10] Converse v. Joslin, 176 Cal. App. 2d 638 (1959).

[11] Justice Stevens concurring in the denial of certiorari in Liles v. Oregon, 425 U.S. 963, 964 (1976).

[12] Kaleva-Norman-Dickson School District No. 6 v. Kaleva-Norman-Dickson School Teachers Ass'n., 52 Mich. App. 433 (1974).

[13] Brown v. Sptiza, 45 Mich. App. 97 (1973).

. . . and because of the structural insufficiency of portions of the court house to bear the weight of books."[14]

Recommendations

Books will remain a substantial if not the chief research resource for lawyers well into the future.[15] So despite the enormous *finding advances* that computers bring and the hoped-for *sharing advantages* that library "networks" promise, law offices will continue to set aside large blocks of space for their expanding book collections.

These recommendations are based on the conviction that the computer is best for *collecting and pinpointing* information. But books are best for, *understanding* and *analyzing* it. The recommendations are really adaptable to individual office needs and preferences. They are based on experience in planning office libraries in building space whose current rent ranges from $12 a square foot in Tampa (where it was only $6) to $50 a foot on Madison Avenue in New York (where the tenants are accustomed to paying half that amount).

Cost and effective utilization of space on one hand and ease of access to the cases on the other are the twin aims.

A. Corridor Shelving. A single self-contained and contiguous area has long been regarded as the best space for a law office library. It helps ensure control over a wandering book collection and speeds service to lawyers. But given high rents and already crowded libraries, the unused office corridors become an appealing alternative for storage of long runs of uniformly bound court

---

[14] State ex rel. Board of Commissioners, 53 Ohio State 2d 56, 372 N.E. 2d 349, 350 (1978).

[15] A strong case for "book" rather than "paperless" libraries appears in an article by Eli M. Oboler, librarian at Idaho University Library from 1949 to 1980 in the Oct. 1, 1981 issue of Library Journal.

> "To my own knowledge, academic libraries which should have known better have traded off hours of opening, book and serials purchases, and even staff for membership in information utilities. I think they—and their patrons—have lost by this exchange. My own private Utopia for the libraries of the 21st Century . . . will include the libraries of America as not linked by any national network, as not obliged to use VDT terminals instead of book stacks, as still maintained by librarians very similar to the librarians of the 1980's—some technology-minded, some management-minded, some user-oriented, some bookmen and even some a mixture of all of these."

reports. For example, each ten feet of corridor space can accommodate 480 volumes, assuming that the older reporters run about six volumes to the foot and shelves are eight high. A total of 100 feet along office corridors provides space for 4,800 volumes—at no increase in rent. The space is "free."

The problem of control is minimized because in most offices demand for the "stored" works is less than for more recent publications. Yet when any one of these books is in fact needed, it can usually be brought back to the library in about two to five minutes.

Most of the early reporters are uniformly bound and highly decorative. They do not require the same degree of control as do the most recent reports because they are called for less frequently. For these reasons, it makes sense to line otherwise drab hallways with books that retain at least some utility.

B. Cellar Storage. Cellar space can often be rented at a far lower rate than above-ground space. When it is available in one's own building, it provides efficient nearby book storage. The round trip travel time even from the fortieth floor of a modern office building to retrieve specific volumes should not exceed fifteen minutes. A space of 1,000 square feet used for book stacks alone should accommodate 17,280 closely packed volumes. A major drawback to cellar storage, however, is that in some buildings, cellars can be reached only after changing elevator banks. Cellars are less accessible than corridors for storage of older volumes, but the use of cellar storage is certainly preferable to off-site storage.

C. Compact Storage. Where the floor load can be increased to permit its installation, compact storage of books on movable shelves provides some 50 percent increased book capacity over standard shelving. It permits a larger number of volumes to remain within the office library where they are more likely to be used than if they were placed some distance away. This form of shelving is expensive. It is heavy; use of compact shelving requires steel reinforcement of library floors, a process best performed while a building is under construction, not after it has been topped out. This kind of storage is more satisfactory for shelving infrequently consulted works. However, at least one Wall Street firm has installed compact shelving for its entire library. Its main disadvantage is that a portion of the shelving must be moved in order that books on interior shelves be taken out or replaced.

D. Warehouse Storage. Low cost warehouse storage used to be the favorite solution to the space problem. The practice was simply to take the old records or books and get them out of sight. There are four reasons why retrieval from a warehouse was never perfectly satisfactory. First, it always took too long to make the trip—even when a full-time warehouse staff was employed. Second, the messengers were often away on "more important" errands. Third, the librarians kept less than perfect records of (a) what they stored in the warehouse and (b) in which numbered cartons or on what shelves in the warehouse particular books were placed. Fourth, lawyers tended to disregard cases that they could not get their hands on quickly. Delivery time was rarely shorter than one hour—when the books could be found at all—and the waiting time often stretched to several hours or into the next day.

E. Computer Storage. The arcane argot of "computographers" goes far toward discouraging lawyers and librarians from embracing the new technology. Terms like ASCII files, Boolean searching, down-drop menu, gigabyte, and system degradation are enough to scare off any novice from getting involved with computers. Nevertheless, the language is necessary. The term "gigabyte," for example, refers to billions of characters. When compact disks begin storing gigabytes—retrievable in seconds and occupying only a few inches of space—they are bound to compete with books. The typical 1,000 page older reporter contains approximately four million characters. A compact disk containing just ten gigabytes could store the entire series of regional reporters, have enough room to include the *New York Supplement*, and still have room left over for some 600 additional volumes.

Despite the argot, library planners can no longer ignore the ways in which computer technology will benefit the law library. Computers may never replace law books, but they are complementary to the more traditional methods of storing research material. Eventually computer storage may replace some of the older, large, space occupying series of bound reporters.

Responding to an apparent demand, "Lexis" and "Westlaw" suppliers are now storing cases decided in earlier periods. For example, in New York, "Lexis" starts with 1884 cases for *New York Reports* and with 1919 for *Miscellaneous and Appellate Division Reports*. In Federal law, "Lexis" has started U.S. Supreme Court opinions from 1790 on, Circuit Court of Appeals opinions from 1789, and District Court

Cases from 1790. "Westlaw" stores *New York Reports* from 1918, *Northwest Reports* from 1885, Federal Court cases from 1789, U.S. Circuit Court cases from 1891 and U.S. Reports from 1754.

F. Republication of Leading Cases. The first series of regional reporters together with *Federal Reporter* were published in 2,000 volumes. Only a small proportion of the thousands of cases reported there are referred to with any frequency. But when needed at all, they may be absolutely indispensable. By republishing the leading cases in those series, West Publishing Company would provide the legal profession with a valuable tool and still save the space that most of those volumes occupy. A choice of only one-tenth of this material isssued in 200 thin-paper volumes would occupy about twenty-eight and one half linear feet of shelf space. They would contain the best of late nineteenth and early twentieth century decisions. An ultra microfiche edition of all 2,000 volumes is not a completely satisfactory alternative.

G. Sharing Collections. "Library co-operation is dead," asserted one prominent law school librarian a few years ago. Today he is a staunch advocate of library networks—a scheme for sharing library resources. Whether he was right in the past or is correct today is unproved. Libraries that are under great pressure to conserve space may join a consortium for the collection of the older law books. But experience shows that the problems of where to store the books and who should control them are still unresolved.

Cooperative libraries are most suitable in buildings that have at least three or four fair sized law firm tenants. The tenants share in the rent of a modest amount of space and agree to store single sets of various series of older legal publications. They then discard or give away any duplicate sets. Such a collection can be compactly stored because none of the sets belonging to individual constituents will grow any further—each set is already complete. Nor does such a library require more than minimal supervision. An obvious drawback to the cooperative library system is that if a firm moves out of the building, it loses its interest in the stored books.

H. Microforms: Microfiche and Microfilm. Without question microreduction has become a popular alternative to storage of the older volumes of court reports, session laws and other serial publications. Its advantages and disadvantages have been repeatedly discussed at library seminars and will only be touched on in this chapter. The "calamitous" microfiche edition of Congressional bills points up the dangers inherent in the hasty substitution of microforms.[16] Microform storage is best used for runs of newspapers and publications like the *Federal Register*. Nevertheless, microforms are likely to be displaced by computer storage.

Currently available on ultrafiche through West Publishing Company are the complete first series of the regional reporters and *Federal Reporter*. Their cost is $16,000. The 300 volumes of *New York Supplement* are listed as $2,400. Also available are the first 450 volumes of *Federal Reporter 2nd Series* at $3,825 and 350 volumes of *Federal Supplement* for $3,050. New volumes are added each year. With office rents zooming, the charge of about $8 a volume for those three series of ultrafiche is not out of line.

University Microfilms will supply *Statutes at Large* from 1789 through 1971 on 35mm microfilm for $1,485. Subsequent years are available for a relatively low charge on microfiche or film from various sources.

The New York "side" reports and session laws have been filmed and are on sale, but they are relatively expensive.

Before exchanging books for film, however, five questions should be considered. First, is the investment in film too heavy to bear at all? Second, how much space is actually saved after steel microfilm cabinets are purchased and microfilm reader-printers set in place? Third, do service companies provide speedy repair work when readers or printers break down? Fourth, will the film

---

[16] Letter of Thomas H. Reynolds, Assistant Law Librarian, Univ. of California School of Law (Berkeley) (Oct. 5, 1981).

"What are you folks doing to cope with the new approach to the Congressional bill service, i.e., the microfiche edition? As far back as I can remember this law library subscribed to the U.S. bill service in hard copy. It was, of course, costly and troublesome to maintain this material current and in order, but it was felt that user needs required such an approach. I was overjoyed when a microfiche version was announced and we were told this was all that would be available on deposit—or for sale as far as I can determine. We have now had a few months experience with the microfiche and it is clearly a calamity of major proportions! . . . . The bills are photographed, if not quite at random at least in such a format as to discourage all but the most determined user. The 'Microfiche user's guide' is of minimal assistance at best and I still haven't figured out how to easily find all amendments. . . ."

or fiche that is purchased be usable ten years in the future or will temperature and humidity fluctuation, dirt or dust and careless handling destroy portions of it? Fifth, will lawyers be so deterred by poor prints or failing machines that they will consciously avoid the older cases? A best guess to these five questions are:

1. Yes, for many lawyers.
2. Less than one might expect.
3. Rarely.
4. No one can guarantee the permanence of film.
5. In all likelihood, yes.

Assuming that law office libraries—like law firms—cannot continue to grow forever, each office must still determine its own optimum use of library space. That determination, should not result in (1) slowing down or curtailing the delivery of library services to lawyers or (2) lowering the quality of their services to clients. Indeed, in a few large offices, library staffs are taking on additional paralegal functions at a net reduction in office costs.

Given a choice among the eight alternative solutions to the space dilemma, there is no reason to shrink library facilities or to limit library services. But it is reasonable to expect the computer to begin solving library space problems in the future

CHAPTER 39B

The Court Reports—Their Accelerating Space Demands

The following material comprises a new Chapter 39B for Legal Research and Law Library Management. *It is intended as supplemental material to the Main text.*

"*. . . it takes all the running you can do to keep in the same place. If you want to get somewhere else, you must run at least twice as fast as that.*"—Through the Looking Glass. Chapter II.

Once every five or ten years, it is useful to verify that the Red Queen is right. Do law book collections really grow as fast as we can run? Do they "run" (grow) faster each year? The answer to each question is still "Yes"—as it was ten and twenty years ago. The accelerating expansion of law books is as unremitting as inflation. Nor has the improvement in microform equipment made any significant inroads on the space requirements of the leading law reports.

This chapter concerns the shelf space occupied by the leading federal court reports and by those of four states in which litigation is widespread: New York, New Jersey, Pennsylvania and California.

What this demonstrates for library planners—and for those who pay the rent of library real estate—is that arithmetic projections of space needs will not work. Those who plan new offices in this way will always underestimate their needs and run out of space too soon. They simply leave out of their calculations the basic "acceleration" factor. Those libraries that maintain two or three sets of federal reporters will have to "run" very fast indeed to keep up with expansion.

A. Federal Law.

Two of the major tenants of library shelving are *Federal Supplement* and *Federal Reporter 2nd Series.* Both sets expanded more than 60 percent faster in 1981 than they did in 1971. In five-year comparisons, they both grow on the average of more than 20 percent every five years.

B. New York Law.

The State of New York is one of a minority of states that requires citation to alternative runs of court reports—both official and unofficial. The cost to users is high, both in the purchase price of the two series of reports and in the rent of the space that they occupy. This is an addition to the time that must be spent in locating and comparing interior references in the two sets. Only the printers and the beneficiaries of free subscriptions to these books appear to gain from the system.

Moreover, the rate of growth of the unofficial *New York Supplement* 2nd Series has been sharply lower during the past few years than the rate for the three official editions of the same cases: *Miscellaneous, Appellate Division* and *New York Reports.* For example, more than twice as many *Appellate Division* 2nd Series volumes appeared during the period from 1977 to 1981 as were issued from 1972 to 1976. The other two official series also showed substantial gains.

Again, this problem is compounded in many libraries by the necessity to subscribe to multiple copies of all these series of reporters.

C. New Jersey Law.

New Jersey is a relatively small state in area. But the volume of its court opinions has expanded at least as rapidly as those of the New York courts across the Hudson River. Moreover, New Jersey lawyers consult both *Atlantic Reporters* and their home state official reporters, *New Jersey Superior* and *New Jersey Reports.* There is considerable overlapping, if less than perfect correspondence, between the official and unofficial editions.

D. Pennsylvania Law.

No state in the United States exceeds Pennsylvania in the variety of its court reports, the number of series of reporters and the acceleration in the volume of their printing. The Commonwealth has a separate series of reports for more than half of its sixty-seven counties, a series of *District and County Reports* that publishes county reports selectively, three series of official state reports and two editions of unofficial reporters.

The *Pennsylvania Superior Court Reports* is a series that leads the country in the rate of increase in the space occupied by volumes issued in the single year 1981 over 1971. These books expanded by some 700 percent. Presumably a change in printing contract awards and a backlog of unpublished cases helped to swell the number of volumes issued. All the same, the reports of the Commonwealth Court itself expanded by 350 percent and those of the Supreme Court by 50 percent in the same period.

Pennsylvania cases are well covered by the *Atlantic Reporter*. In addition, West Publishing Company extracts Pennsylvania cases from the *Atlantic Reporter* and publishes them separately in its *Pennsylvania Reporter*. It is curious that the rate of growth of the latter series actually declined in the five years after 1976 as compared with the 1972-1976 period. All other Pennsylvania reporters shown in the table expanded sharply.

E. California Law.

California runs counter to the trend set elsewhere in the country. The *California Appellate Reports* 3rd Series actually declined in the rate of its growth. The California Reports 3rd Series grew at an even rate through 1983. *West's California Reporters* expanded by a modest 13.6 percent in the same period over the growth of the previous five years. *Pacific Reporter* 2nd Series, however, is a massive set of books that comprised some 632 volumes at the end of 1981.

Conclusion

Librarians who know these facts and library consultants who deal with them daily should be forthright in disclosing them. Managing and "building" partners of law firms should be informed of the mushrooming tendencies of the leading court reporters.

"Most of my clients—approximately 100 of them—grossly underestimated their office space needs," a noted architect reported. The cost of office space—between $35 and $50 a foot in large cities—is a major deterrent to realistic planning. Few law offices volunteer to allot more space than the library actually requires and most—at least in the early stages of planning—allot far less.

The solution lies in (1) analyzing a library's current space requirements, (2) projecting those needs realistically five or ten years in the future and (3) accepting the planning advice that one pays for.

CHAPTER 39C

Seven Fallacies of Library Space Planning

The following material comprises a new Chapter 39C for Legal Research and Law Library Management. *It is intended as supplemental material to the Main Text.*

Library directors and consultants owe it to their employers to use space effectively and economically. Libraries are expensive enough to maintain without wasting space. Yet those who allocate space owe it to their firms to base their decisions on facts not fallacies. Some wrong decisions can be laid to a series of space fallacies that are bedeviling the law office scene.

> FIRST FALLACY: Books are on the way out and our Lexis and Westlaw terminals will soon replace them. Therefore we don't have to allot any more space for books, but only for machines, and we can convert most of our existing library space to "productive" use.

These statements are doubly wrong. The fact is that computer services are superior case and fact finders. But it is wasteful of a firm's or client's money to use them to replace Xerox copiers, or, having found a series of cases on point, to read the full text of those opinions on a screen while the computer's meter keeps running.

Moreover, enough has been written on turning a library into a profit center to persuade most administrators that books, computers and librarians produce income for a firm.[1] They don't waste it.

When his firm installed its first Lexis terminal more than ten years

---

[1]See, for example, "Turning the Office Library into a Profit Center:, Chapter 37B *supra*.

ago, a partner turned to a young associate and jested, "Now that we have Lexis I guess we won't need *you* much longer." Lawyers are no more on the way out than books are. The facts are that this firm now has numerous computer terminals. But it employs nearly twice as many lawyers as it did ten years earlier and its library contains more books than it ever did before.

> SECOND FALLACY: Books are on the way out and microfiche, microfilm and Ultrafiche will soon replace them. Therefore, we can convert the rest of our existing library to 'productive' uses.

The space saving features of microforms are their most appealing asset—particularly to those who don't have to train their own eyes on a micro screen. Long term reading from a screen is inefficient and uneconomical. It is a cause of aggravated eyestrain and a barrier to serious concentration over complex issues.

But when additional space is not immediately available, and books keep arriving, microforms become a necessity in many libraries. This is particularly true if the material to be read can be quickly converted to hard copies.

The fallacy arises in maintaining that as many books can be converted to microforms as are currently being issued and, therefore, libraries can be kept to a constant size, or their space even reduced.

The fact is that it is unsound to weed out the old books as fast as the courts produce new ones. Old precedents are still needed; cases are won and lost because of them. When they are buried by being placed on film, lawyers tend to avoid or reject them.

> THIRD FALLACY: We are taking in six new associates this fall. We need offices for *them*. Therefore, we can't spare any more study space in the library.

There is a direct correlation between the number of lawyers (and in some cases paralegal assistants) in an office and the need for study facilities in the library. A ratio of one seat for each five or six lawyers is an accepted standard. It is shortsighted to actually reduce the number of seats whenever the need for offices increases. Young lawyers—those whose library use is greatest—have friends in competing firms. They are the first to know when their friends have superior facilities. This is not a mere matter of "I want to be top dog." It goes to lawyer productivity, effectiveness and morale. Provide a cramped, noisy, dark library and lawyers will stay away in droves.

FOURTH FALLACY: (This weird example is the statement of a newly named partner in a fast-growing Connecticut law firm). "I don't like to work in the library because to do so might give the associates the impression there is something I don't know. Therefore, don't include any space in the library for me or the other partners."

Not even the Red Queen can top this one.

FIFTH FALLACY: We had to stop buying new books two years ago because we were out of space. Therefore we don't need any more space for the library.

This statement was reported in all seriousness by a court administrator in a fast-growing gulf county in Florida. It is the old fashioned circular argument similar to the one urged by the farmer who was training his horse to gradually reduce the intake of oats to zero. "Just when I almost had him giving up oats altogether," the farmer complained, "the ornery creature up and died."

SIXTH FALLACY: We know only too well that the book collection is increasing in size. But three factors keep us from providing more space: (1) We can't expand to adjacent space because we have more important use for that space; (2) We can't raise the shelf height from seven to eight shelves because that would interefere with the air conditioning equipment; and (3) we can't place the book stacks any closer together because the floor won't take the increased load.

This is a more chronic condition than a fallacy. The flaw is that these three reasons do not cover even half the alternatives. There may be other space for the library on a different floor. The collection may stand rigorous weeding. The cost of shifting the air conditioning equipment or of reinforcing a portion of the floor may be affordable. Corridor shelving or even ultrafiche conversion of early reporters may be acceptable. If a library really needs additional space, ways can be found to acquire it. Librarians must convince management that they have taken all other sensible steps first.

> SEVENTH FALLACY: We don't need our own library at all. We would do just as well to get together with the other firms in our building and operate a jointly owned library. We would save thousands of dollars a year by doing this.

None of the fallacies comes closer to making sense than this one. For one thing, building libraries exist in several cities and they are working almost as well as their supporters claim.

The fallacy is that the library partnership urged *in this instance* would consist of four law firms located in the same building in a thriving eastern city. Partners in each of those firms constantly oppose one another in both federal and state courts there. They appear on opposite sides in corporate takeover attempts, in estate disputes and in a host of other matters. The risk of leaving confidential papers behind in the library is reason enough to question the value of a joint library in this case. The constant demand for the same books to be used at the same time in the same matters by two or more firms is a virtual certainty. So *in this particular instance* the joint or building library might do more harm than good.

But there are other forms of cooperation that competing firms should explore. Not the least of these is the joint purchase of out-of-state codes, with no overlapping individual ownership of any but the home-state code, and the acquisition of expensive treatises that no single firm might buy on its own.

What is more, for non-conflicting firms, the joint library may be entirely feasible—no fallacy at all. These firms need simply measure the kinds and degrees of inconvenience on one side against the savings in rent, books and library management together with the possibility of more sophisticated librarian services on the other.

The answers will usually—but not invariably—still come down on the side of retaining a firm's private office library. Failure to investigate will always leave a nagging doubt, however. In addition, it is bound to hold back support for essential library expansion. Once it is determined that the joint idea will not work, it is easier to obtain whole hearted backing for the enlarged private library.

CHAPTER 39D

Library Planning and the New Technology

The following material comprises a new Chapter 39D for Legal Research and Law Library Management. *It is intended as supplemental material to the Main Text.*

The question whether the "paperless society" will overcome the traditional type of law library is highly relevant when planning to build and operate a law library. Will the little "black box" supplant the architectural behemoths now known as library reading rooms and stacks? Some would like to delay meeting the thrust of the new technology as it pertains to law libraries. Others are more adventurous, to the point of abandoning tested methods of library service and replacing them with untested substitutes based on the new technology.

In this context, it should also be noted that with the advent of the personal computer, an "electronic cottage" industry is rapidly developing. In a comparatively short period of time, many people will be accessing information in the home or office by using electronic retrieval systems transmitted directly to them by independent producers of data bases. How will libraries and library complexes fit into this information dissemination process?

Even traditionalists recognize that there is little time left to face the challenge of an increasing lack of book storage facilities in libraries. The growth of law library collections due to the publication explosion has taken on such proportions that Fremont Rider's prediction in 1944 that research libraries will double in size every sixteen years is close to becoming a reality. As a result, the miniaturization of law library collections in the form of microform and other media, has been expanding rapidly. Most law librarians would now consider microform and eventually the video disc, as an integral part of the law library collection rather than as an unusual medium to be purchased as a last resort. Not only does microform help meet the challenge of shrinking shelf space, but it also plays an important role with respect to preservation, and in the acquisition of out-of-print historical materials. There is little doubt that the developing video disc will eventually accelerate this process.

Professor Betty Taylor, Director of the University of Florida College of Law Legal Information Center, sees the future law library as a computer and audio visual resource laboratory, with a core collection of 100,000 to 150,000 volumes. Most legal research materials will be on line in a data base and accessed through terminals or through microprocessors installed either in library areas or in remote offices and homes of the law school community.[1]

Books stored in the library, according to Professor Taylor, will be those usually read cover to cover. Reporters which collect bits of information will be electronically stored and retrieved. Library users, no longer limited to "in-house" collections, will be able to access legal data bases containing reference resources from every jurisdiction in the country and even from other countries. It is possible that even the Library of Congress collection could eventually be computerized and stored in a few file cabinets.

Similarly, the traditional materials presently used as part of the teaching function and curriculum, and usually housed in law libraries, may give way to computer programs. Computer Assisted Instruction (CAI), electronic publications and communications will become commonplace. Supplements and course books will be in the form of yearly updates published in-house as printouts. Just as the faculty will stress teaching with computers, judges will write opinions so that they can be processed quickly into Westlaw and Lexis data bases and be retrieved immediately by the researcher. Even the future of the book is being questioned. A 1983 Senate Concurrent Resolution authorized the Librarian of Congress, under the auspices of the Center for the Books, to study the changing role of the book in the future.[2] In light of the impact of rapidly advancing technologies on reading and learning, the

---

[1] ABA Section on Legal Education at the McGeorge School of Law, *A Look at Legal Education in the Twenty-First Century* (April 1984).

[2] Senate Concurrent Resolution 59 (Sept. 14, 1983).

continuing utility of the book as an inexpensive accessible educational tool is becoming questionable.

On the other hand, Richard DeGennaro, Director of the New York Public Library believes that "the truth is that libraries are alive and well and adapting to a changing world . . . [Although], it is true that a variety of new and expensive commercial information services are mushrooming to serve the special needs of business and industry, . . . for most of us, libraries are, and will be for years to come, the only affordable information game in town or on the campus."[3]

Although technologists and futurists predict that books and other forms of print on paper are on their way out along with the libraries which stack and service them and that they will be replaced by electronic technology in the form of communication satellites, cable TV, inexpensive mass storage (optical and digital video discs and microcomputers on chips), still experience should teach that such change frequently takes longer, costs more, or comes in ways that are not expected and cannot be forseen. DeGennaro aptly adds that these experts who are predicting the early demise of books and libraries are of the same type as those "who in the 1960's, were predicting the end of books and libraries along with a revolution in education based on teaching machines and new media." DeGennaro concludes that "information technology being marketed by commercial vendors will not make libraries obsolete. Libraries are and will continue to be a critical link in the chain that produces, preserves and disseminates the knowledge that has created and sustains our information society. The information industry is not making libraries obsolete. Rather it is revitalizing them with new technology and services."

In planning a law library today, the prime interests of those who will be serviced by it must be anticipated, at least for the next twenty-five years. Not only is it uncertain what the developing library technology will be capable of accomplishing twenty-five years from now, but just as significantly, at this time, it is not known whether available technology is far enough advanced to lead to the conclusion that libraries will be able to avoid the growth of hard copy publications in the next twenty-five years. It would appear that the only responsible manage-

---

[3] Library Journal p.1045 (June 1, 1982).

ment decision at this time is to assume that growth in library collections will continue at or near the current growth rates.

The full effect of technology in growth of library collections will be evolutionary rather than revolutionary. Books will continue to play a major role in library research. Technology will provide enriched research capabilities, but will not supplant books sufficiently to warrant planning less physical space for their storage. In all probability, an uneasy truce will govern the relationship between technology and books; both will co-exist in support of each other. When talking glibly of the potential use of the optical disc and the developing forms of information storage, their accompanying frustrating problems such as copyright and the need for technical implementation to guarantee a consistent, uninterrupted service, capable of successfully replacing the book are often forgotten.

By the same token, however, the effect of the new technology on libraries cannot be completely ignored—even during this developing period. A decision must be made whether to abandon the traditional central reading room and to employ instead, a dispersed and intermixture of reading spaces and stacks. Then again, multi-media rooms for microform and audiovisual material are being recognized as a requirement in law library planning today. However, it is questionable whether they will be needed after the mid-1990's, which is presently considered to be the time when personal computers could be acquired by most students and adapted to legal research and study. In addition, the computer-based legal data retrieval of LEXIS and WESTLAW will require specific physical provisions to house computer terminals. Consideration should also be given for space for an in-house computer as well as space for personal computers.

The effect of new library technology on library planning usually starts with automation of library housekeeping services, such as circulation and cataloging. It then continues with other related library functions, such as reserve, acquisition and serials, which eventually link up to a utility like RLIN or OCLC. Thereafter the public is introduced to these services by allowing independent access to terminals providing cataloging and circulation information by on-line catalog systems.

Although it cannot be anticipated exactly how technology will affect library service in the future, libraries can still be designed and equiped today to accommodate such changes by providing for additional computer assisted legal research facilities, conduits for personal computers and other automation, and sufficient space per reader to allow each one to use personal computers in carrels or elsewhere in the library.

It is questionable whether automation of library functions will reduce the size of the library staff. Certainly, it will not in the near future. As is characteristic of such library automation, service for acquisitions, serials, accounting, cataloging and circulation will become more accurate, comprehensive and responsive, but rarely is this accompanied by a reduction in personnel. Hence the anticipated growth of the library staff size should be foreseen when planning library space needs. Actually, additional staff may be required to effectuate electronic data base searching, computer assistance instruction and audio-visual services.

CHAPTER 40

Moving the Library: An Updated Blueprint

The following comprises amended material for Chapter 40 of Legal Research and Law Library Management. *It is intended as replacement material to the Main Text. Substitute the following for Chapter 40 of the Main Text, appearing on pages 381 through 385.*

Moving a law library is a mixed work of art and science. The cost varies in inverse proportion to the care and the skills applied. One computer terminal or file cabinet, unlike a book, is much like any other for moving purposes.

But law books are not fungible. They are not so many lumps of coal. Each is different. Those that form series occupy the most space and demand particular attention. Some series, such as the 300 volumes of the first edition of the *Federal Reporter*, are complete and static. This set will forever occupy the same finite amount of shelf space in the new location as it does in its current one, unless it is condensed in a thin paper edition, substituted with microfiche, or eliminated altogether.

Other sets, for example the *Federal Reporter 2d Series*, are "living" and grow like glaciers at *varying*, usually *accelerating* and *predictable* rates of speed. The success of a library move may hang on the accuracy of one's space predictions. Allow too little space and your library may have to be expanded or remodeled within months of the move. Allow too much space and it may resemble an empty warehouse.

The art consists of the total plan: (1) compiling a library inventory; (2) weeding and strengthening the collection; (3) drafting a logical scheme for its arrangement; (4) packing, tagging and moving what remains of it; and (5) unpacking and reshelving the collection. The science lies in the accurate prediction of the collection's rate of growth and in the sensible spacing of its constituent sets.

[1]—Library Inventory

The first step is to compile an inventory of everything that is to be moved: the furniture, equipment (typewriters, copiers, computer terminals, microform-reader-printers and the like), even book shelving, if any of it is to be salvaged, and, of course, the book collection.

The second step is to meet with the moving company personnel and determine who will do what: their personnel, your librarian and staff. The movers should designate a foreman or contact person who should work out all details of the move with the librarian or anyone the firm designates. Both must remain at work throughout the weekend of the move.

[2]—Weeding the Collection

Travel light, but take everything you need! Eliminate first all superseded publications—outdated treatises, replaced digest and encyclopedia volumes. Consider eliminating early reporters, for example the New York side reports or other Pre-regional reporters. Consider exchanging any of the thick older editions of court reports for their thin paper editions or of converting some of them to microforms. Compare the cost of these steps with those of installing track shelving (often requiring floor reinforcement) or of simply paying rent for the editions you decide to keep. Remember always the cost in lawyer time of traveling elsewhere to look at reporters the firm used to keep on its own shelves.

[3]—Strengthening the Collection

Moving to new quarters is an excellent time to evaluate your library resources. Do they represent the firm's current and anticipated practice? This is one step where a consultants advice will reap immediate benefits. Consult also among the younger associates as to how they handle their research assignments. Determine what exists in the fields in which the firm excels or would like to excel and purchase the most useful among the publishers' "wares."

[4]—Scheme of Arrangement

"There is no logic to our library. *Federal Supplement* volumes are split and continued in three different locations. The place is a shambles.

Again, an office move gives a firm the chance to place like things together and regain control over an expanding body of resources that seems to be controlling it. Our preference in a good general collection is a three-way combination of arrangements: (1) by jurisdiction, for the main federal, state and regional publications; (2) by subject, for the treatises, e.g., corporations, commercial law, products liability, environment; and (3) by form, that is the law reviews, looseleaf services, government documents.

Whatever plan of arrangement is agreed to, it should be set out on a floor plan of the new library which should show the location of every major set in the collection. If your planning is accurate, the precise location of each book can be fixed weeks in advance of the move and the diagram circulated to all lawyers the day they move in.

[5]—Projection of Growth

A law book collection may double in size in from ten to fourteen years. One starts with known facts: the shelf space in linear feet of the existing collection, minus space occupied by weeded materials, plus that needed for converted or compressed works and proposed new acquisitions.

The constituent sets of a law collection grow at varying rates. The *Federal Reporter 2d series* which used to add one 1,000-page volume a month now increases by thirty 1,500-page books each year. Its *acceleration* rate can be determined by measuring growth at five-year intervals for the past ten to twenty years. In order to eliminate frequent shifting of books, space should be left clear between sets for a growth period of five or ten years—whichever the firm finds economic to adopt. It will take a librarian one or two months to plot the growth of all "living" sets in the library—particularly since all other services must be maintained while the move is being planned. This is the best way of ensuring a workable plan of arrangement in the new quarters.

[6]—Packing, Tagging and Moving

A first step is to number each section of shelving in the new location and to complete the plan of arrangement for the collection. With that done, packing can begin. It is best to pack no more than one shelf of books in a carton and to tag it with the contents and its destination, e.g., "NYS 2d Vols 1-18—Destination: Sect.21."

Some moving companies use temporary shelving units mounted on wheels, which match in number of shelves and width the equivalent sections of shelving in the new library. These units take a minimum time to pack and unpack and avoid the confusion attendant on misplaced or faultily labeled cartons.

Whether cartons or mobile shelving units are used, the fixed plan of arrangement permits any number of helpers to pitch in and both pack and unpack books in various corners of the library at the same time—without interfering with one another.

[7]—Reshelving the Collection

As cartons or shelving units arrive at the new library, they should be brought to the appropriate shelving sections and unpacked.

Books should be reshelved, preferably by library personnel, or at least under their constant supervision. The worst scourge is the missing book. Imagine reshelving some 400 volumes of *New York Supplement 2d* and *then* discovering that Volume 51 is missing! The entire run from Volume 52 to 400 must be moved a second time. Good practice dictates that a mover's representative and a library assistant each "read" the shelves as fast as books are placed on them to make sure that space has been left for any missing book before they go on to any succeeding section of shelving.

All shelvers should be cautioned not to pack the books too closely, but to leave at least one or two inches of open space on each shelf. Books tend to absorb moisture and in a year or two will expand to fill the shelf. If no space is left, they become jammed tight and attempts to remove one will result in torn bindings.

[8]—Conclusion

One satisfaction in doing a planned, as opposed to a haphazard move, is that the entire library can remain in use until a few days or a week before the move—preferably over the weekend—and then, on the following Monday, all the sets will be in their new places evenly lined up along the forward edges of their shelves. Few adjustments need be made and lawyers can immediately resume the work they had started the previous Friday.

Finally, the cost of a planned move is invariably less than a haphazard one. It take the movers fewer hours—there is less overtime and double time work required—and it takes firm personnel a shorter time to resume routine operations.

CHAPTER 41

Library Scourges—Fire, Water, Smoke

The following comprises additional material for Chapter 41 of the Main Text.

"You can hide the fire, but what are ya gonna do about the smoke."
—Joel Chandler Harris

It is not easy to consume lawyers or librarians in flames. They are hardy and wary. But smoke and water will do in the books every time and panic may cripple the people. The 1984 fire at 666 Fifth Avenue in New York was the latest in a frightening series of high rise office building conflagrations.[1]

Claudette Hunt, who was at work on the 32nd floor in the law offices of Rosen & Reader—29 floors above the source of the fire—reported, "The smoke just hit me right in the face. . . . No alarms went off."[2]

"No one knew anything and no one knew what to do," complained Susan Friedman, an employee in an accounting firm on the 34th floor.[3] She added, "There was chaos when the halls and stairwells filled with smoke. There were no fire marshals. We had wet paper towels on our faces."[4]

A spokesman for the Tishman East Management Corporation, the managers of the building, asserted, "All alarms did go off and the stair-

---

[1] See Chapter 41 in the main text for an account of the fire at 299 Park Avenue in New York that occurred during the summer of 1980. The high rise office building hazards being faced in New York are beginning to alert tenants in similar buildings throughout the country.

[2] Daily News, Feb. 10, 1984, p. 7.

[3] *Id.*

[4] New York Post, Feb. 10, 1984, p. 4.

cases were well-lit. We have the most up-to-date alarm safety system in the city."[5] Curiously, that is the substance of the management statement that was circulated after the *first* fire at 299 Park Avenue.[6] A second fire there merited little press comment.

How Adequate is the Law?

A review of the lingering effects of office fires on law libraries may alert owners, tenants and local lawmakers to precautions that should have been taken but were not taken. Is the problem with the law? Or its enforcement? Or both? The stench of smoke no longer permeates the library books at Baer, Marks & Upham. It is several years since the second and little publicized *second* fire at 299 Park Avenue. Books and documents left on window sills to become waterlogged have long since dried out. But the mop-up and preservation work took many weeks. Moveover, fire insurance has proved to be no substitute for unimpeded work and clean documents. Time cannot repair smoke-scarred lungs.

New York's Local Law 5 (1973), as amended, is the basis for current fire regulation of office buildings in the city.[7] It is regarded as a model prototype for the country. There is an additional overlay of regulation elsewhere in the Fire Department rules and in the regulations of other city departments. But most fire safety matters are covered in just six paragraphs of the regulations entitled, "Fire safety in office buildings—a Fire Safety Plan" and in four further provisions that specify forms of safety signs.[8] There is little problem with the signs. There is every problem with the "Fire Safety Plan."

Every owner and occupant of a New York City office building and every employee who works in a high-rise building should know its six provisions. Moreover, each affected person should be able to answer, "Yes", to the question, "Are those provisions enforced in the building where I work?"

---

[5] *Id.*

[6] *The New York Times*, June 25, 1980, a statement attributed to Charles G. Moerdler, former New York City Buildings Commissioner and then, as now, counsel to the building owners. "The building was in complete compliance with the law."

[7] Codified in the Administrative Code of the City of New York, Sec. C-19-161.2.

[8] *Id.*, Subparagraphs "b" through "e".

It is required that each building subject to this Local Law adopt a *Plan for fire drill and evacuation procedures* approved by the department and distributed, in salient measure, to all employees.[9] Has that been done in your building? Can you put your hands on the plan this morning?

Safety and Evacuation Supervisors. A fire safety director and deputy directors (who are building employees) must earn a Fire Department "certificate of fitness" qualifying each to "conduct fire drills, evacuations and such related activities as organizing, training and supervising a fire brigade."[10] Do you know who those people are in your own building? Are their names and telephone numbers affixed to your phone?

Those safety employees are required to be on the premises during normal business hours.[11] "At all other times when there are occupants in the building, there shall be at least one employee on duty designated as building evacuation supervisor. He shall be capable of directing the evacuation of the occupants as provided for in the fire safety plan. . . ."[12]

Are the safety employees on duty this morning? Do you know who was on duty last Saturday? Are you confident that he knows what to do? Parents tend to take their infant children to the office on Saturdays and let them wander at will while parents work. That is why weekend safety coverage is specially important.

Fire Brigade. "A fire brigade consisting of qualified building service employees shall be selected, organized, trained and supervised by the fire safety director."[13] Do you know these people? Are you confident that they can protect you in case of fire?

Fire Drills. This provision requires the holding of semi-annual fire drills in all buildings subject to the law, except that in new buildings they must be held every three months during the first two years after the issuance of a certificate of occupancy.

However, this provision is virtually emasculated by the proviso that "The occupants of the building other than building service employees,

---

[9] *Id.*, Subparagraph "a-1".
[10] *Id.* Subparagraph, "a-2(a)".
[11] *Id.*, Subparagraph, "a-2(b)".
[12] *Id.*, Subparagraph, "a-2(c)".
[13] *Id.*, Subparagraph, "a-3".

shall not be required to leave the floor or use the exits during the drill."[14]

This is similar to the requirement at the University of Pennsylvania Law School library where students are merely asked to gaze at a fire exit when the alarm sounds and then resume studying. It defeats the purpose of the drill.

The Catch-All Loophole. ". . . where compliance would cause practical difficulty or undue hardship, *the Commissioner may waive or modify the requirements of this subdivision* and accept alternatives fulfilling the intent of these requirements consistent with public safety."[15]

Every tenant wants to use office premises to the full and variances in building codes are routinely granted. But in matters of safety it is foolhardy to downgrade these modest requirements. Do you know whether or not they have been waived for your building and in what respect?

Tenant Fire Wardens. An addition to the regulations in 1978 which gave building owners the power to require tenants on each floor to designate their own employees as fire wardens or deputy fire wardens.[16] The constitutionality of this provision has been upheld.[17]

Has this been done in your building? If so, who are your wardens?

Proposed Remedies

Since the New York law is regarded as a prototype of a fire protection law for the country, it is well to strengthen its provisions so as to better protect people and books from the hazards of fire. This writer makes three fairly modest proposals.

Fire Drills. In most offices fire drills are a joke. The law should be amended to require the holding of *actual* and not *mock* drills. The catchall loophole (Subparagraph 5) should be repealed.

Smoke and Fire Alarms. It is no longer necessary to carry canaries in cages to the offices—as coal miners used to do to alert themselves to coal fumes and to deadly carbon monoxide gas. The most effective smoke detection equipment should be installed in every office. Fire alarms should be *numerous enough and loud enough to do the job*. Recent experience suggests that they are neither.

---

[14] *Id.*, Subparagraph, "a-4".
[15] *Id.*, Subparagraph, "a-5".
[16] *Id.*, Subparagraph "a-6".
[17] McCallin v. Walsh, 64 A.D.2d 46, 407 N.Y.S. 2d 882 (1978).

Fresh Air Access. It may seem revolutionary to ask for real windows and window sashes. Yet ever since the advent of glass-sealed buildings after World War II, the incidence of smoke poisoning and smoke damage has risen.

Everyone wants access to fresh air. On Friday afternoons in summer, lawyers and their employees race to the shore. In winter, they are laden with skis and skates.

Engineers and architects should begin studies to determine how to bring fresh air back into the city's buildings—not only in emergencies, but all the time. They can find a way to avoid scenes of choking and asphyxiation that have become all too common in glass-sealed office buildings.

The alternative is to prohibit sealed windows altogether and return to the practical casement or sash windows.[18] If a simple air vent panel alongside existing windows would solve the problem, then its installation should be required. If a series of air ducts would accomplish the same end, they should be installed.

Unusual risks may require unusual remedies. The builders of a new Madison Avenue building in New York solved a similar problem when the owners of Reidy's Restaurant that occupied part of the proposed building site, refused to sell their lot. The builders agreed to install flues that run some 40 floors above the restaurant kitchen on the street level to the roof. This compromise permitted them to build both around and above the restaurant and allowed the kitchen fumes to escape into the sky.

Equally imaginative means must be found to bring fresh air back into offices and office libraries.

---

[18] Until 1956, a window had to open and close in order to fit the first *Webster* definition: "An opening in the wall of a building for the admission of light or air, usually closed by casements or sashes, containing transparent material as glass, and capable of being opened and shut." *Webster's New International Dictionary*, 2d Ed. 1956.

Ten years later, *Webster* "sealed" its windows with the times and modified its definition to include the words: "*Often* to admit air"—"An opening in a wall of a building or a side of a vehicle to admit light usu. through a transparent or translucent material (as glass) usu. to permit vision through the wall or side, and often to admit air." *Id.*, 3d ed. 1966.

Given the inventive genius of building engineers and a little push by the public, Webster's 4th edition may be able to re-use the old plates and tenants may once again be able to touch snowflakes or feel raindrops outside their own "openable" windows.

CHAPTER 41A

Fire in the Library

The following material comprises a new Chapter 41A for Legal Research and Law Library Management. *It is intended as supplemental material to the Main Text.*

Self protection against injury to law firm personnel and its book collection caused by fire is essential in every law office. A practical protection program falls into four phases:

(1) Fire avoidance steps;
(2) Pre-fire inventory recording;
(3) Concurrent and immediate library evaluation; and
(4) Fire insurance review

[1]—Fire Avoidance Steps

Drafting a checklist of "Do's" and "Don'ts" is the first step and its implementation the second step in any fire avoidance program.

Things To Do (A bare suggested list);

(1) Designate the librarian or a staff member as your library fire warden;
(2) List danger points to inspect daily or weekly, e.g., waste baskets, ashtrays, electric appliances (frayed wires), ventilations ducts; sandwich wrappings and any other flammable material;
(3) Maintain a newspaper clipping book of office fire news stories, covering at least the past five years. Keep that book on the library counter or in a browsing area;
(4) Ensure that *everyone* in the office participates in monthly or bimonthly fire drills.

Things to Discourage or Prohibit:

(1) Don't permit electric coffee warmers or cooking plates in the library;
(2) Discourage smoking in the library;
(3) Don't allow trash baskets to remain unemptied *any* evening, and particularly on the eve of holidays or weekends;
(4) Don't let cartons or equipment block any aisles or exits;
(5) Don't store books or papers on library window sills or office sills, where water seepage can cause irreparable damage. This has occurred in almost every office building fire; and
(6) Don't lock the library doors at any time.

[2]—Pre-Fire Inventory Recording

There is no substitute to satisfy insurance adjusters that can match a well-documented inventory. Furniture and equipment inventory records should be maintained in duplicate notebooks, one kept by the librarian and the other stored off the premises in a fireproof vault. The library copy should be regularly updated, the duplicate two or three times a year. The book collection records should be kept in as compact a form as possible.

[a]—Furniture. A list of library furniture will ordinarily fill no more than a single sheet of paper: Tables, chairs, movable carrels, fixed position carrels, built-in counters, newspaper racks, card catalog cabinets, file cabinets, "kik-stools," carpets and curtains or other window blinds. Accompanying the list should be counterpart invoices and on-site snapshots appropriately labelled and dated.

[b]—Equipment. An equipment list can also be compressed onto a single page or two in most instances: Computer terminals and printers, microform readers and printers, lighting fixtures, including lamps, pencil sharpeners, bindery machinery, paper cutters, drills and the like. Again, copies of invoices and snapshots are useful as evidence of cost and ownership.

[c]—The Book Collection. A shelf list, that is, a list of publications in the order in which they are kept on the shelves, is the most compact form of inventory. Some librarians make microform records of their shelflist and keep the microform copy in a fireproof location outside the library.

In addition, a duplicate checklist of all major or multi-volume sets should be compiled. This need cover no more than twnety or thirty pages and is easily stored in a safe place. In many libraries, copies are furnished as a matter of course to all lawyers in the office—frequently accompanied by a library diagram.

If compilations of transaction papers or "deals" or collections of records and briefs in particular cases are kept in the library, they should be separately listed in duplicate—and, as before, regularly updated.

Strongly recommended are photographs of aisles of library books, both close up and at a distance, that may later be contrasted with pictures of the same books immediately after a fire.

[3]—Concurrent Library Valuation

The invoice totals for furniture and equipment referred to above will furnish the basis for valuation of everything in the library except the book collection.

The book collection valuation is a more complex process. Begin with the checklist of major or multi-volume sets and divide it into two parts: Those still current and in print; and those completed or out of print. *Moore's Federal Practice* would be in the first group, *Abbott's Digest* (the first three series) would be in the second group. Publishers' catalogs provide list prices for books in print (West salesmen will supply the prices not disclosed in their catalogs). Book dealers' price lists and occasional advertisements in the classified columns of the *New York Law Journal* and other legal newspapers furnish prices for many of the out-of-print sets. Repeated reference to these sources will complete the pricing for the major sets. Copies of the publishers' catalogs, book dealers lists and dated newspaper advertisements should be saved as evidence of pricing data.

A valuation of individual monographs is also necessary to get a complete record of costs for the published book collection. In view of the enormity of the task of pricing each of a thousand or more titles, it seems reasonable to strike an average cost. This can be based on a survey of twenty or thirty titles in half a dozen different publishers' catalogs. It will probably turn out that monographs cost somewhere between $35 and $65 a volume. Whatever the average in a particular library, it need only be multiplied by the number of volumes not otherwised priced.

The unpublished lawyers' work products pose a different problem. There is no "market" for these papers. Yet they represent—next to unbilled time and law firm good will—some of the most valuable assets in the office. At a minimum, the number of hours it took to compile the collections of records and briefs, and the collections of transactions, as well as the time spent in indexing or cataloging them, should be recorded. That number of hours times the rate paid to the person doing this work should be added to the cost of binding these volumes. In addition, any lawyer time not paid for by client fees—for example, *pro bono* work—should be added to the value of those compilations.

The total value of a law office library then is the sum of the value of its furniture, equipment, published book collection and unpublished lawyers' work products—with one important addition. That is, the cost of book aquisition, processing, preparation for binding and cataloging.

It is well to know how much it costs to process a book from the moment it is ordered, until it is stamped, book cards and pockets are typed and pasted into it, the book is cataloged, the spine marked and the book placed on a shelf. Estimates from $12 to $16 per title are not far off. One simple calculation method is to determine the number of volumes processed in any year, and the salary for the number of hours spent on this work in the same year.

For example, if a cataloger and a student clerk together earned an average of $7.50 an hour and together devoted 2,000 hours a year, the total is $15,000. If they processed just 1,000 volumes in that year, then the cost is $15 a volume for processing. This, of course, is in addition to the price of the book.

Insurance companies are more likely to accept a valuation reached by an independent expert over one made by a firm employee.

[4]—Fire Insurance Review

Determining whether the library is underinsured is a matter of fairly simple arithmetic. Most law offices fail to insure their libraries to their true value. The advantage accrues only in the event of disaster of course.

My recommendation is to take steps (1) Fire Avoidance, (2) Inventory Recording and (3) Library Valuation in any event first. Step one may help to avoid fire altogether. Steps two and three have inherent uses in the routine running of an office. They also provide the knowledge—the power—to determine when and whether to upgrade one's library insurance coverage.

CHAPTER 43

The Non-book and the Law

The following material comprises an addition to Chapter 43 of Legal Research and Law Library Management. *It is intended to be read in conjunction with the material in the Main Text.*

"At $40 a square foot rental for my office," a lawyer said, "I am having serious reservations about expanding the size of my library. Can these new microform publications help in any way?"

Yes—they can!—for not only does microform allow for the preservation of deteriorating books and periodicals slowly turning to dust on library shelves, it also reduces space used in practitioners' office libraries for the storage of books. In this context, it should also be noted that the dependence on microform will not affect the research methodology used by lawyers today. The lawyer referring to a case in the National Reporter system, for example, reads it quickly to determine whether it is relevant to the research involved, and if so, invariably makes a photocopy of the case for prolonged analysis, along with other photocopied cases and excerpts from statutes, etc., to be quoted or otherwise used in a brief or memorandum of law. A similar facsimile reproduction can be made of the same case, published on ultrafiche by the West Publishing Company. Whether the bound volume or the microform edition is used—the end product is the same—a photocopy or facsimile reproduction of a page.

That microform is generally becoming more acceptable to legal researchers is borne out by the increasing number of law libraries purchasing microform publications today. A recent report of the American Bar Association, dated June 15, 1982, reveals that a predominant number of law school libraries contain more than 50,000 volume equivalent of microforms in their collection. Columbia University Law Library, for example, contains 58,774,

New York University, 61,759, Texas, 55,736, Virginia, 130,587, University of Florida, 107,569, Georgetown, 104,191 and Tulane, 85,613. It is interesting to note in this context, that many law libraries which started later in time to develop their law collection, have a greater proportion of microforms to hard copies of books than the more established libraries. Using microforms is the most economic and expeditious way to acquire legal materials not generally available otherwise, such as out-of-print books, and records or briefs of the Supreme Court of the U.S., the U.S. Circuit Courts and appellate state courts. Microform is also used by those libraries to reduce space required on their stack shelves, as a substitute for hard copy sets of legal source materials infrequently used, such as early state court reports, session laws, attorney general opinions, bar association materials, state administrative documents, as well as complete collections of huge retrospective sets, such as legal newspapers.

Of the more recently developed law libraries, Florida State, for example, with a collection of 207,751, contains 120,191 hard copy volumes and 87,560 volume equivalents of microform. New York Law School with 206,736 volumes has 134,901 volumes and 71,835 in microform, Cleveland State with 195,795, has 118,955 volumes and 76,800 in microform; Oral Roberts with 172,395 volumes, has 110,883 in hard copy and 61,512 in microform; Pepperdine with 150,057 volumes has 75,337 in hard copy and 74,720 in microform; and Hawaii with 121,728 volumes has 55,895 in hard copy and 65,833 in microform.

In 1978, the Law Library of the Library of Congress reported that in 1970, no microform materials were maintained by the Law Library. In 1978, the legal microform collection consisted of 8,600 reels of microfilm, more than 150,000 microfiche cards and 2,400 ultrafiche cards. It then noted that the growth of legal microforms has been so rapid that accurate projections of the size of the collection are not possible.

A few remaining sceptics suggest that these huge microform sales are more a tribute to the salesmanship of the vendors than the wisdom of the librarians.

Microform is a term used for any information communication too small to be read without magnification. In physical appearance they are divided into two groups, roll and flat. Flat microform includes microfiche, ultrafiche and micro-opaques. Roll microform consists of varying lengths of microfilm wound on a reel. They are read on screens of microform readers, which project the micro-image on the screen enlarged to facsimile size. They can then be printed from the screen by reader/printers.

Microfiche is a 4″ × 6″ sheet of film containing micro-images in patterns of rows and columns. There can be sixty, ninety, or ninety-eight images on one fiche card.

Ultrafiche means "ultra high reduction microfiche." One 4″ × 6″ ultrafiche card can contain up to 3000 images. The West Publishing Co. publishes an entire volume of the National Reporter System, up to 1,450 pages on a single 4″×6″ ultrafiche card.

Micro-opaques are rarely used today. They were the earliest format published and are called microcards and microprint.

Microfilm comes in two sizes—16 mm and 35 mm.

Law books generally occupy about ten per square foot. This figure includes aisle space and 7′ 6″ high stacks with seven shelves, one foot apart in height. Thus, a lawyer can easily estimate how much in rental space, a law library can cost when physically stored in law office quarters. If the lawyer is renting the office space at $50 a square foot, 1000 books, occupying 100 square feet will cost in rental alone, $5,000 annually, or $5 annually for each book shelved in the office, whether used or not.

If you maintain any of the regional reporters of the National Reporter system, consider the following: The West Publishing Company is gradually publishing an ultrafiche edition of the National Reporter system to replace the hard copy edition of the first series. Incidentally, many volumes of the first series of the regional reporters of the National Reporter series are now out-of-print, and the West Company is not reprinting them. Eventually, ultrafiche will be the only source for those volumes.

The West Publishing Company has estimated that the shelf space for units of the *National Reporter System.* The estimated annual bound volume increase will affect the need for additional physical office library growth.

The *National Reporter System, First Edition,* consisting of the *Atlantic Reporter* (200 bound volumes), the *New York Supplement* (300 volumes), *North Eastern Reporter* (200 volumes), *North Western Reporter,* (300 volumes), *Pacific Reporter* (300 volumes), *South Eastern Reporter* (200 volumes), *Southern Reporter* (200 volumes), *South Western Reporter* (300 volumes) and *Federal Reporter* (300 volumes) comprises 2300 volumes (nearly 2,500,000 pages) and contain State and Federal Appellate Court cases from the 1870's to the 1940's.

The West ultrafiche edition of these volumes reproduces each of these volumes on a single ultrafiche—clearly labeled by series title and volume number. The pages are arranged in rows of fifty each, making it comparatively easy to locate the exact page. The First Series occupies more than 300 feet of shelving. The ultrafiche edition, housed in plastic cases, occupies less than six feet.

In a similar manner, the West Company is gradually offering an ultrafiche edition of the *Second Series* of the *National Reporter System*. Thus of the 557 volumes published in *Atlantic Reporter 2d*, which presently occupies 110 linear shelf feet, the first 150 volumes are now on ultrafiche, which leaves a remainder of 450 volumes occupying eighty-two linear shelf feet. (The estimated annual bound volume increase is two feet, six inches.)

New York Supplement 2d now has 533 volumes occupying 106 linear feet of shelves. By the end of 1983, the ultrafiche edition of volumes 1-150 became available. That could free an additional twenty-three feet of shelf-space. (The estimated bound volume increase is one foot, nine inches.)

The *North Eastern Reporter 2d* has 537 volumes occupying 106 feet of shelf space. By the end of 1983, the first 150 volumes were available on ultrafiche to make possible an additional twenty-three feet of shelf-space savings. (Estimated annual bound volume increase is two feet eight inches.)

The *North Western Reporter 2d* has 439 bound volumes occupying eighty-seven linear feet. The first 150 volumes are now available on ultrafiche, requiring fifty-nine feet to accommodate the remaining 289 volumes. (Estimated annual bound volume increase is one foot, nine inches.)

The *Pacific Reporter 2d* has 640 bound volumes occupying 120 linear feet by the end of 1983. The first 150 volumes are available on ultrafiche, making possible an additional twenty-three feet of shelf space savings. (Estimated annual bound volume increase is three feet, two inches.)

The *South Eastern Reporter 2d* has 376 volumes occupying seventy-five feet of shelving. The first 150 volumes are now available on ultrafiche, leaving 226 volumes occupying forty-five linear feet. (Estimated annual bound volume increase is one foot eight inches.)

The *Southern Reporter 2d* has 541 volumes occupying 108 linear feet. By the end of 1983, the first 150 volumes were available on ultrafiche, making possible an additional twenty-three feet of shelf space. (Estimated annual bound volume increase is two feet, six inches.)

The *South Western Reporter 2d* now has 769 bound volumes occupying 154 linear feet. The first 150 volumes are now available on ultrafiche, leaving a remainder of 619 volumes occupying 124 feet. (Estimated annual bound volume increase is two feet, ten inches.)

The *Federal Reporter 2d* now has 874 volumes occupying 174 feet. The first 450 volumes are now available on ultrafiche leaving a remainder of 424 volumes occupying eighty-five linear feet. (The estimated annual bound volume increase is four feet, two inches.)

The *Federal Supplement* now has 711 bound volumes occupying 142 linear feet. The first 350 volumes are now available on ultrafiche leaving a remainder of 361 volumes occupying seventy-two linear feet. (The estimated annual bound volume increase is three feet, ten inches.)

The *Federal Rules Decisions* now has 124 bound volumes occupying 25 linear feet. (Estimated annual bound volume increase is seven inches.)

The *Supreme Court Reporter* now has 140 bound volumes occupying twenty-eight linear feet. (Estimated annual bound volume increase is nine inches.)

The *West's California Reporter* now has 252 bound volumes, occupying fifty linear feet. (Estimated annual bound volume increase is one foot, one inch.)

The ultrafiche edition of the *National Reporter* System, alone—can save considerably in rental space.

There are many other sources of the law and legal research materials lawyers can acquire in microform, with considerable savings in space.

Commerce Clearing House publishes an *Ultrafiche Tax Library,* using the same ultrafiche medium introduced by the West Publishing Company. It provides the subscriber the U.S. tax Cases (1913-date), the Tax Court Memorandum Decisions (1943-

date), the Tax Court reports (1943-date), the Cumulative Bulletins (1919-date) and the Board of Tax Appeals Reports (1924-1942 complete). These bound sets also occupy a considerable number of linear feet when shelved, and the ultrafiche edition obviously is also a space saver.

The lawyer maintaining law review subscriptions can now purchase many of the leading American law reviews in microfilm or microfiche from Fred B. Rothman and the William B. Hein Company. For example, Harvard Law Review, Yale Law Journal, New York University Law Review, Columbia Law Review and Cornell Law Review, to name a few, run into long volume runs, and can be converted into microform with considerable space savings.

Many federal and state government publications of significant value in legal research are also available in microform. Oceana/Transmedia offers in microfilm the *Code of Federal Regulations* (1939 to the present). University Microfilms International and Congressional Information Service sell the *Federal Register* in microfiche, from 1936 to the present. University Microfilms International also provides in microfiche the *Statutes at Large* of the United States from 1789 to the present. Prior to Volume 18 (1873-75), the *Statutes at Large* were published by private publishers with official authority. From Volume 18 on—they were published by the Government. After Volume 64, Part 3 (1949), Treaties and other international agreements were dropped from the *Statutes at Large* and independently published in a new series entitled *U.S. Treaties and Other International Acts Series*. All these are also available on microform from University Microfilms International and Congressional Information Series. Incidentally, for those interested in international treaties, the Oceana/Transmedial Co. publishes in microfilm the *United Nations Treaty Series*.

The University Microfilms International and Congressional Information Service also provide in microfilm and microfiche the debates of Congress from 1789 to the present. These have been issued in four series:

Annals of Congress (1789-1824)
Register of Debates (1824-1837)

Congressional Globe (1837-1873)
Congressional Record (1873-date)

All the known session laws of the American states and former territories are also available on microfiche from Congressional Information Series and William B. Hein Company.

Legislative histories of all important federal legislation are also available by subject on microfiche from University Microfilms International and Congressional Information Service and Commerce Clearing House.

Similarly, University Microfilms International and Congressional Information Series provide Congressional Committee hearings, prints and reports, retrospectively and currently, as well as the decisions, findings, orders and reports of the U.S. regulatory agencies, such as the Civil Aeronautics Board, the Atomic Energy Commission and the Federal Trade Commission. They also provide in microfilm and microfiche the U.S. Patent Office Decisions of the Commissioner of Patents and of the U.S. Courts in Patent and Trademark cases, as well as its Official Gazette for Patents and Trademarks, similarly SEC Releases on microfiche.

University Microfilms International sells in 35 mm microfilm the *United States Supreme Court Reports* from Volume 1 to 458 and on microfiche from Volume 423 to 458 (1981) + .

For those lawyers who need access to the various official editions of the United States Code from the 1925-26 editions to the 1976 editions—these too are available on microform.

Also available on microform are the *New York Legislative Documents* from 1919 to the present. They include Attorney General Reports, Banking Department Reports, Commission studies, Governors' messages, Judicial Council Reports, Law Review Commission, Legislative Committee Reports, among others. These are available from William B. Hein & Co.—as are also the *New York State Court of Appeals Records and Briefs.*

Oceana/Transmedia retrospectively has made available on microfilm all the State Reports, prior to the *National Reporter System,* as well as post *National Reporter* state reports and the *Federal Cases* (1789-1879). It also offers on microfilm the *Trinity Series,* consisting of the *American Decisions* (1760-1869), *Ameri-*

can Reports (1870-1887), and *American State Reports* (1887-1911). For the annotated court reports there is also available on microfilm from Oceana/Transmedia the *American* and *English Annotated Cases* (1901-1918) and the *Lawyers Reports Annotated* (1888-1918). Oceana/Transmedia also has published on microfilm the *Presidential Executive Orders* (1845-1936) of the *Presidential Proclamations* 1789-1936, Attorneys General Reports and Opinions of all States and Bar Association Proceedings.

The Annual *Guide to Microforms in Print* (in two parts, author/title and subject) lists all microforms currently in print, their publishers and prices. For information on microform hardware, see the annual *Buyers' Guide to Micrographic Equipment, Products and Services.*

CHAPTER 44

The Emerging Form of Microfilm in Law Libraries

The following material comprises an addition to Chapter 44 of Legal Research and Law Library Management. *It is intended to be read in conjunction with the material in the Main Text.*

Computers are now being used to retrieve copies of selected documents from rolls of microfilm which can then be displayed on a Cathode Ray Tube (CRT) Terminal screen. Known as computer-assisted retrieval or CAR, this system of micrographics allows documents stored on microfilm to be electronically fed into a computer's databank, along with a related index of key words or codes. By typing key words into a video display terminal, the computer allows the researcher to find the document sought in the exact microfilm cartridge where it was originally microfilmed. The microfilm cartridge thus located can be placed into the micro-image terminal which, by means of a microprocessor, can display the specific document or documents on the screen in a period of seconds. This displayed document can then be made into a facsimile reproduction on paper.

As microfilm cartridges usually can obtain up to 6000 frames or images in 100 feet of film, the possibilities of this system can be highly significant in legal research. Now, documents can be stored in random sequence, rather than in logical order, by date or alphabetically, in as much as the computer seeks the document by code. This obviously facilitates the process of microfilming the original documents and cuts down on the costs involved in processing.

The Eastman Kodak Co., the Bell and Howell Co. and the Minnesota Mining and Manufacturing Co. are the largest producers of CAR's. Each has its own system, however, although based on the same concept.

CHAPTER 44A

Microforms and CD Roms in Law Libraries

The following material comprises a new Chapter 44A for Legal Research and Law Library Management. *It is intended as supplemental material to the Main Text.*

The role of microform in law libraries is grossly exaggerated. Despite the evolving technology that appears to be capable of displacing microform for storage and retrieval of legal documentation and information such as CD-ROM, CD-I and on-line electronic data bases, the 1985-1986 Law School Library Statistics Report, prepared by the Office of Statistics, American Association for Law Libraries (AALL), in cooperation with the Consultant on Legal Education to the American Bar Association (ABA), reflects a surprising dependency of Law School libraries on microform to meet American Bar Association library standards. The use of microform in law libraries is actually increasing, and reports of its demise are certainly not borne out by the statistics.

The term microform is descriptive of any form of printing either on film or paper which contains micro-images. Some micro-materials are on a 35-mm roll film, some on 16-mm roll film, some on 24 × fiche, some on 42 × or 48 × COM fiche, and some on 75 ultrafiche. Microfilm in 35-mm is a popular form, recommended by experts in the field for storage of large numbers of pages which run continuously in sequence and are updated infrequently, such as court reports, session laws and serials.

Microfiche is a sheet of microfilm in the form of a card 3″ × 5″ or 4″ × 6″ containing multiple micro-images in a grid pattern. It usually contains identification information of the micro-images on the fiche which can be read by the naked eye. Depending on the reduction, microfiche contains from 64 to 96 pages on each 4″ × 6″ card. Ultrafiche, presently being used by the West Publishing Co., can contain as many as 1,600 microimage pages of a National Reporter System volume on a 4″ × 6″ fiche. Fiche is generally used for single volumes and when updating is necessary.

Beginning with the academic year 1987-1988, the American Bar Association asks all ABA approved law schools to provide a gross piece count of their microform holdings which will be computed according to the following formula:

microfiche: 6:1	Six fiche equals one volume.
Microfilm: 1:5	One roll equals five volumes.

This decision was based on a determination that, for accreditation purposes, a standardized microform equivalency formula which would apply equally to all ABA-approved schools was needed and that the then current dependency on publishers' count did not provide that standardization.

By the use of reader/printers and reader hardware, it is comparatively easy for the user to read the microform on a screen and to make facsimile copies of pages for personal use.

Libraries of all 175 ABA approved law schools are required annually to provide information and statistics about their operations which are analyzed by the AALL statistics coordinator. Whether a law school complies with the ABA accreditation standards depends, among other requirements, upon whether it maintains and administers a library "adequate for its program." The standards require certain types of materials to be part of a core collection of the law library as one of the indicia of "adequacy." The ABA standards do not distinguish between the hard copy book or the nonbook format, such as microform. As long as the library complies with ABA standard 603(d), which reads that "if the library contains materials in microform, tape or similar form, it shall provide the necessary viewing . . . equipment in an area suitable for its use," there is no limitation on the percentage of total microform volume equivalents to hard copy volumes held by the library. This has resulted in the following unusual conditions currently prevalent in law libraries.

Of the total microform volume equivalents (microfiche 6:1, microfilm 1:5) added during the fiscal year 1985–1986 by the 175 reporting libraries as a percentage of total book volumes added during that period, the mean (or average) was 124% and the median (or midpoint) was 78.1%. In other words, on an average, law libraries added more microform volume equivalents to their collection during the period than hard copies.

The total microform volume equivalents held at the end of 1986 as a percentage of total book volumes held by academic law libraries was a mean of 45.3% and a median of 38.5%. It would therefore appear that the growth of hard copy volumes in law libraries is dramatically shrinking. This conclusion is definitely supported by the statistics. The mean number of microfiche held at the end of 1986 was 338,946, and the median 322,435. The number of microfiche added was 37,978 for the mean and 24,332 for the median. The number of microform reels held at the end of the year by the reporting libraries was 2,689 for the mean and 2,027 for the median which adds up to 13,448 volume equivalents as a mean and 10,135 as the median, and those figures are for microfilm alone.

In this context, it should also be noted that the total book volumes and microform volume equivalents held by the 175 reporting libraries at the end of the year as a mean was 264,359 and as a median 220,495. Using those figures as a base, it is interesting to note how microform has assumed such importance in the collection development policies of law school libraries, especially those that have been established since 1960.

Although the total microform volume equivalent held as a percentage of total book volumes in the collection at the end of 1988 was 45.3% as a mean and 38% as a median, the top ranked in this category had much higher percentages of microform to hard copy. The top ranked was the law school of St. Thomas University, Florida, with a percentage of 169.5 of microform to hard copy, followed by:

(1) Detroit College, Michigan—123%
(2) Hawaii—116.7%
(3) Mississippi—114.8%
(4) Thomas M. Cooley—111%
(5) Loyola University of Chicago—107.4%
(6) CUNY at Queens College—103.3%
(7) Pace University—99.4%

(8) Northern Kentucky University—94.7%
(9) University of Puget Sound—94.7%

Many of these are relatively new schools. However, even the more established law libraries are acquiring microform materials.

Columbia University, for example, number two in rank of total volumes and volume equivalents held by law school libraries, adding up to 767,468 volumes, reflects 10.5% of those volumes in microform. Number one, Harvard Law School Library with a combined total of 1,565,962 volumes, contains almost the same percentage of microform at 10.2%. Number three, Yale, with 742,270 volumes, reflects a 13.2 percentage and, fourth placed New York University, with a total of 725,275 volumes, has 15.8% of that collection in microform. Fifth place Texas, with 692,194 volumes, has 19.6% of that collection in microform.

At least sixty-three law school libraries have a greater proportion of their law collection in microform over hard copies and many of these are at the 60% to 90% range.

The librarians heading those institutions are highly professional and sophisticated in their education and experience in the field. They are also, on the whole, highly sensitive to how they should respond to the impact of the new technology on legal research. However, they continue to depend on microform to provide a significant resource in that context. Why?

First, it should be noted that the concept of miniaturization of the printed work on film or paper has been used since the 1830s. As early as 1839, an English scientist named Benjamin Dancer reduced a document twenty inches long to one-eighth inch in length and by use of a 100-power microscope was able to read it. During the Franco-Prussian War, secret messages were photographed on microfilm rolls which were attached to the legs of carrier pigeons to be delivered between Paris and Bordeaux. In the 1930's, microfilm began to be used commercially, especially by banks, for the preservation of records of cancelled checks. By the 1950's libraries began to adopt this microform technology and as microform viewers and viewer-printers became less costly in the 1960s publishers began to edit and publish software and manufacturers began to produce hardware to meet the requirements of library users and readers.

A number of major law publishers have entered the microform publishing field: West Publishing Company, Oceana/Transmedia, CIS, UMI, BNA, Heine, Law Library Microform Consortium, F. B. Rothman, to name a few. These companies provide a plethora of basic and fringe materials of value in law libraries such as law reports, statutes, administrative regulations, serials and out-of-print books. The Public Printer proposed microfiche as the sole form for distribution of major legislative and regulatory documents in order to save money and meet the budget for the depository program. At the October 1986 meeting of The Depository Library Council, it was announced that over 60% of depository titles are now issued in microfiche.

Publishers try to meet the requirements of ANSI/AIIM Standards, and produce a silver polyester-base microfilm. These should last for about 200 years. A non-silver option (vesicular) is also available, for this has a much more limited life span. Many legal serial titles available in microform are listed in the University Microfilms International *Serials in Microform Catalog* (1987). Readers of the *New York Law Journal* are probably familiar with the advertisement, which appears occasionally, offering for sale the past ninety-eight years of the *New York Law Journal* on microfilm.

There are many obvious reasons why microform has been welcomed by law librarians. The increasing cost of book storage and the increasing lack of shelf space encourage the acquisition of legal materials in miniaturized form. It also allows access to materials which are unavailable otherwise, such as out-of-print books, and records and briefs of appellate courts.

Of even more significance, microform allows for the preservation of law books, particularly those published after 1850. Many of them were printed on paper containing self-destructive acid and are crumbling into dust on the library shelves. Dr. Varton Gregorian, former president of the New York Public Library, estimates that 76 million "brittle books," published since 1850 are doomed to that fate. A House subcommittee has found that the Library of Congress contains almost 4 million brittle books with 77,000 volumes being added annually. Many of these are law books. Dr. Gregorian and David Boorstin, the Librarian of Congress, are now advocating a nationally coordinated microfilming campaign to preserve on film copies of those crumbling books until new technologies, including removal of acid content from printed paper, are perfected.

An article in *The New York Times Book Review* (March 29, 1987), by Eric Stange, notes that millions of books are turning to dust; it asks whether they can be saved. Referring to the House Committee report and the statements of Dr. Gregorian and David Boorstin, he notes that "their message was both chilling and overdue. With the program they propose, we can hope to photograph about 3.3 million volumes or about one-third of the books that will be unusable by the end of the century. For the rest, it is too late. *Microfilm is the best method of reproduction.* Accelerated-aging tests have shown that microfilm will last for at least 200 years, plenty of time for preservationists to transfer material to yet another medium if the film begins to crumble. In any case, microfilm will probably soon be supplanted by optical disks and other forms of electronic technology that are far less bulky than film."

CD ROM stands for compact disk-read only memory. Data is stored in CD ROM as three-dimensional, silvered pits, burned into the master by a laser beam and replicated as holes and flat surfaces pressed into the information bearing surface of each copy (over 2 billion pits along a three mile track). This surface is physically sealed off from contact with the disc drive environment sandwiched between the grooved, transparent upper surface and a protective undercoating. Read out is accomplished by a scanning laser beam reflected (or not) from the silvered pits through the transparent upper layer. Read out thus involves no physical contact or wear, therefore, loss or degradation of data hardly ever occurs.

A compact disk can store still or moving images in black and white or color; stereo or two separate sound tracks integrated with or separate from the images; digital program files (word processors, spread sheets) and digital information files (documents, records, catalogs).

Each disk can store 540 megabytes or approximately 540 million American Standard Code for Information Interchange (ASCII) characters in one or more files. A floppy disk can store only three seconds of high quality audio while the compact disk can store an hour. More than 200,000 pages of type, text, or approximately 100 volumes of legal books can be stored on a CD ROM disk. The CD ROM also has the capability of interacting with the user.

The *PC World* Report "CD ROM Goes to Work" (April 1987) notes: "Although expectations run high, mass acceptance still awaits. Unlike the CD, the CD ROM doesn't replace existing technology; this presents some creative challenges to would-be-moguls trying to carve out a market. Unresolved technical and marketing issues similarly cloud CD ROM's otherwise sunny future. Is the CD ROM just a repository for gargantuan data bases? Or is it a means of turning the television into an interactive all-in-one home entertainment and education center? Who owns the information on a CD ROM? Will a standard emerge that embraces the spectrum of optical video products from 5 inch CDs to 12-inch laser video disks? And will truly interactive video applications capture the imagination and pocketbooks of American consumers?"

Compared with microform, the digitized data used by CD ROM is easier to process by machine and therefore retrieval is simpler. CD ROM is more durable and the quality of displayed images potentially superior.

A disadvantage of CD ROM is that you cannot write on, erase or edit files stored on the disk. Information cannot, therefore, be updated by the user. However, as brought out in the *PC World* Report, product developers are creating a host of prototype CD ROM applications "from disk-based encyclopedias to monumental repositories of medical data and stock quotations. In the business world, companies are just beginning to exploit CD ROM to store and manage their records."

It has been noted, however, that custom CD ROM applications "demand a hefty investment"—estimated as costing nearly $20,000 to transfer 100 MB of data on CD ROM from tape or floppy disk. Another contributor, T. J. Byers notes: "The very quality that makes CD ROM so attractive—vast storage capacity, is also its biggest drawback. File directories, the mainstay of magnetic floppy and hard disks, can't effectively cope with the immense number of files a CD ROM can hold. The names wouldn't scroll across the screen for just a few seconds, but for hours. To keep data sorted in usable batches, we need something more than just a faster version of what we use now."

Confronted with the huge storage capacity of CD ROMs, programmers are now looking for "ways to tag and retrieve data." A visionary idea called "hypertext" may turn out to be the most practical approach, according to Byers. Hypertext arranges data storage and retrieval by association; a body of information is referenced within itself rather than to an outside directory. Until sophisticated hypertext legal applications are available, the full potential of CD ROM for law libraries will not be realized.

Law Librarians presently prefer microform to CD ROM because production costs are lower and this factor is reflected in the price.

Moreover, facilities and methods for using microform are already in place and mastered by users, whereas those for CD ROM are in a state of flux.

Law libraries have a huge investment in microform. It is difficult to accept that it is economically feasible to duplicate on CD ROM the staggering mass of legal materials presently available on microform and then offer the CD ROM version for sale to law libraries already possessing the same material in microform. However, that was the very argument which was offered against replacing books with microfilm.

At this time, CD ROM does not replace microform technology. Instead, they compete for the storage of lesser used law books; but neither can entirely supplant the printed book.

CHAPTER 46A

Videotapes and Continuing Legal Education

The following material comprises a new Chapter 46A for Legal Research and Law Library Management. *It is intended as supplemental material to the Main Text.*

Videotapes are taking on an important role as a cost-effective and significant form of Continuing Legal Education. There are some very good reasons for this development. Certainly it is more economical to view a seminar on Bankruptcy in the privacy of one's office than to travel from New York to Chicago for the same purpose. Moreover, a videotape of a seminar on a legal subject of current interest to practitioners can be viewed and reflected on at the convenience of the interested practitioner, rather than at a pre-ordained scheduled time in conflict with the practitioner's other responsibilities. Videotapes can also be used in in-house training programs. In this context they are especially helpful as the means to introduce a topic of interest to the lawyers assembled, stimulate discussion, or to supplement a speaker's presentation, all within the constraints of the firm's other scheduled events.

The increased interest expressed by lawyers in videotapes as a means of upgrading their professional skills and understanding of current developments in the law is reflected in the increasing number of organizations producing professional seminars on legal subjects and then making them available on videotape for private showing.

The American Bar Association is playing an important role in the production of videotapes as part of its Continuing Legal Education program. Recently its Division of Professional Education published the second edition of the *ABA Video Law Seminar Catalog* (1983-84), and it is of interest to note that more that 300 ABA Video Law Seminar tapes are now available on a variety of subjects from Advocacy to Torts.

Similarly engaged are the California Continuing Education of the Bar, The Pennsylvania Bar Institute and the State Bar of Wisconsin. There is also the National Institute for Trial Advocacy, whose purpose is to contribute to the development of an adequately trained professionally responsible trial bar. Additionally, the Association of Trial Lawyers of America has a program of video cassettes stressing trial advocacy and there is the National Practice Institute for Continuing Professional Education which has an impressive catalog of videotapes on the training of lawyers. The Practising Law Institute sells and rents videotapes of some of its seminars. Even the traditional publishers of legal texts are becoming involved in this development. Mathew Bender now features a video library on advocacy as does Little Brown with its Law Films on Evidence.

All these organizations are proud of the fact that so many nationally recognized experts in specific fields of law participate in their videotaped programs.

It should be noted in this context, that some of these seminars are recorded and pre-staged in television production studios and others are recorded live at conferences or seminars held around the country. As a result the quality and effectiveness of a videotaped program can vary significantly. When we note additionally in this context the extremely high prices charged for their rental or purchase, it is wise to take precautions to avoid acquiring a "lemon."

Rental should be preferred to purchase unless the circumstances warrant purchase. Whenever possible try to work out an agreement on "approval." The American Bar Association, for example, will arrange for a preview tape, running for approximately 15 to 20 minutes to be reviewed by a prospective purchaser of the tape, as a sample of the program, prior to purchase or rental. These preview tapes are available for only the cost of shipping and handling.

It has been suggested that the way prerecorded videotapes can be used in a law firm training program depends on the resources and skills of the lawyers in the firm. For example, the tapes can be played without any additional explanatory materials or commentary. Many tapes, however, are accompanied by additional information in the form of study guides or manuals which allow the viewers to compare their own analysis and evaluation of a problem with the opinions presented in the program.

One of the most effective ways to use these tapes, is to supplement them with live discussion, before, during or after the program. The videotape format allows the program planner to rearrange sections and to repeat certain parts to enhance the effectiveness of the information.

It is interesting to note that the attention span for viewing videotapes, while much longer than for audiotapes, is usually less than for a live speaker. For this reason, the Division of Professional Education of the American Bar Association recommends short breaks at the end of a one-hour tape and programs of less than half-day segments.

It is also important to note that the hardware and software of the videotape recording and viewing are varied and often not compatible. As the producers of these tapes market them in all available formats, a specific description of the type of tape or recorder used by the purchaser must accompany the order.

With that thought in mind, it is worthwhile to review the basic equipment being used today in the production and viewing of videotapes. They are a video cassette recorder and a television set. These permit not only the playing of prerecorded videotapes but also of off-air taping as well. With a camera it is even possible to produce one's own video program by, for example, rehearsing courtroom presentations and depositions or even creating one's own training tape.

Video recorders and video cassettes are available in different "formats." It should be noted that the three main formats, ½″ VHS ½″ Beta and ¾″ U-matic, are not compatible. As a result, a Beta tape cannot be played on a VHS recorder/player or vice versa. The most common format at present is VHS. Most TV sets can be hooked up for record and playback with any format of video-recorder. Most videotaped programs are available in all three formats.

Video recorders are used to play prerecorded videotapes and to record with a camera or off-the-air. Video recorders use magnetic tape that allows immediate playback without processing. Prerecorded video cassettes must be ordered in the same "format" as the video recorder.

At present there is a choice available of the new ½″ video recorder, which is designed for home use and the ¾″ machine, designed for industrial use. The ½″ video recorder features an extended record and playback capability. It also has a small mini computer that allows automatic recording of TV programs. The ¾″

video recorder, is generally not equipped for off-the-air recording. It is larger and heavier, and more sturdy than the ½″. It is also much more expensive. It does provide better picture quality, especially when recording with a camera. For most purposes the ½″ recorder (either VHS or Beta) is considered satisfactory.

Videotaped CLE programs are a new concept in continuing legal education. Usually they are timely and informative as well as interestingly presented. The video format allows outstanding experts in selected fields of law to educate and to communicate with the viewer and to reflect through their personalities and highly specialized professional skills, the nuances of style and expression that have made them leaders in the field. By the same token, these videotapes must be used with circumspection and reserve: Remember the advice once given to a law student by his dean "If you do not learn to discriminate you will never be a lawyer."

It can be aptly applied to lawyers seeking to upgrade their skills and professionalism through the medium of videotaped CLE programs.

CHAPTER 46B

Law Libraries in the Twenty-First Century

The following material comprises a new Chapter 46B for Legal Research and Law Library Management. *It is intended as supplemental material to the Main Text.*

What will law libraries look like at the end of the Twentieth Century? Will the "paperless society" overcome the traditional type of law library we are familiar with today? Law librarians are struggling with this problem especially those involved in the planning of a law library facility today, which obviously must remain in use after the year 2000. Some would like to delay meeting the thrust of the new technology as it pertains to libraries. Others are straining at the leash to incorporate the new technological developments in law library administration, even at the risk of abandoning tested traditional methods of library service and replacing them with untested substitutes based on the new technology.

The former Director of Libraries of the University of Pennslyvania, Richard DeGennaro, warns us in an article on Libraries and Technology in the *Library Journal* (June 1, 1982 issue) not to be too precipitous in assuming that hard copy literature will disappear from libraries. He notes that the "thinkers" are more apt to predict the demise of the library as we know it. The administrators who must make the hard decisions involving resources and library users — still have many reservations about the role of the new technology in libraries vis-a-vis "real books." As to predictions of the future, he perceptively remarks: "life is full of surprises, and as a Chinese philosopher said: 'Prediction is very difficult, particularly of the future'."

Occasionally, we do get a glimpse of the future which not only provides more grist for the mill, but which can actually overwhelm you with its significance for library planning. This happened recently when a fascinating interview of Bob Zilch, Acting Director of the Library of Congress's Planning and Development Office, appeared in the June, 1983 issue of *Copyright Notices,* published by the U.S. Copyright Office.

Zilch describes a new "Optical Disk Pilot Program" of the Library of Congress which reveals a revolutionary new technological breakthrough which can have a tremendous effect on library service.

As explained in a Library of Congress release, of the 80 million items of stored knowledge of the Library of Congress (the largest in the world), an appalling proportion of them are in an advanced state of deterioration. Most of the printed materials added to the Library's collections every year are on acidic paper. As a result, they start to deteriorate, actually turning to dust on the shelves, within a period of 25 to 100 years. To preserve items in the original, the Library of Congress is developing deacidification technologies and encouraging publishers to print their books on alkaline paper.

To provide secondary format preservation and to insure public access to high-use material and fragile or rare materials, the Library has instituted a three year pilot program in image presentation and retrieval using optical disk technology.

In contrast to microforms, optical disk technology affords extremely high-density storage of information. Whereas a 4″ × 6″ microfiche can store approximately 96 pages and an ultra fiche of the same size about 1600 pages, a one-sided 12-inch digital disk can store between 10,000, and 20,000 pages of text depending on the resolution required. One side of an analog disk can store up to 54,000 images. This technology represents a potentially efficient and economic way to store and retrieve images. Optical storage also avoids wear resulting from continuous disk usage, since only a beam of light touches the medium during playback. In addition, information on the digital optical disk can be transferred to a new disk without any loss. It is thus valuable as a preservation format. Together these strengths thus make the disk a potentially ideal medium for on-demand retrieval of high-use items.

The Library of Congress has defined equipment and disk specifications and has already entered into two contracts: one with Integrated Automation to supply an experimental digital disk system, and the other with SONY Video Communications Products Co. to supply experimental video discs and commercial players.

The Optical Disk Pilot Program consists of two parts: print materials will be stored on digital optical disks; non-print or image based materials will be stored on analog optical discs, better known as videodiscs.

High-use current periodicals will be given initial emphasis in the digital disk project. Up to 500,000 images per year can be stored, including in addition, selected maps, microforms, manuscripts and sheet music. At the document preparation station, information relating to the printed library materials will be entered by keyboarding via computer terminals into the Library of Congress Information System (LOCIS) database with a document number corresponding to a library retrieval number. Documents will then be sent to the input station where they are scanned and digitized at 300 lines per inch resolution by a high-speed scanner. This digitized information is then transferred by a laser writing process onto the surface of an optical disc. Because of the high resolution of the digital process, the disk will contain substantially all of the information contained in the original item, and therefore will be capable of serving as a black-and-white secondary preservation format for the original items, as microforms are now used.

To recall the information, the user will type in the appropriate identification. The library's computer will tie the request to the image coded on the disk and display the black and white images on the terminal screen. The user stations, which can be located at various places in the library, will have a high-resolution terminal for requests and display of full pages of text, along with a medium-speed printer for single-page printouts. Off-line batch printing will also be available from a central facility.

By the use of analog viodeo-discs, which can store up to 54,000 separate black and white or color images on one of its 12 inch sides, a similar process will be used to store and view motion pictures, photoprints, and other images.

While preservation is the primary objective of the Optical Disk Pilot Program, the disks are also expected to solve the problems of availability of frequently used materials which are not on the shelf.

The introduction to the interview with Bob Zilch in *Copyright Notices* aptly questions, that as libraries turn to optical disks—both to preserve the collections and to provide better reader access, "will we readers be seated at terminals looking at black screens as lasers display *War and Peace* page by page? Will we be able to buy *Time* and *Newsweek* in chip form only? Experts predict that we will be able to carry around book sized terminals, battery run, and insert a chip when we want to read a book! Imagine reading from a chip in the bathroom, on the beach! Will all 30 volumes of the *Encyclopedia Britannica* be available in laser-read optical disk form on two sides of a 12 inch disk!?"

Bob Zilch notes, "digital optical disk technology is seen by some of us as the likely next generation of microfilm," for preservation purposes.

When asked "so you imprint it on the disk page by page and then read it page by page?", Zilch responded: "Yes, that's right. An electronic snapshot instead of a chemical snapshot. We expect that the material on which the image is recorded, is either likely to last a long time, or alternatively, the technology will permit the information, which is to say the electronic snapshot on the disk, to be transferred to the next generation of disk without loss of quality."

Zilch explains what is meant by a print being digitized. "It is the old zero and one kind of concept." When you think of a television screen which has 525 lines and a line made up of dots which glow or don't glow and think of a glowing dot as being yes or 0 and a nonglowing dot as no or 1, you get sort of a picture—each of the glowing dots is called a pixel and the number of dots per images is what defines the level of resolution.

Summarizing some of Zilch's other thoughts on the Optical Disk Pilot Program, he believes that the optical disk may form the basis of the Library of Congress's reference collections by the end of the century. On access, he is concerned with the reactions of the users of the equipment. Will readers be able to sit down and use the machines—will they accept the images, will people with bifocals be able to read the images, etc.?

He expected that by the summer of 1984, there would be a sufficient number of images of a facsimile quality available on disks stored in juke boxes, so that when patrons go up to any of the high resolution terminals, they could, if they have done their bibliographic searching, actually see the first page and call it out in 10 seconds and then page backward or forward in the document they have called up. Everything will be "on shelf"—because readers don't touch the disk. As long as the machine works, as long as what the patron is interested in is in the machines, that level of service will be possible—that is—in 10 seconds.

Of significance too is the fact that the machine is constructed so that it takes each request as it comes through but it has a technique of capturing the data that comes back in response and holding it in its memory called the buffer. Then the juke box can move on to the next chore and provide the same disk and the same material to another patron.

Zilch stresses that "one important point about access is that this technology permits us to distribute these images far and wide; these images could be beamed to homes, to libraries, whatever. So people would not need to come to the library to have access to our collections. It gives a whole new meaning to interlibrary loan . . . It transforms and gives a new meaning to all traditional library services. Whether it's loan, photocopying, or whatever, some would say it calls in question the traditional library organization in all its aspects. Do we need specialized reading rooms, do we need specialized librarians?" And—here is the rub! "Will we need libraries, will we need library buildings?" And how will this technological breakthrough affect the private law firm library and the research habits of its lawyers and of the judiciary?

These are the questions that bother law librarians today—and what about the copyright problems involved? Section 108 of the Copyright law allows the making of a single copy of a library item for preservation purposes only. Obviously, we are dealing with a whole new ballgame now. Perhaps these technological developments will force a solution to the copyright problem which cannot be realized now.

CHAPTER 46C

Electronic Media and Federal Government Generated Information

The following material comprises a new Chapter 46C for Legal Research and Law Library Management. *It is intended as supplemental material to the Main Text.*

"As electronic technology has advanced, so too has the capability improved for the generation, processing, storage, and retrieval of information. Most fedral agencies now use word processing and photo composition techniques in the generation of their publications. More than half of the machine-readable statistical files are produced by agencies, which have no procedures for distributing their data. Often documents distributed to the depository libraries[1] in paper or microfiche are also available in full text in electronic form. In other cases, and particularly with the decrease in federal publishing, much Government information is stored only in electronic media, and often it is less accessible to the public than previously. As more data is computerized and with the increasing use of personal computers to retrieve, manipulate, and display that data, fewer publications will have counter-parts. As the cost of traditional ink and paper rises, and the manipulation of paper documents becomes comparatively more cumbersome, we can ex-

---

[1]There are 1,382 libraries in the United States serving as Congressional Federal depositories. At least one depository library is located in each of the 435 Congressional districts. These libraries receive publications issued by the executive, judicial and the legislative branches at no charge in exchange for providing free public assess. This program is administered by the Superintendent of Documents, U.S. Government Printing Office (G.P.O.) Regional depositories receive one copy of all materials distributed. Partial depositories receive only those materials they select.

pect more government information to be available only through electronic media."

This significant finding made in a Report of an Ad Hoc Committee on Depository Library access to Federal Automated Data Bases to the Joint Committee on Printing, U.S. Congress and entitled "Provision of Federal Government Publications in Electronic Format to Depository Libraries,"[2] suggests how lawyers and other legal researchers will soon be obtaining access to law related information generated by the federal government and its agencies.

The Joint Committee on Printing appointed the Ad Hoc Committee in 1983 with the charge to evaluate the feasibility and desirability of providing access to federal government information in electronic formats to depository libraries. After making a survey to determine how depository libraries currently use data processing equipment, publications in electronic format and participation in electronic networks, the committee found that some government agencies are making their publications electronically available to the public either directly, or through database providers and vendors which provide access to federal data bases.

It should be noted in this context that some of these data bases are more timely than their paper and microfiche counterparts. They also provide a better searching capability because they are based on Boolean logic. In addition they provide indexing and abstracting to the full text, as well as selective announcement services and document delivery either by means of a user profile or as a by-product of the user's search.

Already, many business offices and research and academic institutions regularly use such services. Ultimately, of course, many homes will also have access to these data bases through personal computers. The general public however, will have no access to this data, unless it is provided to them through the depository libraries. It is with this concern that the library community urged the Government Printing Office to work with the Joint Committee on Printing to expand the depository library program to include government publications in all formats such as electronic data files and a variety of other non-print materials.

As part of its findings, the Ad Hoc Committee observed that electronic data bases will become more useful in the performance of gov-

---

[2]U.S. Government Printing Office, 1984, p.1.

ernment business and will increase in depth and breadth as federal agencies find it less expensive to produce information in electronic format.

Although not generally known, there are currently a number of mechanisms in place for the distribution of government data files that could prove useful in law related research. They are:

(1) Sale or lease of Government data tapes, magnetic disks, etc. directly by Government agencies such as the National Technical Information Sevice (NTIS),[3] the National Library of Medicine,[4] the Bureau of the Census, and the Department of Agriculture.[5]
(2) Sale of electronic photocomposition tapes by Government agencies such as the sale of the Federal Register tapes by the G.P.O.
(3) Provision of free on-line access to data bases by Government agencies such as U.S. Patent Office Classification and Search Support Information System (CASSIS) available free to Patent Depository Libraries.[6]
(4) Provision of fee-based, on-line access to data bases by Govern-

---

[3]NTIS, an agency of the U.S. Department of Commerce, is the central source for the public sale of U.S. Government sponsored research, development and engineering reports, as well as foreign technical reports and other analyses prepared by national and local government agencies, their contractors or grantees. It is the central source for federally generated, machine processable data files and software and manages the Federal Software Exchange Center. NTIS is the central source for information on all new U.S. Government owned patents and pending applications, consisting not only of inventions primarily coming out of government laboratories, but also those contractor inventions to which the government has title.

[4]The National Library of Medicine has a program under way to design, develop and evaluate a laboratory facility that serves as an engineering prototype that will electronically store, retrieve and display documents acquired by the library.

[5]In 1981, the Department of Agriculture upgraded distribution of its news releases and perishable or time sensitive material from surface mail and telephone facsimile, to instantaneous transmissions over an electronic message net work. It is also establishing an information base or data base to allow users to access only those items they need. Users are individuals in regional information offices, land grant universities and state departments of agriculture.

[6]This file includes more than 4.6 million U.S. Patents which are classified and cross-referenced among the approximately 110,000 categories of technology that make up the U.S. Patent Classification System. Along with similarly categorized foreign patents and other technical publications, they make up a collection totaling more than 24 million documents. This patent file is increasing in size by 500,000 documents annually.

ment agencies, such as The National Library of Medicine and The Chemical Substances Information Network (CSIM).[7]

(5) Provision of fee based, on-line access of secondary (private) data bases derived from, or extracted from Government-originated data files by commercial organizations such as Lockheed's DIALOG, BRS, ORBIT, LEXIS and WESTLAW. These fee based, on-line data bases often result from value-added activity by the providers. This activity includes re-processing, reformatting, or manipulation of the orignal Government-generated information, and sometimes merging it with data from other sources.

(6) Provision of free or fee-based access to data tapes, disks, on-line data through a Government Contractor, such as a HUD contract with ABT Associates to provide access to American National Housing Surveys, Office of Aging and Bureau of Justic Statistics Contracts with ICPSP.

One of the present difficulties in implementing access to Federal data in electronic format is the wide array of computer equipment already in place in depository libraries or in their parent institutions. Despite the fact that there is no single technology or medium that encompasses all electronic information in the same manner as paper or microform, still with the rapidly emerging technology of computer storage media and telecommunications, most specialists in the field agree with the conclusion of the American Chemical Society that we can anticipate with confidence the technical and commercial feasibility of creating an on-line system for journal/report literature with a print on-demand capability. They also agree that it will be possible in the near future for an author to prepare a manuscript in electronic form using a word-processor and to transmit that manuscript to a vendor via a telecommunications system which can then be selectively accessed electronically by a reader.

They also agree with Dr. Michael L. Dertouzos, Director of the Laboratory for Computer Science at the Massachusetts Institute of

---

[7]The CSIN is a response to the Toxic Substances Control Act (Public Law 94-469) to protect the public and the environment from exposure to hazardous chemicals. The CSIN collects and disseminates data submitted to the administrator of the Environmental Protection Agency (EPA) as required by the Act.

Technology, that electronic information transfer systems would be in general use nationally in approximately five years and that once 10 million microcomputers are in place in a mix of homes, school rooms, work places and laboratories that an avalanche effect will occur, and the use of electronic networks for information transfer will become general among the business, academic and research committees throughout the country.

Dr. Paul A. Strassman, vice-president, Information Products Group, Xerox Corp., cautions, however, that with the evolution of data storage or a variety of disks and tapes, we must look at information differently. The classified library arrangements we use today to provide access to information in print will be supplanted by the new technology in non-print form.

In its report, the Ad Hoc Committee has wisely recommended that the Joint Committee on Printing and the Superintendent of Documents initiate a pilot program in which depository libraries will receive federal information in electronic form and provide it to the general public without charge. This recommendation is based on the survey that the committee conducted which led it to conclude that it is technologically feasible to provide electronic access to federally generated information. In this context, legal researchers will be pleased to note that the publications identified to be electronically accessed in the pilot project will probably include numerous publications of interest to legal researchers. These are: U.S. Public Laws, U.S. Code, Code of Federal Regulations, U.S. Presidential Executive Orders, G.P.O. Sales Reference File, Federal Register, G.P.O. Monthly Catalog, Bureau of Labor Statistics, National Criminal Justice Reference Center, Congressional Record, Census Patents, U.S. Reports, I.R.S., OSHA, LEGIS,[8] SCORPIO.[9]

The report identifies problems and questions which will inevitably arise when electronic accessing of information becomes an acceptable research method. For example, if the user is unfamiliar with the process involved in obtaining access to information in electronic format, obviously there will be a need for a training program equivalent to what is now being done by Lexis and Westlaw.

---

[8]A data bank operated by the House Information System for the internal use of the legislative branch.

[9]A data bank operated by the Library of Congress for the internal use the legislative branch.

Then there are the following basic questions which necessarily arise when we depend on electronically generated information, and which the Ad Hoc Committee plans to address in its pilot program.

"Will having access to information in electronic format increase the usefulness of the information to the users? When comparing former methods used by researchers in obtaining data with the new electronic method, will electronic access increase the users productivity? Does it shorten the amount of time needed to access data? Does it eliminate or create unnecessary information? Is the information more current than that provided under more traditional systems? Is there a greater diversity of information? Is the information of a better quality (e.g. more accurate)?"

The Ad Hoc Committee's recommendations, if eventually implemented, will aid research generally by speeding the work and enlarging the available data bases. However, as noted in Chapter 11A of this Supplement, the government does impose barriers to those needing federally generated information.

CHAPTER 46D

Telefacsimile and Legal Research

The following material comprises a new Chapter 46D for Legal Research and Law Library Management. *It is intended as supplemental material to the Main Text.*

A 1987 National American Bar Journal Subscriber Study, conducted by Don Bowdren Associates, reveals among other trends, a sharp increase in the use of computers by lawyers.

Of equal importance is that 45.9% of the law firms responding to the questionnaire owned a telefacsimile machine. A Library of Congress Report entitled "A Survey of Telefacsimile Equipment" notes in this context that in 1982 there were 350,000 facsimile units in operation in the United States and industry analysts predicted an annual growth of between 13 and 20% to 1.4 million units in 1992.[1] If these predictions are even approximately accurate, the report adds, "fax machines will almost certainly become standard equipment in the Inter Library departments of large and medium size libraries."

As Frederic J. Baum, Director of Library Services of the Association of the Bar of the City of New York simply describes it "For those who are unfamiliar with telefacsimile, it is merely a device that accepts original documents at one end (the Library) and, at the push of a button, allows an 8½″ × 11″ page to be sent electronically (over telephone lines) to a target machine at the other end. It takes less than half-a-minute per page and competition has lowered the cost of equipment to quite affordable levels."

In essence, telefacsimile is a combination of a teletype and a photo-

---

[1] Library Technology Report, "A Survey of Telefacsimile Equipment" pp. 157–187 (March-April 1985).

copier, capable of transmitting not only what teletypes usually do, but also much that they cannot do, such as charts, pictures and graphics. If it can be seen, it can be faxed!

The Library Technology Report on Telefacsimile Equipment notes that "Two conflicting views have emerged on the future of the fax. One is that the technology will soon be superceded by or integrated with new forms of computer-based electronic mail. Other authorities predict ongoing improvements in facsimile, but see serious technical obstacles to any radical breakthrough that would by-pass the basic fax technology. Most of the facsimile equipment sold or leased in the U.S. is now of Japanese manufacture, including almost all the new models sold under American trade names. The Japanese incursion has forced prices down and quality up. Whatever new technology may be developing down the road, it is unlikely to make obsolete fax's presently unique abilities to transmit instantaneously, or to store for delayed transmission, exact photoreproductions of both text and graphics."

The document-delivery potential of telefacsimile has always been of interest to law librarians. Law in the books has become a formidable storage problem and economic factor for law library administrators. This problem has been partially resolved by two dynamic developments: (1) computer retrieval of legal information and documentation; and (2) availability of legal materials in miniaturized form, such as microform and CD ROMs. Much of the legal profession, however, anticipates the time when through these two developments, instantaneous access to all statutes, cases, administrative rules and regulations, law review articles and treatises will be a reality. Still, it is not feasible to plan on it for a certainty. Just to identify and process for electronic retrieval the materials that lawyers and academic legal scholars will require in their research is an immense task. Books and hard cover documentation will continue to be a substantial research source for lawyers well into the future. Many of these books and documents because of age, copyright, and esoteric eccentricities of legal research will be available only from those centers of bibliographic control that have developed programs for their acquisition, particularly books on foreign and international law, legal history, legislative histories and administrative law and regulation as well as books on law-related subjects.

The changing nature of legal research and the growing dependence of lawyers on the sources, analysis and methodology reflected in interdisciplinary research necessitates reference to materials not generally collected in law libraries. Thus they may seek access to apposite materials in economics, sociology, political science, medicine, many of which are issued as government documents. As a result, lawyers will depend on libraries—both legal and nonlegal—for access to these materials.

Here is where the telefacsimile machine takes on importance, especially when time is a factor.

An innovative program instituted by Mr. Baum at the Association of the Bar of the City of New York is characteristic of the significant role the telefacsimile can play in support of legal research. For members of the more than 200 law firms in New York City who use facsimile, he developed a pilot project in the fall of 1986 that allowed journal articles to be "faxed" to association members rather than photocopied on The Bar Association Library's premises and then delivered. "Given crosstown traffic in mid-Manhattan", Baum explained, "it is likely that substantial saving of time and increased convenience will allow faxing to compete well with our photocopy service."

This pilot project turned out to be highly successful because, as Baum pointed out, "Of the 5000 persons who use the Library of the Association each month some 20% make the trip for the limited purpose of photocopying material unavailable in members' Law offices. Associates or other employees are then sent to 44th Street to select a book, walk to a machine, make copies and then return to the office. That it costs minimally $9.00 for the employee to use the Library is one factor. Of greater consequences are the wages, transportation and time involved in sending employees crosstown for photocopies. We thought there had to be a less expensive, more efficient way for members to get hard copies of needed information. Telefacsimile seemed to be the answer."

The Harris/3M lent one of its telefax machines to the Association, and without any official promotion except for a notice in one of the Association's House publications, the program became an instant success. "In short order," Baum notes, "our limited experience allowed dozens of requests to be filled. In every instance, material was "faxed" to the member within an hour of the request. Though some orders came from just a few blocks away, others were phoned to us from Nassau, Suffolk and Westchester. One member from Goshen, N.Y. phoned at 10:50 am and had 13 requested pages on his desk in Goshen fifteen minutes later. The cost? $18.29 (including a 5¢ per page surcharge for area code 914 transmission)."

In addition, Baum pointed out, "With service that gets material to you in minutes, it is fair to suggest that faxing can substitute quite well for your usual practice of sending employees to the Bar Association to make photocopies." Actually, Baum breaks down the costs of a typical faxing transaction as follows:

Five pages of the Federal Register @ $1.25	$6.25
N. Y. State Sales Tax @ .0825	.52
Total cost	$6.77

It should be noted that copyright royalties of $1-$5 may also be applicable and if research is necessary because a citation is inaccurate, the Association reserves the right to impose a $5 service fee.

Small to medium sized law firms which do not have the resources of the larger firms, and single practitioners as well, can make more efficient use of their time by having the Association Library's material faxed directly to their offices.

The cost of telefacsimile machines is quite reasonable, about the same as personal computers—between $1,500 and $6,000 depending upon speed and sophistication. A separate voice-grade telephone line is also required. "Faxing" a message costs the same as making a telephone call.

There is no technical knowledge required to operate a fax. Pushing a few buttons and dialing a telephone number is all that is required. No training is necessary.

There are many vendors and manufacturers of facsimile machines operating in the greater New York area and throughout the country. They include Alden Electronic, Burroughs, Canon, Exxon Office Systems, IBM Corporation, Kentek Information Systems, Harris/3M, Hitachi, NEC America, Panafax, Pitney Bowes, Ricoh Corporation (Robicom) Sharp Electronics Corp., Telautograph Corp., and Xerox Corp. By reason of standards established by the United Nations' Committee Consultative International Telegraph and Telephone (CCITT), all of these machines are compatible with each other for sending and receiving "faxed" materials.

Based on the initiative and business acumen of the Harris/3M Documents Products Inc., which provided its fax machine on loan to the Association, The Harris/3M Co. agreed to sell its machine to Association members at a substantial discount. Thus members seeking telefacsimile service from the Association Library can purchase the Harris/3M machine at a bulk reduced rate. Although the Association does not endorse Harris/3M, Baum notes that the borrowed 3M machine never once failed to operate satisfactorily in over 300 transmissions.

Time involved in legal research can be reduced dramatically with facsimile access to law libraries. Programs similar to that of the Bar Association are being offered by Bar Associations in other parts of the country.

On an experimental basis, John F. Ahlstrom of Harris/3M has provided one of its telefacsimile machines to the St. John's Law Library in Jamaica, New York, to allow it to fax its library materials to St. John's Law alumni who own or rent their own machines. For those alumni who are interested in the service, but do not own a telefacsimile machine, Harris/3M is prepared to sell their latest model machines at a bulk rate discount to them, similar to its arrangement with the Association of the Bar of the City of New York.

This development is yet another exciting advantage the new technology offers the legal profession. Law libraries serving academic, bar, state and practitioner law libraries should attempt to develop similar projects in support of the research activities of their clientele. Certainly the telefacsimile machine can play a prominent role in interlibrary loans, especially as part of a regional network of law libraries.

Over 160 of the libraries listed in the 1987 edition of the *Directory of Law Libraries* now have telefacsimile equipment. The Mid-America Consortium of Law School Libraries reported in 1987 on the success of a telefacsimile pilot project funded by the American Association of Law Libraries. In this project, ten law school libraries installed high speed (Group three) telefacsimile equipment and used it to improve interlibrary borrowing and for quickly transmitting other documents. The study cited by the *The New York Times* predicts a drop in cost of telefax equipment which should eliminate the need for store front telefacsimile centers in office buildings. It also predicts an increase in the number of telefax machines in libraries.

Of equal importance is the development of the "Fax Board" that can be installed in a personal computer. This allows files to be sent directly to a FAX machine without the need to create a hard copy first.

CHAPTER 46E

The Impact of Technology on Legal Research

The following material comprises a new Chapter 46E for Legal Research and Law Library Management. *It is intended as supplemental material to the Main Text.*

Now that the impact of technological change upon legal information storage, retrieval and delivery and in legal research generally has been officially recognized by the American Bar Association,[1] what do librarians and others in academia believe its effect will be on the future of research, law libraries and fiscal planning in the last decade of the 1900s and the 2000s?

A research project, sponsored by the Council on Library Resources, entitled *The Twenty-First Century: Technology's Impact on Academic Research and Law Libraries Including Projections for Fiscal Planning*, addressed this problem, and a summary of its findings bears a message of interest to the legal community.

The data that supports these findings and analysis is based on a survey instrument of approximately 150 questions completed by 224 respondents. The respondents were selected from law librarians, law deans, scientists, library science professors, networkers and members of the Association of Research Libraries. Professor Betty W. Taylor, Director, Legal Information Center, College of Law, University of Florida, Associate Professor Elizabeth B. Mann, School of Library and Information Studies, Florida State University, and Robert J. Munro, Law Librarian, Legal Information Center, College of Law, University of Florida, featured the following six areas in drafting the questionnaire: (1) impact of technology on information publications,

---

[1] See the article in the New York Law Journal p. 4 (Oct. 21, 1986).

(2) library collections and automated information access, (3) budgeting, (4) payment for automated information access (faculty, students, library patrons), (5) personnel, and (6) computer equipment. Analyzing the opinions of the respondents, the authors of the report suggest the present reality and the possible response of law libraries to developing technology. The questions and answers reflect the sophistication and understanding of knowledgeable professionals in the field and provide significant information about the potential impact of technology on the future of law libraries and the services they will provide.

For example, as to whether publication of printed books will continue to increase in the future despite the increase of publication of information in computerized and multimedia formats, most of the correspondents agreed with this premise for the period up to the year 2000; although not so strongly after the year 2000. However, a concomitant perception as to whether the book collections of the libraries of the future will be reduced in size as more information becomes available in computerized and multimedia formats did not reflect the same consensus.

In this context, twenty-seven (12.2%) *strongly agreed*, ninety-nine (44.6%) *agreed*, eleven (5.0%) were *undecided*, seventy-seven (34.7%) *disagreed*, and eight (3.6%) *strongly disagreed*. Of interest too is the disagreement as to when this event would occur, twenty-nine (14.5%) believing it would by the year 1990, fifty-eight (29.0%) believing it would be the year 2000 and eighty-six (4.3%) believing it would occur after the year 2000. Twenty-seven (13.5%) believed it would never occur.

Whether law library book collections of the future will be reduced in size by reason of the new technology is worrisome to the legal profession, especially those planning new law library facilities. Obviously, any building constructed in the late 1980s will probably be in use in the 2050s. As Professors Dan Henke and Julius J. Marke wrote in a Law Library Information Report, entitled "Planning the Law Library as a Legal Information Center" (1986) "The challenge in planning for future law library or legal information center space is to assure that the investment made today in capital improvements will not be lost by obsolescence in the near future. Experience with traditional types of libraries guides library planners with general concepts in book and user spaces but the new technologies are changing the concepts applicable to the access of information and these in turn impinge upon physical space requirements and arrangements for information-gathering activities."[2]

Obviously, a basic need in legal research is accessibility to information and documentation, past and present. As the traditional tools of research give way to the hardware of the new computer assisted legal research and computer assisted legal instruction, what should the average law library look like in the future? Law librarians have been struggling with this problem for years. Some would like to delay meeting the thrust of the new technology as it pertains to law libraries. Others are more adventurous, to the point of being prepared to abandon tested methods of library service and to replace them with interested substitutes based on the new technology.

It is interesting to note in this context that the ambivalence of law librarians and others involved in legal research on the effect of the new technology on law library space planning still continues. One hundred and twenty-six believe that book collections of the libraries of the future will be reduced in size as more information becomes available in computerized and multimedia formats. Eighty-five disagree and eleven are still undecided. There is little doubt that such perceptions will be reflected in the type of law library buildings they play a role in planning.

Characteristic of this indecision is a news article by Judith Axler Turner that appeared in the *Chronicle of Higher Education*, February 4, 1987, under the heading: *"Drive to Require Students to buy computers slows, many colleges awaiting lower costs, development of more software and hard data on effectiveness.*" Turner notes that although a faculty committee of Villanova University seriously considered requiring all of its engineering students to buy their own microcomputers, the dean of the college of engineering turned it down because it would have been too costly to implement and would also be "inefficient." Turner added that similar recommendations are being turned down with "increasing frequency at both technical and liberal arts institutions across the country. It wasn't always thus. For several years, institution after institution announced it would require students to purchase microcomputers. But in 1986 the announcements stopped. Except for the

[2] Henke, Marke, Law Library Information Report, "Planning the Law Library as a Legal Information Center" p.1 (1986).

three service academies—which had made their decisions almost a year earlier—no college or university last year joined the 14 institutions that already required students to buy computers."

Some of the reasons computers are not being required are:

(1) No studies yet prove the educational value of computer ownership, or of computer use in higher education.

(2) The costs of supporting required computers has turned out to be far greater than institutions expected.

(3) There is not enough educational software in most subjects.

(4) The principal use of computers on most campuses, whether or not students have their own machines, is word processing, and many institutions are reluctant to require students to buy what one computer-science professor calls "Fancy Typewriters."

Turner also quoted Daniel Updegrove, a Vice-President of EDUCOM, a consortium of colleges and universities interested in computing as saying "many institutions have chosen not to increase dramatically the number of computers on their campuses—whether by requiring them or by establishing more computer laboratories—because the associated costs are so high . . . [in fact] the costs were much higher than anyone had expected." The dearth of software has been a deterrent to many institutions considering a computer requirement. Another barrier to the development of higher education software is that material written for one manufacturer's computers cannot be used in every other manufacturer's computers. "It's as though every university had its own printing presses and its own language for text books," says Richard M. Cyert, President of Carnegie Mellon University.

Until computer operating systems will become compatible so that software can run on all computers and be "portable," it is questionable how soon the new technology will replace the hard copy, if ever, on the university campus. In essence, these barriers to adoption of computers in research are similar to those faced by law libraries. As indicated in the New York Law Journal article on "Revised ABA Standards for Law School Libraries," "Deans of law schools and law librarians are reevaluating the accepted concepts about how library funds should be spent. For a new library to be cost effective and provide professional service in this transitional period, it must balance allocation of these funds between, a) equipment and skilled staff needed to draw on outside information resources, or required for data base access fees, and b) the traditional use of funds for books, additional building space and for continuing fixed costs to keep current and preserve the integrity of the law library collection."[3]

Although none of the conclusions was unanimous, and some were subject to vigorous dissent, they offer much grist for the mill in planning the law libraries of the next century. Respondent conclusions included the following:

(1) In the future, more people will buy the information they want to read in a computer-based or computer-generated format and will borrow less from a library.

(2) Microform will be replaced by a form of computer-based or computer generated technology.

(3) In the absence of published hard copy, automated information viewable only on a computer screen (with print-out available for permanent retention) will be widely accepted as a readable format.

(4) Use of on-line public catalogs will significantly increase demands for document delivery.

(5) By the year 2000, disks (compact, digital, laser, optical, video) will replace hard copy information by 26% to 50%.

(6) Other technologies will be developed that will permit access to information even faster and cheaper than interactive television, cable systems and on-line systems.

(7) By the year 2000, automated library technology will be characterized primarily by video-disk technology, networks of personal computers or terminals, and access of full text data-bases, such as LEXIS and WESTLAW.

On the subject of payment for automated information access, respondent conclusions included:

(1) Faculty will have to pay for some of the costs to access online information beyond a pre-determined, reasonable, limited amount.

(2) By 1990, most research university or law school student fees

---

[3] "Revised ABA Standards for Law School Libraries, New York Law Journal p.4 (Oct. 21, 1986).

will cover the costs of automated information retrieval, word processing, and other related computer costs in the library.

(3) The library will furnish computer terminals to patrons to access information and will collect the costs through coin or card operated machines or legal tender.

(4) In the future, as there are changes in the library collection format and increased automation, the number and composition of library staff will change. Although the number of administrative librarians will remain the same, the number of public service librarians will increase, the number of technical services librarians will decrease, the number of support staff will decrease; and the number of library trained professionals will increase.

(5) By the year 1990, each faculty member will own or be furnished a personal computer or a terminal for information access and word and data processing.

(6) Most students enrolling in college will own personal computers.

It is interesting to note, that on the question whether, by 1990, each student will be *required* to have a personal computer, 106 (48.4%) of the respondents *disagreed*, fourteen (6.4%) *strongly* disagreed, fifty (22.8%) were undecided, forty (18.3%) agreed and 9(4.1%) strongly agreed. This perception appears to be in line with the Chronicle of Higher Education report.

CHAPTER 46F

How Practitioners Support Their Research With the New Technology

The following material comprises a new Chapter 46E for Legal Research and Law Library Management. *It is intended as supplemental material to the Main Text.*

A revealing study of the subscribers to the American Bar Association Journal, conducted by Don Bowdren Associates in 1987, points out not only how the dynamics of the legal profession continue to change but also how lawyers are adjusting to the new technology in the implementation of their research requirements. In this context it also notes that "lawyers comprise an increasingly important and influential market of serious buyers of business and consumer products and services." This is especially reflected in the markedly increased use of computers at the office, actually up 34.9% from 1985; 30.4% of the ABA Journal subscribers own personal computers as well. Don Bowdren's editor also anticipates that all indications are that these numbers "will continue to soar as more young lawyers (their average age is only 38) reach their middle years of professional prosperity and affluence."

When asked "which brands of computers does your firm own or release?" the 447 ABA Journal subscribers of the 718 asked to fill out the questionnaire (a recovery of 60%—the equivalent by interpolation to a potential random sampling of over 200,000 households) revealed that IBM, as anticipated, has been dominating the lawyer's market although other companies, such as Apple are beginning to be acquired as well.

Lawyers are using a variety of computer brands to support their research and housekeeping functions.

IBM	51.3%
ATT	6.3%
Apple	7.4%
Digital	7.4%
Wang	16.9%
Data General	1.1%
Harris Lanier	3.2%
Texas Instruments	2.9%
Zenith	1.4%
Hewlett Packard	4.3%
Barrister	1.7%
Alpha Microsystem	0.3%
Epson	3.7%
Radio Shack	4.6%
CPT	4.0%
Sperry	0.6%
Panasonic	0.9%
Compaq	6.9%
NCR	2.0%
NEC	1.1%
Fortune Systems	0.6%
Computer Consoles	.0%
Altos	0.3%
Kaypro	2.3%
Xerox	5.2%
Other	22.3%

Of this group 78.1% own or lease one or more computers; 59.7% own or lease microcomputers (P.C.'s); 23.5% mini computers; and 26.6% Main Frame Computers. Interestingly, 27.8% own or lease more than eleven computers, 13.9%, six to ten, 28.4%, two to five and 16.3% own or lease at least one computer.

Lawyers are now using a diverse selection of software:

Employee benefits	13.2%
Accounting/general ledger	51.0%
Accounts payable	33.5%
Billing	53.3%
Business analyses (spreadsheet)	30.1%
Communications with databases	21.8%
Database management	21.8%
Docket and diarying	25.5%
Financial on line	6.3%
Financial planning	6.6%
Tax expert systems	6.9%
Property and real estate	10.9%
Probate and estate planning	6.3%
Law firm practice management	10.6%
Legal databases on line	17.8%
Legal trust accounting	6.6%
Litigation support services	21.5%
Other on line	6.3%
Payroll	28.1%
Timekeeping	36.7%
Word processing	81.4%
Desk top publishing	5.7%

Lawyers are also becoming aware of the potential in their practice of computer assisted legal research and law related services. Following are the statistics on those services:

Total answering	100.0%
ABA/net	5.7%
Lexis/Nexis	33.0%
Westlaw	26.1%
Compuserv	2.9%
Dialog	5.7%
I.T.T. Dialcom	0.3%
Dow Jones News Retrieval	6.6%

Disclosure	2.0%
Phinet	1.1%
The Source	1.7%
MCI Mail	1.7%
Western Union Easylink	4.0%

Westlaw is beginning to catch up to LEXIS; only seven percentage points separates them.

Word processing, in a sense, is also characteristic of the computer age for lawyers and 66.9% use it.

The types of equipment lawyers are using for word processing were brought out as follows:

We don't have a word processing function	33.1%
Barrister	1.6%
CPT	4.9%
DEC	3.8%
Exxon	1.3%
IBM	37.1%
Lanier	7.4%
NBI	4.0%
Syntrex	2.9%
Wang	16.3%

As previously indicated, 30.4% of the lawyers questioned own their own computers, paying from $500 to $5,000 for the terminals and required peripheral equipment. As the cost for computers dramatically diminishes and the bar admits the thousands of law school computer-trained young lawyers (a good number of them actually acquiring their own P.C.'s while attending law school), there is little doubt that the ownership of computers by lawyers should double in number in the near future. This trend eventually should subsequently change the manner in which lawyers conduct legal research, since there will be remote access from a home base, or otherwise, to legal information and documentation. Dependence on the firm's law library collection will give way to a greater dependence on the guidance of the firm's librarian on how to identify and use the software commercially available and, even more so, the firm's separately developed computer data.

As to the brands of home computers lawyers personally purchase, it was not surprising that Apple led the list because of its competitive cost and ease of handling. The breakdown by brand for the 134 ABA Journal subscribers who own home computers was as follows:

Apple	35.8%
AT&T	1.5%
Commodore	16.4%
Compaq	4.5%
Digital Equipment	0.7%
Hewlett-Packard	.0%
IBM	13.4%
Tandy/Radio Shack	10.4%
Other	16.4%

Under the caption "Other Firm Equipment", the study reports about 45.9% of the firms owned or rented telefacsimile machines, 36.5% video equipment, and 36.5% photographic equipment. All these items, of course, can play a highly supporting role in obtaining access to documentation and know-how. The telefacsimile machines, particularly, are proving to be highly effective for interlibrary loan transactions of documentation and related information.

Many lawyers today, when involved in legal research, photocopy relevant pages of cases, statutes, law reviews, articles, treatises, government reports, administrative rules and regulations, etc., so that they can be referred to as part of the file, whether in the office or elsewhere. As a result, the photocopier, also a product of the new technology, has become practically standard equipment for the active law firm.

In this context, it was interesting to note that 96.9% of the law firms questioned owned photocopiers, 41.2% owned at least one, 5.4% owned twenty or more, 11.3% owned ten to nineteen, 4.9% owned four, 11.3% owned three, and 16.7% owned two.

Many law firms bill their clients for photocopies as well. Of the 447 firms responding, 60.5% do and 39.5% do not do so. The lawyers involved estimated that their firms produced in an average month, an average of 15,252 photocopies. Actually, 14.7% of the firms produced 50,000 or more photocopies in an average month, 6.8% produced 25,000 to 49,999, 14.5% produced 10,000 to 24,999, 19.7% produced 5,000 to 9,999, and 42.5% produced up to 5,000 copies.

It would have been helpful if the survey had also brought out how lawyers have adapted to the use of microform and CD/ROM in their research. Unfortunately, this data is not reflected in the report.

Law in the books has become a formidable storage problem and economic factor for lawyers. The document-delivery potential of telefacsimile and computer retrieval of legal information and documentation, along with the availability of legal materials in microform and CD/ROM, have played significant roles in bridging the gap. Some lawyers are now purchasing microform reader-printers and microfiche to solve the problem of book storage and availability of legal sources such as the National Reporter Series and legal periodicals.

CHAPTER 49

Law Library Consultants

The following material comprises an addition to Chapter 49 of Legal Research and Law Library Management. *It is intended to be read in conjunction with the material in the Main Text.*

Why use law library consultants at all?

What do they accomplish?

How do they go about their work?

The answers cut across all phases of law library work.

Why Use Law Library Consultants? Overcrowding is the chief reason for calling in a consultant. Bookshelves are virtually full. Study facilities are cramped. Lawyers stay out of the library and instead turn their own offices into satellite libraries, frequently failing to sign for books. Meanwhile, the missing-book problem becomes the chief lawyer complaint. In most cases, staff work areas were designed for a different purpose. They are too small and too noisy. Rarely is poor library service the primary reason for employing a consultant.

What Does a Consultant Accomplish? If space is the problem, the consultant will project the office needs over a period of years and recommend its optimum use. If library service is the problem, he will detail the duties that librarians perform, including duties of which they can relieve lawyers, and estimate the number of employees needed, the cost of their services and the dollar savings in lawyer time.

The consultant confirms what lawyers already know but need to have confirmed: *The fact that there is a serious problem.* Frequently, the problem is one of poor communications between librarians and other employees. The advantages that the consultant brings to his work are his trade secrets.

How Do Consultants Solve Library Problems? They do it by applying four trade secrets. The four may be summed up in one word: *Experience.* It is impossible to visit scores of law office libraries across the country and fail to recognize the variation in quality in the use of space, in the development of book collections and in staff services. They may range from excellent to good to mediocre to poor. It is in the application of these four trade secrets that a consultant helps turn a poor library into an excellent one.

First Trade Secret—The Use of Space. The consultant maintains a unique collection of law office library floor plans and photographs. They represent many configurations in the use of space, large and small, contiguous and gerrymandered. Each office has its own style of practice and that style should be reflected in the library design.

Too often libraries are not planned. Instead they are forced to react to crises. As the simplest illustration, firm partners will keep major sets of looseleaf services in their offices. The reason: There is no room elsewhere. The result: Associates who need these publications most have no access to them if (1) a conference is in progress in the partner's office, (2) he is dictating or speaking on the telephone or (3) he prefers not to be disturbed. This is a waste of lawyer time and an unwise economy in the use of space. Shared books belong in a freely shared library.

In a total library plan, the consultant attempts to satisfy the interests of the greatest number of library users—equated to the degree of their use. He tries to resolve conflicting interests—especially as they relate to satellite collections. He also projects libraries of a sensible size—given the estimated rate of firm or department expansion, the nature of its research needs, the cost of space and the advantage of computer assisted research.

Second Trade Secret—The Opinions of Lawyers and Librarians. The consultant maintains records of verbatim interviews on library matters with hundreds of practicing lawyers and librarians. He knows research habits, the peeves and gripes of lawyers and librarians alike, the kinds and quality of services that lawyers need and appreciate most.

The library profession was established long before the term "paralegal" was coined. Those librarians who keep abreast of new technological and management developments are among a firm's most valuable employees. The consultant helps to bring the two professions together and in the process to raise lawyers' expectations.

Again and again lawyers exclaim, "But we would never ask our librarian to do that." Invariably *that* is precisely the kind of service that lawyers down the street or across the state enjoy every day. This is a trade secret that lawyers learn in the course of interviews.

Third Trade Secret—Book Collections. The consultant has a file of checklists of book collections of scores of law libraries in offices with varied specialties. He has a sense of which books are used heavily and which only rarely. He makes recommendations for weeding existing collections and adding to them.

Fourth Trade Secret—Library Standards. The consultant has a knowledge of library "averages." They relate to (1) size of budget, (2) kinds of law practice and kinds of matching library services and (3) overall library excellence.

(1) The size of the budget for salaries, books and space is measurable. So too is the lawyer population. Comparisons are useful. Budgets give an office a sense of relative costs and relative returns for the library investment.

(2) The kinds of services are best set out in the library's "S.O.P.," its manual of standard operating procedures. Some libraries may be so well run that a manual is unnecessary. Some are so poorly run that a manual has never been heard of. The consultant can quickly learn what tasks the librarian and staff perform and whether those tasks are too few or too many in number for the staff size.

It comes as a shock to lawyers to learn that successful library work is the culmination of many hundreds of tasks that are performed behind the scenes. It is apparent that the replacement sheets in the CCH *Federal Securities Law Reporter* were filed in place by some human being. It is not apparent what efforts librarians exert to claim missing issues of advance sheets—those that the Post Office may lose or the ones that the publisher fails to send, the efforts made to locate publications that the office does not own and to collect background information about industries, companies or other law offices. No firm or office cares to lag behind comparable organizations.

(3) The consultant judges excellence by talking to lawyers about their work and librarians about their libraries. He observes both groups at work.

Overall excellence is a judgment based on tangible and intangible factors, on comparisons in which the law practices may be similar but the libraries are different. The tangible library factors include the size and distribution of the collection, the qualifications and accomplishments of the librarian and staff, the floor area occupied, the library's arrangement and convenience of use. The intangible factors relate to quality of staff performance, individual ability, drive, imagination and morale.

The mere presence of a consultant causes lawyers to focus attention on the library and to enhance lawyer recognition of what constitutes library excellence.

In summary, (1) the consultant collects facts through interviews and observation; (2) he persuades through the examples of other firms and departments; and (3) he advises through written reports and follow-up visits. Anemia and obesity are the twin scourages of law libraries. They can be controlled only by regular attention and sensible supervision.

CHAPTER 49A

Choosing and Using a Law Library Consultant

The following material comprises a new Chapter 49A for Legal Research and Law Library Management. *It is intended as supplemental material to the Main Text.*

Four factors have broadened the need for library consultants: the growth of law office size, the diversity of practice, the advent of computers and word processors and the increasing cost of operations.

When should consultants enter the picture? What do they do? How good are they? What are their shortcomings? This chapter offers a blueprint for their selection.

When Is a Consultant Needed?

The signals that a consultant is needed often assail the eye and ear at the library's very entrance—overcrowded shelves and files; inadequate space for study; noise from typewriters and telephones; the traffic of those who turn the library into a passageway; and cramped work space for librarians.

One law firm partner complained recently, "When the books are shelved at all, it looks as if they were hoisted with a pitchfork."

The less obvious symptoms may be harder to pin down. The cost of operations aside, the main problems are the quality of the book collection and the level of service to lawyers. In many cases, the needs of lawyers have outgrown the expansion of the office. The library staff has failed to expand in proportion to those needs. The book collection cannot meet the changed demands of practice.

How much space is really required? How much staff? Has anyone projected that growth? Lawyers need professional help in reaching decisions today that will affect their practice ten or more years in the future.

A consultant may be useful in these specific situations: The office is planning to move to another building or expand in its own quarters. Where should the library be placed? How large should it be? What shape? Our firm or company is merging. We will soon have two libraries.

Library valuation is required in connection with the retirement of a partner, a major fire or dissolution of a firm.

The shelves are 95 percent full or will soon reach that point. Sets of "Federal Supplement" and "Federal Reporter" have had to be split and shelved in three places. The most recent volumes cover tables and chairs.

The librarian is underpaid, underutilized or underappreciated—or the contrary.

Library expenses appear to be too high or may be too low; and there is an uneasy feeling that no one in the office really knows which is true. A consultant can explain what other offices are doing and paying and what is sensible for a particular practice.

The library is overcrowded in the winter. When the summer associates arrive, it is unbearable. There is simply no place to study.

A consultant helped re-organize the library five years ago. Is the situation better? What needs to be done now?

Dispersed throughout the office are memos of law, opinions, corporate precedents and litigation forms. Each lawyer has a private collection, but there is no central file. Nor is there any index. A consultant can make sense of these papers and achieve some order among them.

We now have automated our billing and most typing operations. How can we mechanize our library routines?

We may or may not have all the best books for our practice. We don't even know what we have, and frequently can't find what we own. There is no catalog or checklist, nor any effective circulation control.

We spend thousands of dollars a year for books and serial publications. Is it too much or too little? Some partners complain one way, some another. What should we do?

What Do Consultants Do?

Consultants diagnose library problems and offer solutions. They compare your situation with library facilities and practices in the best run offices. They evaluate your routines and your library performance. They draft layouts for more effective and more economical use of space.

They take the pulse of the office in these ways: they interview representative lawyers and the librarian; they inspect the existing library and proposed new space; they evaluate the book collection, making recommendations on what to weed and what to add; and, finally, they analyze costs.

An effective consultant produces a blueprint for future action in a detailed report. Step by step, his report advises what to do, how to go about it and what return your investment should bring.

How Good are Consultants?

Consultants vary from the ablest and most experienced to the most inept. How do you chose one? The Buick slogan is best: "Ask the man who owns one." In the case of a consultant, ask the lawyer who has employed one. A 10-minute telephone conversation will tell how good he or she is, what results were achieved, and what it cost.

A consultant's work suffers most if he has any of five shortcomings. These are the inexcusable traits; avoid those who have them: inexperience comes first; ineptness in execution of a library plan and clumsiness in describing it constitute the second shortcoming; next are insularity, rigidity and its opposite, waffling.

Inexperience

The library that one plans today may have to last 10 years. It is wise to use utmost care in hiring a consultant for it. The inexperienced consultant, like the beginning architect, learns at your expense. The seasoned consultant already knows his profession. He knows the ways of law firms and corporate legal departments because he has worked in them and planned their libraries.

Ineptness

Consulting consists of nearly equal parts of planning, advising and persuading. Advice should be rejected if a proposed plan fails to make sense, is unclear or is apparently illogical. Even if the plan is a good one, it should be rejected if its presentation is awkward and it cannot be understood. A consultant should be able to marshal his arguments with precision.

Insularity

It takes many lawyers and other specialists to make a law office operate successfully. A consultant is ineffective if he misunderstands the problems or is insensitive to the interests of all who participate in achieving that success. They include two groups, each with different perspectives: first, the librarians, office managers and administrators who perform and supervise the services; and second, the lawyers who consume and benefit from those services.

For example, both lawyers and librarians need adequate space in which to study or work. The entire firm is handicapped if the consultant proposes a librarian's office or a study carrel that is barely the size of a telephone booth. Yet each is all too common.

The effective consultant demonstrates balance. He understands the role and acknowledges the contribution of each participant in the enterprise.

Rigidity

Issues arise in planning or running a library on which lawyers are bound to disagree. Two such issues are library size and the choice between a central library and several satellite libraries. Office rent in New York ranges close to $50 a square foot. It can bar major expansion. Strong personalities in an office sometimes rule the roost, making decisions that may be right for them, but plainly wrong for the firm.

The consultant is hired to do the best job he can under the circumstances. For example, experience shows that one central library is usually the best law firm arrangement. Experience also shows that most lawyers want the library right outside their own offices. The rigid consultant is inflexible and yields to no arguments. The wise consultant is a good negotiator. He knows when and how much to compromise in order to achieve a workable library. He knows that satellite libraries should be avoided where possible and kept to a minimum where necessary.

Waffling

Waffling or wishy-washiness is just as damaging. The consultant has only his experience and advice to offer. He must be able to look at any proposal impartially and judge which is the best of several alternative plans.

Waffling enters the picture when the consultant fails to give his best advice because a strong personality sweeps his proposals aside. The waffler, for example, agrees with the last or most decisive partner he talks to. He caves in at the very moment when his client starts to test him with counterarguments, merely waiting to be persuaded.

Rigidity and waffling rarely show up in the same person. But inexperience, ineptness and insularity abound.

It is worth hiring a consultant. But it is worth even more to exercise care in selecting one.

CHAPTER 49B

Long Term Library Planning

The following material comprises a new Chapter 49B for Legal Research and Law Library Management. *It is intended as supplemental material to the Main Text.*

Every law firm has the need to study its actual and potential library resources and services. Both inside talent and an outside consultant are useful sources of information. Above all, partners should be listening to the librarian and the young associates. They are the troops who work in the library. Some seniors may have forgotten, or pretend to have forgotten, where the library is. But they know what it costs.

Goals should be set in a five year or ten year plan based on a detailed analytical study. The report should then be submitted to the firm's partners for their consideration and action. The study, at a minimum, should address four basic topics:

(1) The use of space;
(2) Computer applications;
(3) The book collection; and
(4) Professional support services.

[1]—The Use of Space

The library frequently occupies a significant portion of the firm's real estate. In total, it may take up more space than most of the other support services combined. Consideration must be given to how the space is used, whether it is efficiently planned or whether it contains bottlenecks, crowded conditions, noise or poor lighting; whether the library is strategically located and its size or growth contained; and the means of solving any of these problems which may exist.

[2]—Computer Applications

Research by computer has been hailed for its speed, scope and thoroughness, but not always for its economy. The firm must determine how to take full advantage of Lexis, Westlaw or any other computer resources.

The use of computers for storing and coordinating lawyer work products has been long promised, but not often realized. The report should include the current state of the art and what will it be five and ten years from today.

Some libraries are using computer applications in their day-to-day routines. Computers control book circulation records; they list book catalog entries; they maintain subscription records; and they compile and revise routing lists. The report should include an analysis of the extent to which these services are used, and should be used.

[3]—The Book Collection

The book collection is a mass of diverse publications. It may contain only a few or many thousands of volumes and cover most fields of law and law-related subjects as well. Questions the report should cover include: Is the collection used; is it used enough; are "hot" subjects effectively covered; is there a systematic way of reviewing and acquiring worthwhile new publications; are looseleaf services renewed and paid for whether they are used or not; and what is the frequency of cancellation? Most important, does the collection accurately reflect the needs of the practice?

[4]—Professional Support Services

Library services range from housekeeping (merely holding the fort) to sophisticated time-saving research and continuing in-house lawyer education. For example, services cover compiling federal and state legislative histories; updating federal regulations or tracing one to its source. The firm must determine the extent to which such services are desired and supplied.

[5]—Recommendations and Implementation of the Study

The report should contain specific recommendations and its implementation should depend on the tenor of discussion, preferably at a firm retreat, and the determination of the firm to act.

Following discussion, the best way is to submit the report as a whole to a vote. If it is accepted, means should be adopted straightaway to act on it. If some recommendations are agreed to, but others are not, then those approved should be implemented and the others referred to a committee for immediate rethinking, amendment and possible future action.

The very submission of the report will clear the air and help eliminate frustrations that firm members may have hesitated to mention before. The most important results of the study should be:

(1) Knowledge that the firm library is operating at a high level of proficiency and, if not, that a blueprint to make it so is at hand; and
(2) Knowledge that the firm is on the way to realizing a five-year or ten-year library plan that is directly keyed to its practice.

CHAPTER 49C

The Designer's Role in Law Library Planning

The following material comprises a new Chapter 49C for Legal Research and Law Library Management. *It is intended as supplemental material to the Main Text.*

The law library is full of objects, including chairs, tables, carrels, book stacks, lighting fixtures, a circulation counter and a number of machines—more each year. The law library designer may assemble them so as to give the library clean lines—the utmost simplicity—or he may reproduce the clutter there already, and make an obstacle course of the library. Designers can help in the realization of one's dreams—but sometimes at enormous expense.

The designer knows many of the suppliers of the objects that law libraries need. To give the firms a fighting chance to buy their needed equipment at competitive prices, the *Library Journal* lists most of those suppliers in its "Buying Guide" issue each April. It enables both designer and client to respond to most library planning concerns. This periodical is found in most college and large public libraries, but rarely in private law libraries.

[1]—Chairs

One chair is the most comfortable, durable, economical and the safest of any other. It is the "Bank of England" chair and is usually made of maple or oak. "The most comfortable chair on earth" is how the librarian at New York University Law School describes it.

Lawyers can comfortably sit on these chairs many hours a day. They enjoy its back support and its low center of gravity. Many claim that they can think only when their feet are higher than their heads. By contrast the upholstered swivel-type chair has a dangerously high center of gravity. It often tips over when feet rest on tabletops.

The supplier of the "Bank of England" chair is the Krug Furniture Company of Ontario, Canada. The *Library Journal* Buyers Guide lists many other chair makers, but most have discontinued this style because there is much more profit in the kinds that wear out.

[2]—Tables and Carrels

Three features should be stressed about tables and carrels:

(1) the working surface should be large enough—at least four feet wide and probably wider and two feet deep—so that each lawyer can keep several books at hand and still write on a legal-size pad without knocking elbows or knees with his neighbor;

(2) a raised storage shelf is highly desirable (it permits the storage of an additional dozen or more books and leaves the writing surface free);

(3) the lighting on the tabletop must be unblocked. If the table has a storage shelf mounted on it, the angle at which the shelf is mounted will determine whether or not the writing surface is in shadow. If so, either recessed lighting will be needed or the angle must be changed. Ceiling light is frequently insufficient.

The "Buying Guide" offers a wide choice among tables and carrels. One attractive preference for carrels is to build a row of small, partly enclosed alcoves against a long wall—and not buy readymade carrels. They are rarely large enough.

[3]—Lighting

In addition to the study areas, the *poorest lit* place in most libraries is between rows of book stacks. There the lighting is the most feeble. Researchers should not have to get down on their haunches and wear a miner's cap to beam light at the lower shelves of books. Yet in many cases it is only the books on the middle shelves whose spines can be plainly read. The volume numbers are virtually invisible on the backs of books kept on top or bottom shelves. The solution is to make sure that the ceiling light fixtures cast an even beam from the top to bottom. Failing that, lighting fixtures can be mounted out from the top shelf—the way some museums highlight their paintings.

[4]—Traditional Book Shelving

Book shelves occupy about one half of the library's real estate. Despite the development of Lexis, Westlaw, microforms, compact disks, optical scanners, and facsimile transmitters, books will remain the prime component of law office libraries for many years into the next century. The most useful method of book storage is on open book shelves where one can browse and choose.

Law libraries grow at an annual rate of about six per cent. Growth can be controlled and kept in bounds, but it cannot be stopped so long as the courts issue opinions and issue them at an accelerating rate.

To start with, consider the typical shelving unit—either seven or eight shelves high. At a three-foot width and seven-shelf height, the single section contains twenty-one feet of shelving or about 116 books at 5½ volumes per foot. By adding an eighth shelf—raising the section to 102″ or103″, the section is enlarged to twenty-four linear feet and holds 132 books. Each 10,000 volumes require 76 eight-shelf shelving units even when crammed to capacity. An additional eight units are needed if you leave space for ten per cent growth.

At rentals of $40 or $50 a foot it is downright wasteful to stop below eight shelves—or to keep books that are never used. Short people can reach the top shelf with the aid of a Kik-stool.

First choice for shelving features is the case-type storage unit with eight openings, each shelf adjustable at one-inch intervals. A pull-out shelf is essential because it enables lawyers to consult a score of books in minutes—without dragging them back to a table and without causing more clutter for the shelvers to clear.

About ten per cent of the collection will require deep shelves—twelve inches deep. The rest will require eight- or nine-inch-deep shelves. There are two main factors governing safety. First, an entire range of sections of shelving has been known to collapse in a domino-type disaster. This can be avoided by anchoring the shelving to ceiling and walls. Second, lawyers who cannot reach the top shelf and don't immediately see a Kik-stool are likely to step onto the first or second shelf to remove the books they need. The harm is that the shelf bends like a barrel stave under their weight and the books come tumbling down. Sometimes, the lawyers fall with them. The solution is to be generous in suppling very visible Kik-stools, but not where people will trip over them.

The main supplier of this form of shelving is Adjustable Steel Products Company, Inc. in New York City. The *Library Journal* "Buying Guide" lists numerous competitors, but few other companies can fit shelving into any size space. This company also furnishes wood end panelling and wood wrap-around panelling.

[5]—Compact Book Shelving

It is possible to store twice as many books in compact as in traditional shelving. A number of firms have taken advantage of compact shelves for storing long runs of infrequently consulted court reports. Others have gone to "Ultrafiche" storage. In either case it can be frustrating to lawyers when active portions of the collection are stored in those ways.

Compact shelving can slow down research and reshelving, and it may be a nuisance for every day use. However, it is a *real bargain* for the least used portions of the collection. A good rule of thumb is to store no more than one-fifth of the books in that way. The Adjustable Steel Company's compact line is called "Compac Trac." It has several competitors, as shown in the "Buying Guide." One caution: It is heavy, very heavy equipment. It requires reinforced flooring and the clearance of a building engineer before installing it.

CHAPTER 49D

The Effect of New Technology on Law Library Planning

The following material comprises a new Chapter 49D for Legal Research and Law Library Management. *It is intended as supplemental material to the Main Text.*

First we had the publication explosion. Then came the information explosion. Now we have the video explosion. As a result of these breakthroughs the concept of a law library as a depository of books is giving way to the concept of the law library as an information transfer network.

The impact of technological change upon storage, retrieval and delivery of legal information has become so significant in legal research, that it is now recognized even in the standards of the American Bar Association as they pertain to law school libraries. As amended two years ago, they are designed "to reflect current and prospective use of electronic and other technology in legal research." As a result, by reason of ABA interpretation of the standard 405(b), law schools in order to be approved by the American Bar Association "should make reasonable provision for faculty access to automated information systems suitable for scholarly research." Then in Annex II of its *Standards for Approval of Law Schools*, which refers to the types of materials which should be in the core collection of the library, law libraries are required to provide "computer assisted legal research services of national scope and broad subject coverage."

Although limited to law school libraries at present, inevitably they should affect similar services and law library planning in bar libraries, court libraries, and private law firms.

In this context, it should also be noted that ABA standard 603(c) reads that "the library shall provide adequate access to commonly used materials by additional copies or nonprint means for use by the faculty and students." As the core collection library schedule listed in Annex II does not distinguish between the hard copy book or the non-book format, such as microform, it appears that any format will be acceptable provided the library complies with ABA standard 603(d) which reads that "if the library contains materials in microform, tape or similar form, it shall provide the necessary viewing and listening equipment in an area suitable for its use."

Note too, ABA standard 704 relating to seating in law libraries which requires "adequate numbers of study stations with suitable facilities for the use of automated information retrieval equipment."

A leading information systems consultant, commenting on the dramatic changes that have taken place in library automation since the 1960's [*Technology and the Modern Library* Library Journal, June 15, 1984, p. 1183] believes that, despite library dependence on microcomputer technology rather than on the large mainframe computer, libraries both large and small in the future will rely on multi-user microcomputers that can support up to fifteen terminals with several functions being performed concurrently.[1] These functions will pertain to on-line integrated systems on which a single bibliographic file supports acquisitions, serials, cataloging, circulation and other library related functions.

In the not too distant future the majority of medium sized and large libraries in North America will be automated and a majority of all but school libraries will have implemented systems.

> "Libraries will not be paperless, however. Acquisition decisions will be based on extensive management information about library users and patterns of collection use, ordering will be done on line, and funds accounting will be done automatically. Shared cataloging will be a by-product of shared bibliographic databases, mounted on bibliographic utility systems, such as OCLC [Online Computer Library Center] and RLIN [Research Libraries Information Network] or distributed on video disk or optical digital disk. Online patron access catalog and circulation control functions will be commonplace

[1] Boss, "Technology and the Modern Library," Library Journal, p. 1183 (June 15, 1984).

because they have the greatest potential value for users. The user will be able to access both the holding and current availability status of materials in an entire library system from a terminal in any library location or from the home or office using a computer terminal or a television receiver adapted for videotex."[2]

As a videotex system can operate in a two-way or interactive mode, the user will not only be able to receive information, but also to transmit data back to the system.

Another prediction is that "libraries will continue to have collections of printed books and journals, but a significant percentage of statistical and directory data will be accessed through computer terminals, as will almost all bibliographic data."[3]

Characteristic too of this development is the realization that librarians become highly effective managers of technology and will have to be skillful in both the printed and electronic media to serve their patrons and to compete effectively with commercial electronic systems such as videotex to information brokers who respond to telephone queries for a fee.

Whether law library book collections of the future will be reduced in size by reason of the new technology is a concern of the legal profession, especially those planning new library facilities. As has been pointed out: "The challenge in planning for future law library or legal information center space is to assure that the investment made today in capital improvements will not be lost by obsolescence in the near future. . . . The new technologies are changing the concepts applicable to the access of information and these in turn impinge upon physical space requirements and arrangements for informational-gathering activities."[4]

It is also relevant to note that even traditionalists recognize the challenge of an increasing lack of book storage in libraries, due to the publication explosion. As a result, the dependence on microform and CD Rom disks to reduce the physical size of the book collection has increased rapidly.

---

[2] *Id.*

[3] *Id.*

[4] Henko and Marke, *Planning the Law Library as an Information Center* (1986).

Note too the implications of the "Optical Disk Program" of the Library of Congress on image presentation and retrieval using optical-disk technology. While presentation of existing hard copy materials was initially the primary objective of the program, the disks are also expected to solve the problems of availability of the Library of Congress materials in various parts of the building complex and even more significantly—outside of the building. As noted by the director of the program, "one important point about access is that this technology permits us to distribute these images far and wide: These images could be beamed to homes, to libraries, whatever. So people would not need to come to our library to have access to our collections. It gives a whole new meaning to interlibrary loan. . . . It transforms and gives a new meaning to all traditional library services. Whether it's loan, photocopying, or whatever, some would say it calls in question the traditional library organization in all its aspects. Do we need specialized reading rooms, do we need specialized libraries?"

Along with microform and CD-ROM, the document delivery potential of telefacsimile and computer retrieval of legal information and documentation have significantly contributed to surmounting the formidable storage problems and economic factors involved in finding law in the books.

The spreading use of telefacsimile technology provides a significant breakthrough in library cooperation. By expediting the delivery of documents from library to library through the simple medium of the telephone, it is now possible for libraries to reduce delivery time and promote resource sharing. The 1988 edition of the AALL *Directory and Handbook* lists 401 law libraries and their telefax telephone number. It is now possible to locate which libraries possess a desired book or other document by referring to automated cataloging networks such as RLIN or OCLC, and then asking by telephone for it to be faxed to the requesting library. The costs are modest, reflecting the telephone charges and the transaction fee of the providing library. It is for good reason that fax machines are described as "long distance copiers." The use of telefacsimile equipment for interlibrary exchanges has become so popular, that between New York University and Columbia alone more than 2000 pages per month are "faxed." A number of law firms in New York have also arranged with Columbia for library materials to be faxed to their offices as part of a law library fee based reference service. Group 3 fax machines are currently considered to be the standard one to use, for they can send or receive a page of type, or picture (or as the fax salespeople say "If you can see it you can fax it"), in as little as nine seconds over voice-grade telephone lines.

The advent of the computer age has dramatically affected Law Library service and operation. Lexis, Westlaw, RLIN, OCLC and other bibliographical utilities have proven to be not only a boon to legal research but have raised basic issues on law library planning such as whether libraries can build new computer-based information capabilities at the expense of their traditional collections and services. The basic premise today is that "The library's traditional book, journal and manuscript collection are and will continue to be the mainstay of our library and its services to users throughout this decade and the next.[5]

There is a split among law librarians over how fast the nature of the law library will change. Technologists and futurists predict that books and other forms of print on paper are on their way out along with the libraries that stack and service them. According to these authorities, standard print material will be replaced by electronic technologies in the form of communication satellites, cable TV, and inexpensive mass storage, such as optical and digital video disks and microcomputers.

The traditionalists, on the other hand, argue that experience teaches us that electronic replacements take longer to develop than is usually predicted, cost more, or are produced in ways that are unforeseeable.

The technologists see the law school or bar library of the future as a computer and audio resource laboratory with a collection of some 150,000 volumes. Most legal research materials will be on line in a database and be accessed through terminals or microprocessors installed either in library areas or in remote offices and homes of the law school community. Books stored in the library will be of the type usually read from cover to cover as opposed to those used only in part for research purposes. Case reporters will be electronically stored and retrieved. Library users, no longer limited to "in-house" collections, will be able to access legal databases containing reference sources from every jurisdiction in the country and even from foreign nations.

Similarly, they argue that the traditional materials presently used as part of the teaching function and curriculum and housed usually in law

---

[5] De Gennaro. "Into the Information Age" (a draft of a five-year plan for the University of Pennsylvania Libraries, 1985-1989).

libraries will give way to computer programming. Just as the faculty will stress teaching with computers, judges will write opinions so that they can be processed quickly into Westlaw and Lexis databases and retrieved by the researcher shortly thereafter.

In light of the uncertainties involved in timing when the new technology will predominate in planning a law library, the only responsible management decision is to assume that growth in library collections will continue at or near current growth rate, and that the full effect of the new technology will be evolutionary rather than revolutionary. Traditional library holdings will continue to be the basic library core collection. Technology will provide enriched research capabilities, but will not supplant books sufficiently to warrant planning less physical space for their storage.

In all probability, an uneasy truce will govern the relationship between technology and books—both will coexist in support of each other. Glib talk about the potential use of the optical disk and the developing forms of information storage often overlooks the accompanying frustrating problems such as copyright limitations on their use and need for improved technical implementation to guarantee a consistent uninterrupted service, capable of successfully replacing the book.

Some of the planning issues that will have to be resolved are:

- Should we abandon the traditional, oversized main reading room and replace it with a dispersed inter-mixture of reading spaces and stacks?
- Do we need multimedia rooms for microform and audio-visual service?
- Should we plan a library without walls in light of the capability provided by the new technology to obtain access to the library's resources electronically from remote stations off the library environs through personal compters?
- Once library housekeeping functions such as cataloging, circulation, reserve, acquisition and serials are automated, when should they, or can they be linked up to a utility such as OCLC or RLIN, and when should the public be allowed independent access to terminals providing cataloging and circulation information by on-line catalog systems?

Although there are uncertainties as to how the new technology will affect library planning, there is a need to provide, mechanically and architecturally, for computer assisted legal research facilities, conduits for personal computers and other automation, and sufficient space per reader to use personal computers in carrels and elsewhere in the library.

Part of the uncertainties involved in planning a law library is the anticipated effect of the new technology on the size of the library staff. The consensus is that automation will not reduce the size of the staff, but will expedite, enhance and improve service for acquisitions, serials, accounting, cataloging, circulation and reference work.

In planning library space for staff, it may actually be necessary to anticipate that automation will require additional staff to service the machines and train in their use.

In planning for multi-media services, a great concern is the large variety of hardware, its initial expense and the fact that some of this equipment cannot be used interchangeably. New developments and changes in this hardware must be addressed as they relate to premature obsolescence of expensive capital investment. For example, the compatibility of computer technology with both microform and compact disk technology and storage procedures in operating a library is still not clear.

A significant cost factor in providing for automation is the construction work required for heating, ventilating, air conditioning, conduit, cable and related construction to accommodate computers and computer terminals. Sound proofing and electrical outlets sufficient to provide for the needs of the many microform readers, audio-cassettes and video equipment must also be provided. In essence we are dealing with library features reflecting systems for video-study carrels, audio laboratory centers and computer accessibility to Lexis and Westlaw, including public online access to the library catalogue.

In this context, it should be noted that whereas only twenty-five to thirty feet must be set aside for each reader using conventional library facilities, approximately fifty to sixty square feet should be assigned for each reader using multimedia equipment.

In summary, a flexible building structure and layouts should be contemplated to provide for computer wiring, computer terminal facilities, microform and optical and video disk viewer stations plus audio and video research carrels to enhance the legal education and legal research process. Modern information technology requires provision for special purpose seating stations for Lexis and Westlaw, student-owned portable microcomputer terminals, audio-visual reception and microform and optical and video disk viewing. Because of the equipment involved, cathode ray terminals, typewriter or word processing terminals, printers, TV screens, audio earphones, microviewer printers and duplicators, these stations are not adaptable to general reading research and study. Yet they must be located adjacent to legal materials in written form for coordinated legal research.

CHAPTER 51

Revised ABA Standards for Law School Libraries

The following material comprises a new Chapter 51 for Legal Research and Law Library Management. *It is intended as supplemental material to the Main Text.*

The impact of technological change on legal information storage, retrieval and delivery and on legal research generally has been officially recognized by The American Bar Association. The House of Delegates of The American Bar Association, at its August 1986 Annual Meeting, adopted the recommendation of the Section of Legal Education and Admissions to the Bar that the ABA Standards for Approval of Law Schools as they pertain to law school libraries be amended "to reflect current and prospective use of electronic and other technology in legal research."

The American Bar Association (ABA) from its very beginnings over 100 years ago, has been concerned with the improvement of the legal education of those who apply for admission to the bar. That interest is implemented by the Accreditation Committee of its Section of Legal Education and Admissions to the Bar. The Section's activities, amongst others, have been directed to promulgating and refining the standards law schools must meet to become accredited. The American Bar Association is the accrediting agency for law schools which are recognized by the United States Commissioner of Education for Governmental Grants and Funds. The Supreme Courts of forty-three states and the District of Columbia Court of Appeals require, either by court rule or board of law examiners' administrative rule, graduation from an ABA approved law school as a requisite for taking the bar examination. Incidentally, in this context, the ABA must meet the same U.S.

Department of Education standards as other national accreditation agencies.

Whether a law school complies with the accreditation standards of the ABA depends, among other requirements, upon whether it maintains and administers a library "adequate for its program." In this context, the Council of the Section of Legal Education and Admissions to the Bar has interpreted ABA Standard 201, which requires a law school to have the "resources necessary to provide a sound legal education and accomplish the objectives of its educational program . . ." to mean that "an approved law school should seek to exceed the minimum requirements of the standards." Hence, the ABA standards pertaining to the law library are merely minimum standards.

All the standards and requirements recommended by the Section and approved by the House of Delegates are printed and distributed to law schools, universities, libraries, boards of bar examiners, professional groups or associations and others concerned with legal education. The standards for the approval of law schools were adopted by the House of Delegates in February 1973. The standards pertaining to the law school library were amended by the House in February 1977.

In March 1982, the Law Libraries Committee of the Section concluded that those portions of the standards for the approval of law schools pertaining to the law school library be amended "to reflect current and prospective use of electronic and other technology in legal research." A subcommittee was appointed to review the existing standards and to prepare proposed revisions. An initial draft was circulated for comment in 1983, a second draft in 1984, and a third in early 1985. After review by the Council of the Section, a fourth and final draft was approved by the Council at its December 14, 1985 meeting.

The subcommittee, on December 5, 1982, recommended changes be made in the library standards, noting that the legal profession is "in a period of rapid change in the ways legal information is preserved, transmitted and retrieved. For example, the full text of much primary legal authority now is stored in computer databases, transmitted electronically, and printed on demand for a user almost anywhere in the United States. Books continue to be heavily used, but automated search and retrieval methods can be more cost-effective in some circumstances. In many law schools the library user now sits, as it were, in a library without walls and can draw upon the legal information resources of a city, a region, or a continent. Law School faculty and students are becoming increasingly aware that their libraries can or could provide such services. In this context, library service focuses more and more on providing access to information needed, rather than on accumulating a giant storehouse of volumes awaiting some possible future use."

In addition, the subcommittee stressed that these changes have obvious economic implications. Deans of law schools and law libraries are reevaluating the accepted concepts about how library funds should be spent. For a law library to be cost effective and provide professional service in this transitional period, it must balance allocation of these funds between (1) equipment and skilled staff needed to draw on outside information resources, or required for data base access fees, and (2) the traditional use of funds for books, additional building space needs and for continuing fixed costs to keep current and preserve the integrity of the law library collection.

The subcommittee also observed that "urban and regional networks among libraries of all kinds are now commonplace. These networks utilize current technology to locate needed information and deliver it to a library user. Some libraries now deliver documents electronically. Increasingly, schools must share the costs of acquiring and maintaining their legal information resources. Each year the average price of a volume increases and, year after year without pause, more volumes are published. The economic pressures to participate in resource sharing are very strong. Technology is available to make such resource sharing effective and reliable. Thus, the duplication in many law schools' libraries of little-used materials is inevitably brought into question. The advisability of acquiring and storing such materials in microform has been demonstrated by newly established law schools. Dependence on significant amounts of source material in alternative forms now seems a reasonable expectation for all approved schools, perhaps with infrequently needed materials held by only one of several cooperative libraries."

The subcommittee obviously was challenging the concept of the law library standards which explicitly identified the materials law libraries had to make available to their users in order to comply with the standards. Although the use of precise quantative measures in this context could guarantee compliance with the standards, it was problematical whether library service was improved by such observance. Instead the subcommittee recommended that new standards be established which would reflect qualitative rather than quantitative values, thus giving more emphasis to quality of services and access and less to rigid quantitative measures. To meet the thrust of this approach, the standards should be appropriate for both manual and automated systems in any context. The important test in evaluating a library would be a combination of (1) the types and depth of information and materials made accessible and usable, (2) the quality of access for all faculty and students, and (3) the extent and dependability of financial resources made available to the library.

These newly approved standards should significantly affect the delivery of legal information resources in law school libraries, for they incorporate a recognition of the value of the new technology in legal research and they deemphasize quantitative criteria. Although limited to law schools at present, inevitably, they should affect similar service in bar libraries, court libraries, and private law firm libraries.

The importance of a law school library has always been measured by the number of books in its collection. The greater the number, the more important the law library. The volume count has been featured in the annual statistics compiled by the ABA on law school libraries and the competition is keen to be in the top ten in the number of books held, or the top twenty, and so on. To be number one, as has been the achievement of Harvard Law School Library, puts a school at the pinacle of success. To be last in number of the 170 or so law school law libraries reflects badly on the law school image. However, often the total number of books in the library does not guarantee the type of service required by the ABA, namely that it be "adequate" for the program and objectives of the law school. As one law librarian has commented, "If there is one thing we librarians know, it is that volume count doesn't really matter. You can have every book published within your walls, but if you don't have access to these books, the collection is useless. We also know that you can have a librarian with a telephone book and a telephone (or its modern equivalent, the computer terminal) which provides good service with no books at all" (Kathleen Price, Law Librarian, University of Minnesota Law School).

These standards reflect the importance of the new technology in legal research by interpreting Standard 405(b) ("The law school shall afford faculty members reasonable opportunity for . . . scholarly research"), to mean that "an approved law school should make reasonable provisions for faculty access to automated information systems suitable for scholarly research." In Annex II, which refers to the types of materials which should be in the core collection of the library, it requires law libraries to provide "computer assisted legal research services of national scope and broad subject coverage."

In addition to these computer assisted legal research (CALR) services required to be provided by the library, the new technology is also reflected in Standard 603(c) which reads "the library shall provide adequate access to commonly used materials by additional copies or nonprint means for use by the faculty and students." As the core collection library schedule listed in Annex II does not distinguish between the hard copy book or the nonbook format, such as microform, any format will be acceptable provided the library complies with Standard 603 (d), which reads that "if the library contains materials in microform, tape or similar form, it shall provide the necessary viewing and listening equipment in an area suitable for its use."

Law school libraries will now have the opportunity to provide their users through CALR, videodisks, microform, and by networking with other law school libraries, with access to a wide range of legal, and law related materials. Previously, high costs prohibited many libraries from providing certain materials; the ABA Standards required the maintenance of many materials in hard copy.

Law school libraries are also sensitive to some of the problems that necessarily will arise from this development. How will the money be found? Who will bear the cost of providing direct CALR instructional programs for legal researchers or for on-line reference librarians who then will control access to legal information? Not only will increased staff costs be involved in providing the instructional program, but there will also be additional costs for hardware, software and communications. Although the ABA standard permits the law school librarian to decide independently to what degree to become involved in CALR, the question of automation costs will still have to be analyzed beforehand.

More significantly, law librarians will also have to address the problem of hard copy versus nonbook library materials. Although law school libraries will save shelf space and upkeep costs through CALR, they realize that a purchased book becomes the property of the library. However, once a subscription to LEXIS or WESTLAW is discontinued, there is nothing the library can depend on for access to the materials reflected in their data bases. Law Librarian Price has noted, "when the computer subscription ends, there is nothing left but the box." It is also obvious that there must be a sufficient number of terminals to provide access to the data base for a variety of users at the same time.

How many will meet the test of "adequate access to commonly used materials by additional copies or non-print means for use by the faculty and students" as required by Standard 603(c)?

Another problem has been clearly raised by Anita Morse, Law Librarian of the University of Wisconsin, which is supported by public funds. Writing in the Law Library Journal, she notes:

> "We must face the issue of public access. Law school libraries—at least public law school libraries—consider it part of their mission to supply legal services to the community. In many geographic areas, the law school library provides the only access to international and foreign law materials, federal agency documents, and specialized legal series. Most CALR services in law schools are on a restricted education contract; only law school faculty and students (in some cases, university faculty or student) use is allowed. Under these conditions, continued substitution of CALR for book format means less public access to the law. Practically, this means that only those few law firms with CALR will have access to such items as IRS private letter rulings or unpublished court opinions. Other lawyers, outside researchers, or community action groups will not. Libraries must consider their obligations to provide the best legal information to every one, whether this means using public terminals on a charge-back basis or paying subsidies for computer information. It could be ironic if law libraries abandoned their duty to provide public access to legal information in the name of efficiency and increased information resources."[1]

The greater dependence on CALR by law school libraries may radically change the physical features of the space they occupy. Instead of book shelves, there could be more need for carrels, and areas for equipment and services such as audio-visual programs, computer stations, microform readers and printers. When many of the library's authorized users of the collection (i.e., faculty, students, alumni, legal aids, lawyers, judges, public officials, and even the public) can be served at P.C. terminals located in remote areas far from the law library's physical plant through CALR, what should the average law library look like in the future?

---

[1] 78 Law Library Journal p. 487 (1986).